THE
DEMOCRATIC
IMAGINATION

THE DEMOCRATIC IMAGINATION

ENVISIONING POPULAR POWER IN THE TWENTY-FIRST CENTURY

James Cairns & Alan Sears

UNIVERSITY OF TORONTO PRESS

Library and Archives Canada Cataloguing in Publication

Cairns, James Irvine, 1979–
    The democratic imagination : envisioning popular power in the twenty-first century / James
Cairn & Alan Sears.

Includes bibliographical references and index.
Issued also in electronic formats.
ISBN 978-1-4426-0528-2

    1. Democracy—Textbooks. I. Sears, Alan, 1956– II. Title.

JC423.C24 2012   321.8   C2012-905270-1

We welcome comments and suggestions regarding any aspect of our publications—please feel free
to contact us at news@utphighereducation.com or visit our Internet site at www.utppublishing.com.

North America
5201 Dufferin Street
North York, Ontario, Canada, M3H 5T8

2250 Military Road
Tonawanda, New York, USA, 14150

ORDERS PHONE: 1–800–565–9523
ORDERS FAX: 1–800–221–9985
ORDERS E-MAIL: utpbooks@utpress.utoronto.ca

UK, Ireland, and continental Europe
NBN International
Estover Road, Plymouth, PL6 7PY, UK
ORDERS PHONE: 44 (0) 1752 202301
ORDERS FAX: 44 (0) 1752 202333
ORDERS E-MAIL: enquiries@nbninternational.com

This book is printed on paper containing 100% post-consumer fibre.

The University of Toronto Press acknowledges the financial support for its publishing activities of
the Government of Canada through the Canada Book Fund.

Typesetting: Em Dash Design

Printed in Canada

This book is dedicated to Mary-Jo Nadeau, our model for the democratic imagination. She is a tireless activist and an acute analyst who is deeply committed to social justice and to the value of laughter.

Contents

Exercising Your Democratic Imagination Textboxes

Acknowledgements

Anne Brackenbury from University of Toronto Press has been much more than an editor for this book. We counted on her insightful reflection from the early moments of conceiving this book and relied on her feedback along the journey. Our sense of the democratic imagination has been bolstered by the households we've lived in. James would like to thank Eroca, Mom & Wendy, Dad & Beth, Simon, Teresa, Kyla & Lexi, and Kate & Corey. Alan would like to remember his father Henry, and thank his life partner Ken, mother Doreen, brother Joel, and nephew Jed. Coffee shops have long been home to heated political debate, and we are grateful for Amelia & Kristjan and all the fine folks at our favourite, Saving Gigi, where many of the ideas in this book were developed through conversation.

We consider this book to be an outcome of our scholarly work and our activism, and we would like to thank those who sustain and enhance our political commitments in these challenging times: Abbie Bakan, Kate Cairns, David Camfield, Sue Ferguson, Todd Gordon, David McNally, Mary-Jo Nadeau, Cynthia Wright, and Rafeef Ziadah. We are fortunate to work with amazing colleagues who nurture creativity, including Tarah Brookfield, Chris Cachia, Doreen Fumia, Rebecca Godderis, Colin Mooers, Kate Rossiter, Charles Wells, Glen Weppler, and Kenneth Werbin. Finally, as teachers, we learn from our students; they really drive our democratic imaginations, and we want to mention Lin Abdul-Rahman, Mary-Katherine Boss, Kyle Brown, Michele Cybulski, Daniel Donovan, Kris Erickson, Matt Feagan, Laura Hartnell, Jo-Anne Lawless, Azar Masoumi, Lali Mohamed, Susanna Quail, Sarah Serajelahi, Amandeep Singh, Shannon Sterrett, and Dorothy Vu.

1 DEMOCRACY AS AN OPEN QUESTION

In a debate during the 2011 federal election in Canada, Prime Minister Stephen Harper said, "I don't think this kind of political bickering, personal attacks back and forth, is frankly going to do anything for Canadians." Liberal Party leader Michael Ignatieff replied, "There he goes again with this word 'bickering.' ... This is a debate, Mr. Harper. This is a democracy" (CBC News 2011).

Democracy might seem like bickering from several perspectives these days. Many people on the **conservative** end of the **political spectrum** argue that political give and take is just so much noise interfering with the core mission, which is the implementation of measures to support a profitable economy. During the election debate, Prime Minister Harper asked, "Do you want to have this kind of bickering, do you want to have another election in two years? Or do you want a focus on the economy?" Generally speaking, conservatives think that sensible economic policy is pretty obvious and that the role of government is to implement policies to provide the basis for **profitability** and productive investment. These policies, which at the present time tend to focus on tax cuts and the downsizing of government, will ultimately benefit everyone, they argue.

From a very different perspective, some **radical** activists saw the election debate as bickering over small differences among politicians who fundamentally agree about the big questions and share a commitment to preserving the current organization of society. For example, a campaign calling itself "Boycott the Elections 2011" argued that most people understand that "elections will not change their lives." In the run-up to voting day, there was no serious discussion among political leaders about foreign policy; poverty; the rights of women or lesbians, gays, bisexuals, or transgendered people; the role of police; worker rights; or immigration policies. The dominant parties largely agree in these areas, so official debate tends to focus on personal integrity, leadership style, or minor divergences in policies that share an overall framework, according to radicals. The borders surrounding legitimate topics for debate are narrow and difficult to break open when the major parties share the same basic views.

In between the radicals and the conservatives are many people who might see politics as the meaningless exchange between dishonest politicians who say whatever they need to say to get elected and then do whatever they need to do to cling to power. Voter turnout rates are falling in many countries, a trend that we examine in this book. A poll in the *Guardian* shows that "only 9% of Europeans think their politicians—in opposition or in power—act with honesty and integrity" (Glover 2011). The mistrust of politicians fits with an overall approach to government: "only 6% of people across Europe say they have a great deal of trust in their government, 46% say they have not very much and 32% none at all" (Glover 2011). This poll was taken in the specific context of an economic recession and sharp **austerity** policies supported by politicians across the spectrum, policies that have led to service cutbacks, wage reductions, and layoffs. It suggests that "political anxiety appears to be fuelled by deep economic worries" (Glover 2011).

Democracy is facing challenges from across the political spectrum, intensified perhaps by the recent global economic slump. At the more conservative end of the spectrum, elected officials increasingly claim that politics clouds issues and impedes good technical decisions that must be taken on a sound economic basis. Chicago Mayor Rahm Emanuel introduced an austerity budget containing sharp cutbacks and said, "Almost every one of these ideas has been discussed and debated before. But politics has stood in the way of their adoption" (Friedman 2011: 11). The idea that the role of government is to align policies with perceived economic necessity, convincing the population to swallow the bitter pill of cutbacks, layoffs, and user-pay strategies to improve the business climate, can undercut ideas of democratic decision making informed by political debate.

At the more radical end of the spectrum, people disillusioned with the system are organizing new protest movements outside established political spaces. An important example of this in 2011 was the Occupy movement that focused on the takeover of public space, ranging from the mobilization of the indignant (los indignados) in Spain to the Occupy Wall Street activism that spurred actions across North America. These movements argue for a more profound democracy, and, in fact, they practise it through rejecting traditional ideas of leadership in favour of regular general meetings where all can participate in decision making. These movements raise important questions about the limits of existing democratic forms of government. It is an important time, then, to inquire into democracy: what it is, where it comes from, and where it is going. This probing means challenging the way democracy is often taken for granted in those societies where the election of representatives is firmly established.

Democracy is everywhere, or at least the word is. It is taught to children in schools and to immigrants seeking to become citizens. The word is chanted by protestors in the streets, and it is promised in election campaigns and political speeches. It is exalted from points across the political spectrum. Democracy is a cornerstone of foreign policy, or at least that is what presidents and prime ministers claim. In fact, democracy is one of those words that gets used so heavily that we do not often pause to think about what it means. However, probing into words and concepts we take for granted can prove valuable. Words have histories and complex layers of meaning that continue to resonate in everyday usage. In some cases, even the core meaning of the word is hotly contested. Anthony Arblaster (1994) describes democracy as an "inherently debatable and changeable idea" that therefore deserves careful consideration (p. 6).

The *Oxford English Dictionary Online* defines democracy as "government by the people." The term is derived from the Greek *demos* (the people) and *kratos* (rule). The Greek origins of the term already tell us something about the specific history of its usage, tracking back to particular historical events to which we will return shortly. It becomes obvious very quickly that, if democracy means government or rule by the people, that phrase can be understood in many different ways. A form of government organized around the periodic election of representatives is only one of those possible meanings.

We approach democracy in this book as an open question whose future has not yet been defined rather than as something already established whose trajectory is known to us. Rather than saying Canada is a democracy and Burma is not, we want to probe more deeply into what actually makes up democracy. George Elliott Clarke (2011) recently wrote that radicals must take over the Canadian state democratically "to begin to utilize its awesome power to democratize Canadian society" (p. 57). To at least some readers, who might presume that Canada already is a democracy, this statement might look odd. In his article, Clarke points out the deep-set nature of racism and other inequalities in Canadian social, political, and economic life. His democracy, then, includes certain kinds of equity; and without equity, democracy is incomplete.

It is our goal in writing this book to encourage readers to define for themselves what characterizes meaningful democracy, to assess the extent to which existing political institutions might meet those criteria, and to consider what actions might be required to achieve or safeguard **popular power**. The "democratic imagination" in the title of this book is the capacity to envision what democracy looks like and to work toward actually achieving it. This conception draws on the important work C. Wright Mills (1959) did on "the sociological imagination," which aimed to develop the capacity of people to understand their own private troubles in the context of the broad social-economic relations that frame their personal experiences.

Expanding the Democratic Imagination

James Laxer (2009) writes that "the appetite for democracy arises not from political theory but from the tangible needs of millions of people" (p. 113). This perspective is an important counterpoint to approaches that treat democracy as though it were a great idea dreamt up by ancient Greek philosophers and then passed down through the generations by professional thinkers, mainly white males, from Plato to John Locke to John Rawls. The idea that human beings deserve freedom, meaning that they ought to govern their own lives and communities, has indeed emerged from the resistance of the downtrodden to the experience of domination. It is this actual resistance, in the form of **collective action**, and not simply the power of an idea, that has led to the development of different forms of democracy at key moments in history. Regardless of the particular ways in which democracy is imagined, it is fundamentally about the daily practice of living together as humans. Safeguarding or improving democracy, therefore, involves action in the real world.

Yet, at the same time, though democracy emerges from everyday practices, it is also an ideal: a conceptual map designed to guide the organization of human life. The effectiveness of political action can be enhanced by analyzing competing conceptions of democracy to clarify how the word is being used in particular contexts. The definition of democracy can shape the aspirations that lead people to take certain actions, playing an important role in shaping how "rule by the people" gets done in practice.

At the start of the twenty-first century, many citizens and political leaders from across the political spectrum are expressing serious concerns that democracy, however you define it, is getting weaker. Many protestors in the Occupy Wall Street movement carried signs declaring that democracy is broken. The political theorist John Keane (2009) has gone as far as to write about the "death of democracy." Other scholars have focused on what they call the growing "democratic deficit" (Norris 2011; Zweifel 2002). This term has been coined to capture the sense that democratic institutions have grown less responsive to popular influence and that citizens are becoming disenchanted with and disconnected from political institutions. A variety of evidence supports these concerns.

For example, in addition to falling voter turnout rates across most **Western** democracies, the number of people joining political parties has also been declining for decades (Whiteley 2009). Formal democratic institutions appear to be less meaningful than they once were in the eyes of citizens. When growing numbers of people turn away from society's core institutions of democracy, it raises questions about the legitimacy of the democratic system as a whole. A variety of explanations have been offered for the apparent cynicism of the electorate, ranging from the "horse-race" style mass-media coverage of politics in which complex issues are reduced to a sports-like account of winners and losers (Cappella and Hall Jamieson 1997) to the increasingly negative election campaigns waged by politicians themselves, who defame their opponents and replace political disagreements with contending claims to morality and upstanding character (see, for example, Kahn and Kenney 1999).

Laxer (2009) suggests that one reason large numbers of people feel alienated by electoral politics is the enormous sums of money that are spent campaigning for office and lobbying politicians. In his words, twenty-first-century democracy "is morphing into plutocracy"—or rule by the wealthy—"a system in which the power of wealth and money plays an ever-increasing role in determining political outcomes" (p. 102). Individuals and groups without access to massive resources to support campaigning and lobbying can reasonably ask what influence they can expect to have within a political system in which wealth matters so much. Other activists go further, rejecting the very legitimacy of Western democracies by pointing to "the brutal history of occupation and genocide of Indigenous peoples that **settler societies** have been built on" (Walia 2011).

We believe that addressing these and other problems in the practice of contemporary democracy requires developing the democratic imagination. There is general agreement among radical activists and mainstream politicians alike that democracy is in trouble. Our main argument in this book is that in order for democracy to be reinvigorated and raised to new heights—regardless of where you come down on the political spectrum—people need to be able to see it freshly in relation to their own expectations, aspirations, and actions.

Activist and historian of black liberation Robin D.G. Kelley (2002) writes, "the dream of a new world ... was the catalyst for my own political engagement" (p. 3). Our hope is that reopening some key debates about what democracy means and what it might look like in the future will help you to develop your own dreams of a better world. Not all democratic dreams will look the same, but starting a conversation about what these dreams might look like can help clarify the nature of current political problems and assess what might be done about them. Imagination alone will not change the world; but it is an essential part of deliberate action intended to improve the ways that human beings live together. Of course, reflection on our democratic aspirations leads quickly to debates, as people map out different visions of what is possible and desirable.

Debating Democracy

The idea of democracy in a country like Canada or the United States with long-established forms of representative government can seem at once perfectly obvious (as everyone already know what it looks like) and horribly obscure (as it quickly breaks down into complicated disputes). This book uses two key frameworks—official democracy and democracy from below—as contrasting lenses on the current state of democratic theory and practice. We do not believe that a neutral descriptive approach to questions of democracy is either possible or desirable. We, the authors of this book, have views about questions of democracy, as do you, the readers. One way for discussion and debate about democracy to rise above the "bickering" mentioned previously is for participants to be more rigorous in understanding the ways their views on particular issues are founded on sets of conscious or unconscious assumptions about human nature, the environment, and societal structures. The use of these frames in this book is designed to help readers become more cognizant of where they stand on certain questions and, perhaps more importantly, to reflect on why they might hold those views. Frank Cunningham (1987) makes an intriguing point when he says that there are different "degrees" of democracy (pp. 25–55). However, this phrase risks implying that there is such a thing as pure democracy, against which all existing and imagined forms can be measured. Rather than providing a spectrum that measures "more" or "less" democratic models, our frames are used to help you reflect upon the fact that what counts as democracy in the first place is defined differently depending upon the perspective from which you approach the question.

For many readers, the "official democracy" framework will be most familiar. It is the way democracy tends to be portrayed in the most powerful political, educational, and communications institutions in **liberal** democracies such as Canada, Chile, India, or the United States (see Chapter 2 for a fuller discussion of the term "liberal democracies"). In the official frame, democracy is seen primarily as a form of government—one marked by the election of representatives and by specific rights and freedoms such as freedom of the press, freedom of speech, and the rule of law.

The "democracy-from-below" perspective will likely be less familiar to many readers. It is associated with political and social movements that seek to radically change the world. In this framework, democracy is not about being governed but rather about achieving a society based upon the active, collective self-government of all members. Despite the vitality of the democracy-from-below tradition, even the most hopeful and devoted activists from this perspective acknowledge that real people power rooted in genuine equity has yet to be accomplished. This lack of accomplishment raises questions both about the democratic character of the political and social institutions that qualify a country as "a democracy," in the official sense, and about how "realistic" it is to work toward establishing more radical models of democracy.

In practice, democracy often takes different forms even within the two main frames. For example, with respect to the official framework, different countries use different electoral systems, and officials follow different processes for making and enforcing law. Social movements working within the democracy-from-below frame have different critiques of society and employ different organizing techniques to change the world. Although we recognize the significance of differences in form, our goal in this book is not to detail the various forms democracy has taken or might one day take. Instead, our core mission is to open up debates about the meaning and practice of democracy by comparing the fundamental points of contrast between these two opposing frames of democracy. We believe that debates will be richer through comparing the official-democracy frame, in which rule by the people is practised through achieving mass consent to be governed over, and the democracy-from-below frame, in which rule by the people is practised through efforts to achieve mass self-government. In the chapters that follow, we generally present the more familiar "official" framework first and then critique that perspective "from below," to cast issues of democracy in a different light that opens up important questions.

OFFICIAL DEMOCRACY

The official version of democracy, the one that is taught in schools and by government agencies, focuses on a particular form of administration in which "the people" elect representatives who have specific decision-making powers (such as presidents, congresswomen, members of parliament, senators, and so on). We deem this version of democracy "official" as it is fundamentally government policy, treated as part of the expected knowledge of all citizens. Students are required to learn it in school, while immigrants who seek to become citizens must learn this official version of democracy as part of the process of naturalization or attaining citizenship. This is not to say that official democracy is unchanging but rather that change occurs within specific parameters based on a commitment to government as the guarantor and protector of the dominant social order.

The citizenship test that immigrants to Canada or the United State must pass as part of the process of naturalization assesses their knowledge of the official version of democracy, among other things. The study guide to help people prepare for the test in Canada is called *Discover Canada*. The guide describes Canada as "a constitutional monarchy, a parliamentary democracy and a federal state" (Government of Canada 2011b: 3). The workings of parliamentary democracy are more fully described: "the people elect members to the House of Commons in Ottawa and to the provincial and territorial legislatures. These representatives are responsible for passing laws, approving and monitoring expenditures, and keeping the government accountable" (Government of Canada 2011b: 28). A similar study guide for those seeking to become citizens of the United States contains similar concepts, though in the specific language of the American presidential and congressional system (US Citizenship and Immigration Service 2011). In both cases, the fundamental principles of democracy are presented as being rooted in the selection of representatives who will act on behalf of the people.

While immigrants seeking to become citizens must learn the official view of democracy through the naturalization process, people raised within the country are exposed to the official version of democracy not only through popular representations of it in television and movies but also through the school system: for example, in the civics education course that was made compulsory in all high schools in Ontario in 1999 (Schweisfurth 2006). A core goal for that course is to teach students "the fundamental principles of democracy and of active, responsible citizenship" (Ontario Ministry of Education 2005: 4). The core principles that are taught in the course reflect the existing constitutional and institutional arrangements that shape government in Canada, focusing on representative democracy in which the people elect politicians to office and then hold them accountable through subsequent elections.

The approved textbooks used in Ontario's required civics education courses identify democracy with the practice of voting. In the words of one textbook, "The democratic method gives each individual equal input into decisions through a vote" (Ruypers and Ryall 2005: 4). This orientation around voting is tied to a specific sense of politics as "a human activity in which one individual or group opposed to another mobilizes support to obtain power to govern" (Ruypers and Ryall 2005: 5). Thus, while "democratic governments make decisions based on the will of the people" (Ruypers and Ryall 2005: 7), normally, it is through electing individual representatives that the people have their say.

The official view thus casts democracy primarily as *a form of government*. Within the official frame, one frequent way of defining democracy is by distinguishing it from authoritarianism. The contrast between authoritarian and democratic regimes includes several dimensions. It begins with the attitude toward opposition: "In contrast to authoritarian governments, democracies tolerate opposition" (Ruypers and Ryall 2005: 7). It also includes a "free press" as opposed to a "government controlled press," "two or more parties" rather than "one party" and "equal legal rights" not "unequal legal rights," reflected in "courts free of political control" not "courts under political control" (Ruypers and Ryall 2005: 7–8).

The official version of democracy includes the rule of law, grounded primarily in citizen consent and not coercion. "Most Canadians obey laws because they respect the government and their fellow citizens, not because they fear the police" (Ruypers and Ryall 2005: 10). The role of coercive police and military power in a democracy is "to arrest lawbreakers and to preserve public order if it is threatened" (Ruypers and Ryall 2005: 10).

Finally, the official view of democracy includes the commitment that the power of the majority must be tempered by guarantees of minority rights. Democracies based on majority rule "have not always treated minorities well" (Ruypers and Ryall 2005: 13). Therefore, "majority opinion must not always triumph, especially if it might crush the rights of minorities" (Ruypers and Ryall 2005: 13).

Required civics classes address high school students as citizens in formation, who must be taught the principles of official democracy to find their place within it. The exercise of citizen power is central to democratic government, and "civics is the study of how to use that power effectively and responsibly" (Ruypers and Ryall 2005: 10). There is an assumption in civics education that sound knowledge is a prerequisite to democratic participation. Indeed, this premise is at the core of the official view of democracy. Education is seen as crucial to pump up responsible participation in the system. Rudyard Griffiths argues that "lacklustre civic participation" in Canada would be addressed if students were required to "pass a civics literacy test to receive their high school diploma—specifically the recently enhanced and expanded version that newcomers to Canada must take to become citizens" ("How to redesign" 2011: A8). Compulsory civics education ensures that citizens are taught a particular official version of democracy during a critical period of their political development.

Although required citizenship education through civics classes is relatively recent in Ontario, it dates back to the early twentieth century in the United States. This new mode of education was introduced in response to the rise of nationalism associated with the Spanish-American War and World War I, a large wave of immigration from new sources (primarily southern and eastern Europe), and a sharp growth in radical (**socialist**, **anarchist**, and **feminist**) movements driven by militant protests (e.g., strikes). These threats to social order led to a rise of "Americanization programs that ... demanded outward signs of loyalty and social cohesion" (Butts 1978: 185). At the same time, a social, reform-oriented, progressive movement sought to increase civic engagement, encouraging democracy education among some of the disenfranchised (immigrants, white **workers**, women) though not others (African Americans). Civics education thus combined a set of values ("Americanism") with practical skills to promote engagement. Richard Battistoni (1985) describes these dual goals of citizenship education:

> Citizens need to possess the cognitive skills and abilities necessary to responsibly participate in democratic politics. In addition, the right and freedoms accorded in a democracy make it especially imperative that democratic states teach citizens the public responsibilities that go along with democratic rights, as well as the moral and cultural foundations which bind the political order together. (Pp. 3–4)

The textbook *Magruder's American Government*, originally edited by Frank Magruder, appeared in 1917 as part of the emergence of the new civics education in the United States and is still revised annually. A note before the preface of the 1975 edition said, "*American Government*, first published in 1917 ... is an enduring symbol of the author's faith in American ideals and American institutions" (McClenaghan 1975: iv). Note that, from the very beginning, the very first edition of the book reflects a commitment to a specific set of American values.

At the same time, there is a commitment to the development of foundational knowledge for citizenship. "As were each of its fifty-seven predecessors, this edition is based upon the conviction that it is absolutely essential that *all* Americans know and understand the nature of the American system of government." The book emphasizes "the supreme and fundamental characteristic of that system: the fact that government at *every* level in the United States is government *of* the people *by* the people, and *for* the people" (McClenaghan 1975: v).

The book holds up the American system as a global ideal: "We are proud, too, that our system of government is, and has been for generations, the envy of other peoples the world over" (McClenaghan 1975: 5). Others have tried to emulate this system, but "none of them has lasted for so long a time nor been developed on such a scale" (McClenaghan 1975: 5). Certainly, there are debts to previous experiments in England and Athens, but American democracy is held out as the sustainable gold standard. Of course, Canadian civics education, though introduced later, is also nationalistic in its framing of democratic government (see Richardson 2005).

In *Magruder's,* democracy is defined by the fact that "supreme political authority rests with the people. The people hold the sovereign power and government is conducted only by and with their consent" (McClenaghan 1975: 11). Consent is a lower standard for popular power than active self-rule, as it is about willing and informed participation in a particular process but not about the design, selection, or collective self-management of the process itself.

The official-democracy frame guides a great deal of research in political science aiming to identify which countries are democracies and which are not. For example, in their classification scheme, Alvarez et al. (1996) define democracy as "a regime in which some governmental offices are filled as a consequence of contested elections" (p. 4). According to Lenski's (1966) definition, democracies must include both free and fair elections to government office, as well as the protection of political liberties that allow for organized opposition, such as freedom of assembly and free speech. Although these sorts of definitions use slightly different language, what they have in common, and what defines the official-democracy frame, is the assumption that democracy is primarily about a system of government whose authority is based on the majority of the population's consent to being governed.

There is considerable dispute among political scientists about existing models of democratic government and the extent to which they meet criteria for popular consent. The American political scientist Robert Dahl (1989) has developed the term "polyarchy" to distinguish the election-based form of government from "a 'higher' stage of democracy" (p. 223). We have not used his technical language in this book, but we do recognize that there is much debate about the limitations of official democracy and many possibilities for improving its practices.

Democracy is presented in the official view as a characteristic of particular states in the contemporary world and not others (for example, Canada but not Burma, the United States but not North Korea). Of course, even this characterization is contested. Both sides in the **cold war** claimed to be defending democracy (Macpherson 1965). Indeed, North Korea's official name is the "Democratic People's Republic of Korea," and its official ideology is called the "Juche Idea," which "means, in a nutshell, that the masters of the revolution and construction are the masses of the people" (Democratic

People's Republic of Korea 2011). Clearly, the Canadian and North Korean governments have very different views of democracy, but in neither case are the people seen as direct participants in key decision-making processes. In the view of one influential strand of official democracy, "governments are elected on the understanding that they will have a nearly free hand in governing as they see fit" (Cunningham 2002: 126).

In the official view, then, democracy looks like election-campaign signs and buttons, conventions, candidates' debates, documents outlining constitutional rights, motions passing in legislative assemblies, public opinion polls, and media coverage of issues as they develop. At the same time, it is the judge in the courtroom, the police officer on the beat (to serve and protect), the idea of equality before the law, and a "free" (that is, not state-controlled) media system. In many quarters, this view of democracy has developed into common sense, perhaps even coming to seem as though it is the natural way of doing democracy (see Chapter 6). It tends to be shared by politicians of all parties, the powerful media outlets, the judicial system, the schools, and other authorities.

The official view of democracy seems fairly uncontroversial once you have been taught it. In a large and complex society, it seems obvious that the only efficient way to administer things is to select a small number of representatives who are granted decision-making powers through election to specific positions (Catt 1999). Thus, being ruled over and being democratic are equated, provided we have some role in the selection of who will rule. Equality exists as long as everyone has the same rights and minority rights are protected.

DEMOCRACY FROM BELOW

The official version is, however, a fairly limited version of rule by the people. There is another sense of democracy, in which the people exercise effective power themselves rather than simply participating in the choice of who will govern over them. The historian Howard Zinn said in his film *The People Speak*: "Democracy does not come from the top, it comes from the bottom ... The mutinous soldiers, the angry women, the rebellious Native Americans, the **working people**, the agitators, the antiwar protestors, the socialists and anarchists and dissenters of all kinds—the troublemakers, yes, the people who have given us what liberty and democracy we have" (quoted in Le Blanc 2010). During the height of the Occupy protests in 2011, a newspaper columnist in the UK wrote, "democracy has broken out" (Graeber 2011). He saw the movement's rejection of the existing political system, its deep dedication to collective self-government, and its willingness "to stand firm against the state's inevitable violent response" as the latest steps in the long and uneven history of democracy from below.

The writer and activist Hal Draper (1974) distinguishes official democracy—"which stops with governmental forms and does not extend to the 'social question'"—from "popular control from below," which works toward "the democratization of socio-economic life" in general (p. 121). Draper's suggestion is that democracy from below is dedicated to transforming human relations in all areas of society, including schools, the workplace, and personal relationships.

This version of democracy is sometimes briefly discussed in textbooks and then generally dismissed as impractical in large and complex societies (see, for example, Weale 2007). Because Dahl (1989) considers himself a champion of "the maximal achievement of democracy and its values" (p. 322), his dismissal of the democracy-from-below perspective is especially relevant. In Dahl's words, a society based on collective self-government in the interests of all "has never existed in historical times ... and try as hard as I may I can discover no way by which it could be made to exist in the foreseeable future" (p. 323). In other words, concludes Dahl, democracy means government from above. "A world consisting only of very small and highly autonomous political units is out of the question. Countries requiring large-scale governments are bound to exist" (p. 322).

Certainly Dahl and others believe that citizens have a crucial role to play in democratic society. Indeed, there is an important tradition of discussions about "participatory democracy" that emphasizes the active role of citizens, though generally within an overall frame of consent to being governed. Catt (1999) defines participatory democracy as a "distinct form of decision making" (p. 39). The dominant view within the official-democracy perspective defines political participation narrowly as "those voluntary activities by citizens that are intended to influence the selection of government leaders or the decisions they make" (Mishler and Clarke, quoted in Dyck 2008: 258). One of the core arguments is that participatory democracy is limited by the scale of contemporary societies. The critical political scientist Benjamin Barber (1984), who develops a comparatively strong version of participatory democracy, assumes that "a form of government in which all of the people governed themselves in all public matters all of the time ... could hardly be expected to function efficiently in a nation of continental proportions with millions of citizens" (p. xiv).

By contrast, we use the term "democracy from below" to refer more expansively to processes of self-government that are based on the establishment of popular power in all areas of life. Wald's (1992) from-below conception of democracy urges people "to participate in the political movements required to organize and cohere struggles for the self-emancipation of humanity" (p. 219). Chomsky (2011) articulates his view more simply:

"It's basically a skepticism about any form of authority, or domination, or submission." If these can't be justified, Chomsky says, "then they should be dismantled. And that covers everything from personal relations to international affairs" (p. 237). The scholar and activist bell hooks (2000) suggests that feminism is a crucial part of broader struggles for liberation because "it is necessarily a struggle to eradicate the ideology of domination that permeates Western culture on various levels, as well as a commitment to reorganizing society so that the self-development of people can take precedence over imperialism, economic expansion, and material desires" (p. 26). Ness and Azzellini (2011) point to the recurring appearance of "workers' councils and self-managed enterprises" over the past 150 years in all parts of the world in arguing that "instances of workers' control have often enlivened activists' imaginations and raised new possibilities for the democratic organization of workplaces and of communities" (pp. 2–3). Democracy from below is driven by that familiar activist slogan: another world is possible.

Unlike the official version, there is no fully formed example of democracy from below just sitting there to be used as a model. Activists from this perspective embrace Anthony Arblaster's (1987) argument that "democracy is still 'unfinished business' on the agenda of modern politics" (p. 99). They argue that full democracy is a long way from being accomplished, though there are some examples of moments when this kind of democracy flourishes, generally in periods of insurgency when large numbers of people are demonstrating, striking, or occupying spaces that are not normally under their collective control. The American sociologist Frances Fox Piven (2006) argues that, in the United States, "the mobilization of disruptive power" in strikes, demonstrations, riots, boycotts, and other tactics by huge numbers of "ordinary people" is what won the country's most cherished of democratic advances, including "political participation in government, the end of chattel slavery, and the right to unionize and to social welfare protections" (p. 21). Those who focus on democracy from below see it as a potential that is present whenever people get together and act on the world: "power from below is there for the taking" (Piven 2006: 26). The core of democracy from below is direct decision making by those who will be affected by choices about how to organize social life. This does not mean that democracy from below imagines a future society free of all problems (Chomsky 2011: 238; Eagleton 2011: 64–106). It means that problems are addressed within a system based on a more expansive conception of freedom, voluntary association, and collective self-government.

Clearly, democracy from below is not merely about the form of decision making or the style of government but about the control of all aspects of life by the participants. The democracy of Athens in ancient Greece provides an instructive example of this direct control. The origins of the word "democracy" that describes democracies we know today lie in a specific form of self-rule that developed in Athens for a period of time more than 2000 years ago. In order to provide some context for contemporary debates, it is worth taking a moment to reflect upon the unique conditions in which Athenian democracy emerged.

Athenian democracy emerged in a society that was predominantly agricultural, meaning that the greatest source of sustenance and wealth was in the cultivation of land. The largest single **class** of the population consisted of peasants, who worked on the land but did not own it, and therefore were required to turn over a "tribute" (portion of their production) to the nobility who were the landowners. Athens was therefore a **tributary** state in which a small class of aristocratic landowners ruled society, extracting a portion of what was produced by those who worked the land as tribute for access to it (Wolf 1982).

This transfer of wealth from the direct producers, those who worked the land, to the aristocracy who controlled it took different forms. In the case of slavery, the landowner directly owned the slaves and commanded all of their production. Of course, at least some small proportion had to go back to the slaves to keep them alive, as it is a fairly obvious requirement of any system based on living labour that those who do the work must be given at least the most basic level of sustenance to stay alive.

In contrast with slaves, the bodies of peasants were not directly owned by landowners. However, because the nobility controlled the land, peasants were compelled to hand over a part of what they produced in order to gain access to it. This system worked in very different ways in particular settings, ranging from serf relations in which the producer was bound to work a particular piece of land and was not free to move through to systems that taxed peasants, compelling them to hand over a particular portion of what they produced to the landowner.

The role of the state in these tributary relations was crucial. It is hard to imagine a situation in which the people who work on the land voluntarily hand over a portion of what they produce to some member of the nobility living the good life in the big house or in town. Rather, "tribute is extracted from [the direct producer] by political or military means" (Wolf 1982: 80).

In most tributary states throughout history, the aristocracy was the only group of people that held formal decision-making power, so aristocrats exclusively and directly controlled the apparatus of government. However, in ancient Greece and Rome, the peasants obtained certain political rights as citizens (Wood 1995: 188). These rights went furthest in Athens, where the peasants rose up to take over the effective control of the state through a system of *rule by the people.* The state controlled democratically no longer used its political or military power to force peasants to hand over tribute to the landowners. Athenian democracy provided peasants with the means to resist the extraction of tribute, and to control the results of their own productive work (Wood 1995: 202).

This freedom did not apply to slaves, who were not citizens and could not resist tribute extraction in the same way. Indeed, in the face of peasant resistance expressed democratically, landowners sought their tribute primarily from the work of slaves who constituted roughly 20–30% of the population (Wood 1995: 185). Athenian democracy, which excluded slaves and women as citizens, is clearly no ideal model to emulate. But it does provide a powerful example of democracy as insurgency, a popular uprising seeking to place political and economic power in the hands of the masses. "The Athenian citizen claimed to be *masterless,* a servant to no mortal man" (Wood 1995: 204).

Central to the idea of democracy from below is the struggle to be master-less, to escape from being ruled. Over the past 200 years, various anarchists, socialists, radical feminists, Black Power activists, and others have proposed different ideas about what a society based on *not being governed* would look like. Despite differences among these perspectives, they tend to share the view that self-government is ultimately about "dismantling mechanisms of rule while winning ever-larger spaces of autonomy" in which people collectively control their own lives (Graeber 2002: 68). To be masterless is a very old idea, and, indeed, most human societies over time have lived without rulers. Hunter-gatherer societies that lived off the harvest of nature (including many indigenous cultures in what is now North America) and simple horticultural societies in which people did basic planting but did not turn the soil were broadly organized around mechanisms of general access to productive resources and sustenance combined with methods for shared decision making (discussed in Chapter 5). Unequal class societies in which a small layer dominates access to the **key productive resources** and centralizes power arose relatively late in human history, though they are now generally dominant.

Official democracy could be understood as a way to administer unequal class societies, while democracy from below actually challenges their limits. But it is not quite that simple, as the two streams often coexist in a contradictory way in actual movements for change. The struggle for "democracy" in reality has often included vital strands of official and from-below perspectives, sometimes deeply interconnected. Indeed, the accomplishment of official democracy can be seen as a real, if limited and contradictory, step in the direction of achieving democracy from below.

The rise of official democracy, for example, tends to be dated back to the American **Revolution** of 1775–1783 and the French Revolution of 1789–1799 (which we discuss in Chapter 3). While these revolutions did produce new forms of administration, they grew out of insurgent situations in which the people took over the streets with demands for access to power (see Chapter 3 of Piven 2006 for a description of the revolutionary situation in early America).

George Rudé (1964) argues that the French Revolution was just one crucial example of the insurgent crowd, the predominant form of militant activism by employees, artisans, and rural peasants from roughly the 1730s to the 1840s in France and Britain. The crowd engaged in riots, often immediately addressing the sources of injustice by "breaking windows, wrecking machinery, storming markets, burning their enemies of the moment in effigy, firing hayricks, and 'pulling down' their houses, farms, fences, mills or pubs, but rarely by taking lives" (Rudé 1964: 6–7). After the 1840s, the impact of **industrialization** and the gains of previous rounds of activism in these countries made possible new forms of organization, such as the trade union and the political party or formation (e.g., anarchist, labour, or socialist), and consolidated emerging forms of protest (e.g., the strike, the general strike, the legal demonstration).

The uprisings of the crowd did not develop with clearly defined goals or a precise program but rather out of rage against injustice often triggered by a specific event. In France and Britain, the character of insurgency began to change as ways of work and life shifted because of widespread industrialization and the gradual expansion of political rights resulting from earlier activism. The "crowds" fought their way into democracy—but did not necessarily win the robust democracy they sought.

The revolutionary wave of 1917–1927 saw democracy from below and official democracy often emerging side by side in what was called "dual power." This term refers to "a situation in which the oppressed create an alternative center of popular power, one based around mass democratic assemblies and/ or workers' councils in opposition to the sites of ruling class power—the government, the army, and the courts" (McNally 2011a: 165). Throughout North America and Europe, official democracy took the form of elections to parliamentary or congressional bodies, while the more insurgent democracy emerged in various types of workers', soldiers', sailors', and neighbourhood councils composed of delegates from workplaces, military units, or geographic communities (see Eley 2002, especially Section II).

As we discuss in Chapter 3, a new wave of radical movements emerged in the 1960s. It focused largely on the limits and exclusions of official democracy, including colonialism, discrimination, and economic **marginalization**. The language of participatory democracy was associated with these new forms of activism. This language challenges the limits of existing forms of democracy based on representation. The massive global movement of the 1960s and early 1970s was associated with a commitment to expanding dramatically the creative input of all people into key social decisions and to democratizing all areas of life.

One of the defining features of democracy from below is the celebration of insurgency. The act of collective protest itself contains the seeds of a more democratic world (McNally 2006). The British art critic, author, and activist John Berger (1968) has described mass street demonstrations as "rehearsals for revolution" (p. 11). The provocative phrase helps us to envision how forms of organization that people create in struggles themselves provide a glimpse of transformed **social relations**. For example, as we describe later in this chapter, the organization required to sustain protest against an authoritarian crackdown in Egypt in 2011 created new relationships and provided a workshop for the development of new capacities. The question about whether new capacities developed in moments of insurgent mobilization can

---

EXERCISING YOUR DEMOCRATIC IMAGINATION
Promising the World

When the Occupy Wall Street movement emerged in the fall of 2011, it was widely criticized for lacking clear proposals for social change. Politicians and media pundits repeatedly asked, "What do these people actually want?" When protestors said they demanded participatory democracy, an end to corporate greed, and more responsible stewardship for the environment, critics responded that these proposals were either too vague or unrealistic.

One of the key differences between the official-democracy and the democracy-from-below perspectives is the kind of social change each proposes. Official democracy favours incremental change: small, gradual shifts within the existing democratic framework. Major political parties may emphasize different policy priorities and propose slightly different tweaks to the tax system, but they all agree that change must happen within the existing democratic frame. As we discuss in Chapter 2, this fundamental assumption imposes strict limits on what kind of social change is possible to imagine and work toward.

By contrast, democracy-from-below activists who demand total social transformation do not restrict their proposals to new government policies or revising mechanisms of rule. They seek instead the radical reconfiguration of social relations in ways that cultivate self-government throughout all areas of life. Because these are proposals to develop political, social, and economic relationships that do not yet exist, they are much more difficult to describe in detail. Subsequently, activists and scholars in the democracy-from-below tradition often face criticism for not formulating clear and realistic demands.

How does "realistic" politics frame your understanding of official democracy and democracy from below?

What "unrealistic" demands might you support?

be turned into sustainable forms of social organization in the contemporary world with large, complex societies is certainly one that we will engage in this book.

In practice, democracy has never existed exclusively in the pure form of either *official democracy* or *democracy from below*. It has always been produced in part through struggles from below; but these struggles have been constrained by official political and economic institutions, as well as by dominant cultural norms. Life within actually existing democracies, therefore, is contradictory. There are forces pushing the official democratic order deeper into society, yet there have always been contending forces from below resisting this trend and pushing for a different democratic future.

Making Democracy in the Twenty-First Century

The opening up of the question of democracy seems to be taking place in practice in the second decade of the twenty-first century. Consider the wave of popular uprisings that swept across North Africa and West Asia in 2011. Countries that had long suffered under brutal dictatorships suddenly saw millions of people risking their lives by taking to the streets to demand greater freedom and a better life. It was a massive struggle for democracy. But there were heated debates about the meaning of the uprisings and the best ways for them to move forward. These debates are easier to understand and therefore to contribute to if we recognize the role played in them by competing assumptions about what democracy is.

The massive protests started in Tunisia after a 26-year-old street vendor named Tarek el-Tayeb Mohamed Bouazizi lit himself on fire to protest the lack of economic opportunities under the corrupt government of Tunisian dictator Zine el-Abidine Ben Ali. Bouazizi's act of desperation, which for so many Tunisians encapsulated painful but familiar feelings, inspired huge numbers of people to band together and fight in open battle against the Ben Ali regime. People described losing their fear, and masses pushed back against the government's violent response. Within a month, the popular uprising had achieved its primary goal: Ben Ali fled the country on January 14. The dictatorship had fallen.

In the opening months of 2011, similar protests broke out in Egypt, Jordan, Yemen, Algeria, Libya, Bahrain, Syria, and other countries, all of which had also long suffered under repressive dictatorships and poor economic conditions. The people of Egypt were the next to overthrow their dictator. The Egyptian activist Mostafa Omar estimates that "between January 25 and February 11 at least 15 million people out of a population of

80 million—more than 20 percent of the population—took part in the mass demonstrations and mobilizations that forced [President Hosni] Mubarak. to resign" (Omar 2011).

The Egyptian protests were centred in Tahrir Square in Cairo, the capital city. The square was the "nerve center of the Revolution" in which the massive crowd engaged "in direct decision-making, sometimes in its hundreds of thousands," to establish processes needed for building the struggle against the government (McNally 2011b). Inside Tahrir, people with medical know-how helped to establish temporary hospitals to treat sick and wounded protestors. Others helped to establish childcare centres and day schools for young people. Food distribution centres were set up to make it easier for people bringing food into the square to share it widely, and a jail was formed to house the thugs who were caught attacking the protestors. In Omar's (2011) words,

> When you walked across Tahrir Square you saw throngs of poor workers, poor peasants, struggling government clerks; you saw poor housewives who fight every day in order to keep their children somewhat fed and alive; you saw thousands of disabled people on crutches and in wheelchairs ignored by the government for decades; you saw thousands of retirees who cannot afford meat and even certain kinds of vegetables; you saw men and women, Muslim and Christian. All of these groups came to participate, came to support and to protect the youth against the regime's crackdown. (Par. 4)

From the perspective of Omar and many others, these uprisings provide a sterling example of democracy from below: insurgent populations taking power with their own hands. Yet, through the lens of official democracy, the very same uprisings look like the spread of rational and effective democratic administration.

In 2011, US President Barak Obama delivered a speech on the Middle East that supported the uprisings in the Arab world, which he saw as bringing new nations into the reach of official democracy. Many Western leaders, including President Obama, did not fully support the demands of revolutionaries until it was clear that the balance of power had shifted decisively. However, once substantive change became imminent, President Obama argued that Egypt and Tunisia could "set a strong example through free and fair elections; a vibrant civil society; accountable and effective democratic institutions; and responsible regional leadership." He said that the role of American foreign policy should be to support these developments, and the United States was one of several Western nations that sent money and military force in an effort to shape events in Libya. Indeed, the prime minister of Great Britain said that, although the Libyan people want a new democratic future, "the Libyan people cannot reach that future on their own" (Cameron 2011).

The goal of Western leaders is to produce a particular model of nation-state meeting the criteria of official democracy. Thus, in Obama's words, "even as we promote political reform and human rights in the region, our efforts cannot stop there. So the second way that we must support positive change in the region is through our efforts to advance economic development for nations that transition to democracy" (Obama 2011).

Obama's views align with those of economists such as Mancur Olson, who argues that the conditions needed for capitalist growth "are exactly the same conditions that are needed to have a lasting democracy ... the same court system, independent judiciary, and respect for law and individual rights that are needed for a lasting democracy are also required for security of property and contract rights" (quoted in Lynn-Jones 1998). From this perspective, then, the push for democracy in North Africa and West Asia is inevitably also a push for the development of more fully **neo-liberal** capitalist economies.

Moreover, a report published by the Belfer Center at Harvard University argues that, in addition to making life better for people in other parts of the world, "spreading democracy also will directly advance the national interests of the United States, because democracies will not launch wars or terrorist attacks against the United States, will not produce refugees seeking asylum in the United States, and will tend to ally with the United States" (Lynn-Jones 1998). The revolutionaries in Egypt, Tunisia, and other countries did not frame their democratic dreams in terms of enhancing the international profile of the United States of America. However, from the perspective of official democracy in the United States, this effect is indeed a core potential part of the 2011 uprisings. Debates about the results of the revolutions have also emerged, with some arguing that the path to mass liberation remains open despite the troubles faced by movements from below and others arguing that a democratic society is actually less likely to take shape in the immediate future because of the conflicts that have opened up.

The process of sorting through these interpretations and arguments and deciding which ones are more persuasive becomes easier when thinking is guided by the frameworks of official democracy and democracy from below. These frameworks don't decide political disputes in a machine-like fashion, taking information in at one end and popping out answers on the other. However, they can help to reveal the hidden elements of events and debates in the real world and, therefore, make it possible to identify patterns of thought within the different sides of an issue. In this respect, these frameworks are tools that help broaden the democratic imagination.

Reopening Democratic Debates

The career of democracy over the past 250 years has seen it pass from a subversive and scary idea to the taken-for-granted system of government in large parts of the world. C.B. Macpherson (1965) argues that democracy has gained "full acceptance into the ranks of respectability" (p. 1). With this respectability, democracy as it is practised in nation-states today is becoming naturalized: made to seem as though it is the only option, the natural outgrowth of history. The problem when existing democracy is naturalized is that it frames our vision and limits our ability to think and act in ways intended to change the present state of affairs. This book is written with the fundamental assumption that there is a danger when the democratic imagination becomes rigid or contracts.

It would be difficult to argue that life in democracies today is universally satisfying. Growing numbers of people are losing their jobs, living in poverty, and turning away from the institutions of official democracy. To seriously challenge the naturalization of official democracy—to question whether democracy can become more equitable and politics more inclusive—requires reopening some of the fundamental debates around what democracy is, discussions that have been narrowed in recent decades.

To reopen the democratic imagination, each chapter in the book focuses on a basic democratic concept and raises questions about the various ways in which it has been interpreted by political observers and activists from different political perspectives. Chapter 2 focuses on questions about what aspects of life ought to be governed democratically. It examines debates over where the limits of democracy should be drawn in relation to political, economic, and social activity. Chapter 3 describes key historical moments in the development of citizenship in order to ask questions about the ways in which this basic unit of democratic government both includes and excludes. Chapter 4 highlights debates about the tensions between representation and participation in democracy. Chapter 5 examines the sprawling power of bureaucracy in contemporary democracies and compares two contrasting interpretations of the role of the state. Chapters 6 and 7 discuss the role of knowledge and bodies in democracies. Embodied experience and ways of knowing the world are not topics typically found in textbooks on democratic government, but we believe that they are essential parts of more expansive conversations about what democracy means today and how it might develop in the future. Chapter 8 offers some concluding integrative reflections on how thinking about the debates in the previous chapters can help to reopen the democratic imagination.

In introducing some of the key issues and debates related to democracy, we have tried to make the book both accessible and engaging. Our tone is more conversational than what you'll find in traditional textbooks, and the evidence we draw on throughout this book comes from a variety of places: scholarly writing, popular culture, political journalism, and personal experience, for example. We take this approach in the hopes of shining light upon the multidimensional character of important issues that can seem flat if approached in a different way. We also believe that communicating clearly is a crucial part of doing democracy.

The book focuses primarily on the contemporary experiences of official democracies in the **Global North**, and particularly in Canada and the United States. The goal of the book is to open up the question of democracy in places where it is regarded largely as closed because it has already been established. We do this in part by examining both the historical development of those forms of democracy and the experiences of popular power in different places in the world. Neither the historical nor the global accounts here are comprehensive, and we do not claim that a fully inclusive story of democracy is possible in this book.

In contemporary democracies, government can easily seem distant and unresponsive, the terrain of expert politicians, bureaucrats, and academics. One of the aims of this book is to suggest that democracy is broadly relevant in ways that are not always clear on the surface of everyday life. This book will have achieved its main goal if reading it helps you reflect upon the ways in which your own life is already embedded in democratic politics—and on what is at stake in how democracy is defined. You will be the one to decide what to do with the growing power of your democratic imagination.

2 POLITICAL, SOCIAL, AND ECONOMIC DEMOCRACY

Democracy is often seen as a form of government, an alternative to dictator-ship or **absolute monarchy**. A democratic government is characterized by elections, the rule of law, and certain protections for citizens' rights, includ-ing freedom of speech. If the government of a specific state meets these standards, then it is classified as "a democracy." And democracy is seen as so important that it is worth dying for—the idea that military service is largely about personal sacrifice for democracy having become a central feature of contemporary armed forces. As President of the United States Ronald Reagan (1984) said in a speech on the 40th anniversary of the D-Day landing on the beaches of France during World War II, "One's country is worth dying for, and democracy is worth dying for, because it's the most deeply honorable form of government ever devised by man" (par. 13). Indeed, the willingness to die for one's country is seen as one of the central responsibilities of citizenship in the official conception of democracy.

Yet, even in "a democracy," there are many areas of life that do not seem to be governed by even the most basic features of people power. The idea, for example, that employees should elect management seems ridiculous in the context of most workplaces, and freedom of speech for employees, such as the entitlement to criticize management, does not exist. Workplaces are basically dictatorships, though they are certainly regulated by employment law standards and human rights codes established by governments. The employer rules without seeking any mandate from the employees. Similarly, students do not elect their teachers or professors or the administrative managers of schools, colleges, or universities. They do not participate in decisions about what will be taught and how learning will be assessed.

At first glance, it might seem quite natural that standards of democracy should apply only to practices of government and not to other of life's arenas, such as workplaces, schools, families, personal relationships, or organized sports. As we will see, some analysts argue that the sphere of government has its own dynamics, making it uniquely suitable for democratic practices. It is also likely that many of us are quite simply used to the official conception of democracy as a political system in which people willingly give their consent to be governed over. The expectations people have are framed by the existing social relations they live in day to day, as well as by the way these relations get explained by friends and family and authorities such as politicians, teachers, or media pundits.

In this chapter, we will look at the limits of actual existing practices of democracy, highlighting debates on the meaning of these limits. The official view of democracy that we described in Chapter 1 tends to characterize these limits as necessary and logical. It assumes that the best mode of governance is achieved through efficient public administration directed by democratically elected leaders and through meritocratic rule in other areas of life. In contrast, advocates for democracy from below tend to see these limits as a sign of an incomplete project of popular power and seek to extend collective self-government into all areas of society. We want you to assess whether you really live in "a democracy" and to reflect on what criteria must be met to classify a given place or institution as democratic.

Democracy as a Form of Government

In general, the official view takes for granted the idea that democracy is a form of government based on the consent of the governed. This perspective is characterized by the definition of democracy as "that form of government in which the sovereign power resides in the people as a whole, and is exercised either directly by them (as in the small republics of antiquity) or by officers elected by them" (OED Online 2011). In this model, the power in a democracy is vested in the people, who then exercise it either directly or through electing leaders (the common practice in modern times).

The democratic form of government has specific characteristics that extend beyond choosing leaders through election. Victor Sebestyen (2011) spelled out key aspects of democracy in discussing what was missing in the post-Soviet transition in Russia, which falls short of democratic ideals: "In Russia today, there is no concept of loyal opposition, no separation of powers, no mass participation in political life and a news media that is far from free" (par. 15). Democracy, then, is a form of government characterized by elections in which the opposition accepts the legitimacy of the ruling party or group; in which the power of those who make the laws is separate from those who enforce them; in which people make their mark on the political system by joining parties, campaigning at election time, joining protests, and signing petitions; and, finally, in which the press is "free" to criticize the government and investigate issues. David Beetham (2005) summarizes the three "main institutional features of a working democracy" as follows: "the framework of basic citizen rights, the institutions of representative and accountable government, and the associational [or community-oriented] life of civil society" (p. 42).

Within the official view, the applicability of democracy to the realm of government does not mean that democracy is necessarily appropriate in other areas of life. Albert Weale (2007) writes that government is "a significantly distinct institutional realm" and claims that "it is simply intellectually confusing not to distinguish issues that arise in the practice of government from issues that arise from other practices" (p. 21). The sphere of government is unique: it shapes the public realm in which all private interests intersect and common interests are forged. Yet, in other areas of life, private interests and personal conscience shape action. It would be wrong, in the view of official democracy, to organize decision making in these realms according to the same principles that govern the public sphere.

Rather than assuming that democracy is the suitable mode of administration for all areas of human life, Weale argues that people need to take into consideration the particular conditions in which democratic procedures fit:

> Participatory democracy in, say, the university need carry no implications about the form of democracy in the nation-state in the absence of any special argument to show how the former could be a model of the latter. Conversely, democracy in the nation-state need not imply, again in the absence of special argument, democracy in the workplace or the church.... Unless we wish to say that members of churches whose government is non-democratic cannot be good political democrats, we have to acknowledge that arguments about the principles of government do not have straightforward application to other spheres of activity and vice versa. (Weale 2007: 22)

Democracy might not be applicable in all areas of life within the official view, but it is seen as the preferable form of government in a modern society.

Democracy is considered the best method to achieve the administration of our common affairs through the state because the people can use elections, free speech, and certain legal and human rights to have a say in the way they are governed. Indeed, it is a central premise of the official view that the market or capitalist society works best when it is paired with democratic government.

Democracy and Capitalism

In the official view, **capitalism** is the only economic system compatible with democratic government based on the principle of rule by the people. In the words of the Austrian economist Friedrich Hayek, "If 'capitalism' means here a competitive system based on free disposal over private property, it is ... important to realize that only within this system is democracy possible" (quoted in Berger 2002: 13). The freedom of the individual, which democracy both requires and promotes, is thought to find its economic match in democratic capitalism, an economy in which the bulk of goods and services are bought and sold on the free market. Political freedoms, in the sense of democratic rights, and economic freedoms, in the sense of unconstrained market participation, are limited only by how much money individuals can access. In the language of political theory, the belief that free markets and political rights are codependent is called liberalism, and a democratic government based upon the combination of individual political rights and a free market economy is called a **liberal democracy**. Myers (2010) explains that, from the point of view of liberal democracy, "markets are the exemplary realms in which the free development of each is the condition for the free development of all" (p. 49).

It is logical, therefore, that in the foreign policy of a liberal democracy like the United States, the spread of capitalism and democracy are seen as two sides of the same coin. After the United States invaded Iraq in 2003, President Bush argued that bringing capitalism to the Middle East would create democracy: "Free markets will defeat poverty and promote the habits of liberty" (quoted in Youngs 2003). The philosopher Robert Dahl has said that "it is an historical fact that modern democratic institutions ... have existed only in countries with predominantly privately owned, market-oriented economies, or capitalism" (quoted in Stimmann Branson 1991). The most radical pro-capitalist activists have criticized even limited government policies to redistribute wealth (such as an unemployment insurance program) "as an instrument of political repression" (Callaghan 2000: 44). This perspective essentially equates market practices with democracy, seeing the choice between goods for sale as a fundamental freedom and a core basis for real democratic participation.

Yet the relationship between capitalism and democracy is not simple or causal. Capitalism does not cause democracy to rise, nor does democracy inevitably lead to capitalism. There is no automatic association between democracy and the market economy, as capitalism has proven to be compatible with fascism and other forms of dictatorship while democracy has been a feature of anarchist and socialist experiments. There are lots of examples of market economies thriving in the absence of liberal democracy. China is perhaps the most important of the contemporary examples: there, a one-party state has led the transition from a bureaucratic, state-controlled economy (which some might label "socialism") to a market economy, as will be discussed further.

Although democracy and capitalism are not inevitably linked, we can discern, in the modern age, a clear historical relationship between the spread of market economies and the development of democratic political systems, though this relationship is a bit more complex than some advocates of the official view might suggest. The political theorist C.B. Macpherson (1965) argues that the historical relationship between democracy and capitalism broke down into two distinct phases: first, the rise of the liberal state compatible with the market economy and, second, the democratization of the liberal state. The liberal state, which emerged first in Europe, ended the monopoly on key economic and social activities that was exercised by the nobility in the old absolute monarchies.

In the system of absolute monarchy, the nobility had tremendous control over economic activity. To begin with, nobles had a lock on most of the land, which is where the bulk of the wealth that built their great houses and palaces originated. Of course, the land itself did not generate wealth; that came only when peasants worked it and handed over a portion of what they produced to the landowners.

The nobility also tended to have great influence on other areas of economic life. Nobles could levy various taxes and tolls on all who crossed their lands, meaning that they influenced trade. Royal monopolies were granted in key areas of exchange, so that, for example, the Hudson Bay Company was a private corporation granted the unique right to trade furs in the British colonies of North America.

The opening up of the market economy, which would give individuals greater access to land and wealth previously controlled by the state, required the end of the monopolistic political and economic power of the monarchy and nobility. In some cases, these changes were accomplished by overthrowing whole political systems; in other cases, they were achieved through rapid reforms that ultimately undercut the basis of monarchical and noble power. The regimes that consolidated a new form of state to support the burgeoning market economy tended to be non-democratic, either authoritarian or based on a highly restricted franchise, meaning that only a small proportion of the population could vote. Indeed, these early liberal states feared democracy, as they were concerned that real power in the hands of the masses would threaten the unequal power structure of the emerging capitalist order. They were liberal inasmuch as they gave individuals the right to control their own wealth and property, but the principle of popular power had not yet taken root.

In Germany, for example, the conditions for the liberalization of the economy were introduced in rapid and brutal form by an authoritarian bureaucratic state under the direction of Otto von Bismarck who ultimately became the first chancellor of the unified German Empire. The old nobility remained in control of the state apparatus in this period, but nobles were forced by competitive pressures to create the basis for a more fully capitalist economy. As Colin Mooers (1991) argues, "we can only fully appreciate why Bismarck's violent reordering of the state was an imperative forced upon the Prussian state ... if we understand that the competitive compulsions of the world market and military competition between states set definite limits on ruling-class choices" (p. 141). Democratization in Germany came only later, as the people who were excluded from power gradually fought their way in, most importantly through the uprising of workers, soldiers, and sailors in 1918–1923, which overthrew the monarchy and effectively ended German participation in World War I.

In this view, democracy was "forged" from below, through a massive 150-year struggle for economic, social, and political rights (Eley 2002). Popular struggles for inclusion (such as the women's suffrage movement and the African American civil rights movement) broadened the base of democracy. Yet the liberal basis of the state—private control over key productive resources—was consolidated, even as the franchise expanded. The result was liberal democracy, the combination of the capitalist-oriented liberal state with the democratic form of government. C.B. Macpherson (1965) argues that the character of democracy changed through this process: "Democracy has been transformed. From a threat to the liberal state it had become a fulfillment of the liberal state" (p. 10).

This process of economic liberalization followed by democratization (or, at times, associated with it) seems to be ongoing. An important example of its continuation is the period from 1974 to 1995, when a large number of countries adopted democratic forms of government. These included the former Soviet-bloc countries that had operated as one-party bureaucratic states and had described themselves as "communist," as well as several countries that had been governed by right-wing dictatorships, including countries in Europe (Portugal, Spain, and Greece), South and Central America (Argentina and Chile), and Asia (South Korea and the Philippines). This trend toward the adoption of democratic government was often explained in terms of the spread of market relations and the maturing of capitalism.

Prezworski (1991), however, argues that the transition from dictatorship to democracy is not automatic, even where a market economy might be developing. Indeed, emergent democracies are fragile and must be consolidated so that "politically relevant forces subject their values and interests to the uncertain interplay of democratic institutions and comply with the outcomes of the democratic process" (p. 51). This compliance will not happen if the state structures are serving the narrow interests of some, either those who control armed force or those who control the key economic resources: "The strategic problem of transition is to get to democracy without being either killed by those who have arms or starved by those who control productive resources" (Prezworski 1991: 51).

Mission Accomplished?

One of the boldest statements about this spread of democracy and the apparent maturation of capitalist relations was the American political scientist Francis Fukuyama's (1989) declaration of the "end of history." Fukuyama argues that the spread and deepening of capitalist relations in combination with the global extension of democratic rights created a situation in which fundamental disputes about the character of society were outmoded. He argues that the end of the cold war and the fall of the Soviet bloc marked "an unabashed victory of economic and political liberalism" (Fukuyama 1989: par. 2). This victory does not mean that all political dispute will vanish but that the fundamental realm of disagreement will be narrowed to questions of how to improve the functioning of the market economy and how to best administer the democratic state—or how to foster the development of a liberal economy and political system in those places where these were not yet established.

> What we may be witnessing is not just the end of the Cold War, or the passing of a particular period of postwar history, but the end of history as such: that is, the end point of mankind's ideological evolution and the universalization of Western liberal democracy as the final form of human government. (Fukuyama 1989: par. 4)

Certainly conflicts were possible, but there could be no fundamental historical alternative to democracy and the market economy. In the period since he wrote his original article and the book that grew out of it, Fukuyama has continued to hold to this view, though he now sounds less triumphant. In a 2011 interview about his most recent book Fukuyama says,

> That's one of the things that is in this book that wasn't in my original book—the possibility of political decay. I don't think there's any particular reason why, if you are a liberal democracy, you can't decay. Your institutions can get too rigid; your ideas can get too rigid. (Fukuyama, quoted in Moss 2011: par. 7)

The "end of history" thesis does not provide a simple map to triumph, however. Indeed, the increasing inequalities in the period since the 2008 economic slump present serious challenges to liberal democracy and the market economy:

> It is much easier to run a democracy and a capitalist economy that produces inequalities if you have long-term growth because, even if it's not evenly shared, at least everybody is benefiting down the road. Without growth you return to a … world where it's more zero sum. One person gets rich at the expense of another person, and then it becomes much harder to maintain democracy. (Fukuyama, quoted in Moss 2011: par. 10)

Nonetheless, Fukuyama sees only one track for the future development of government: that of liberal democracy (which includes market capitalism). If the train seems to be veering off the tracks, the only sensible goal is to do our best to get it heading in the right direction. In this model, there is a deep connection drawn between the freedom of democratic participation by the population (or at least those who have the vote and other rights) and the economic freedom to invest, trade, and market goods. The "free" circulation of goods in the marketplace and the political freedoms associated with liberal democracy are seen as ideal complements.

In summary, Fukuyama views the long political phase unleashed by the democratic revolutions of the 1600s to 1800s to have ended about 200 years after the French Revolution with the final victory of democratic government and the market economy. These same events can, however, be interpreted very differently using another lens. One challenge to this perspective is that it seems to reduce the rise of liberal democracy to a single story in which capitalism and democracy develop in complementary forms in parts of Europe and North America and then permeate the rest of the world, whose best option is to emulate that model.

Yet, in reality, there seem to be different models of capitalist development, governed in a variety of ways depending on circumstances. China, for example, is becoming a capitalist economic superpower while being administered by a one-party state run by the Communist Party. Democratic participation is highly constrained, but that is not impeding the explosive growth of market capitalism. Although leaders of Western democracies have at times noted concerns about human rights in China, these modest criticisms have not stopped Western governments from actively pursuing stronger trade and economic relations with China's authoritarian government. Fending off charges that Canada is allowing its economic interests to override democratic values, a Canadian government official explains, "It's critical for our success going forward as a country, economically, to engage with one of the world's most important and fastest growing economies" (Leblanc 2011: par. 6). The human rights group Amnesty International has raised similar concerns about the British government's approach to China. In 2010, Kate Allen, the group's United Kingdom director said, "It is unbelievable that the largest UK government delegation to China in a generation will put trade before human rights" (Amnesty International 2010: par.2).

Indeed, China's role in the world economy is increasing dramatically with no indication that substantial political reform is on the agenda. In the global slump that began in 2008, the Chinese economy has been the high point of global capitalism. As an article in *The Globe and Mail's Report on Business* states,

> The great recession was China's chance to shine. The Asian economic superpower led the world out of the downturn, as its breakneck growth sparked global recovery and helped Europe and North America get back on track. (Marlow, Hoffman, and Ebner 2011: par. 5)

Any simple equation between capitalism and democracy is certainly challenged when one of the leading economies is in a place where there have been few signs of democratization. China has seen some important worker resistance over the past number of years, but, although some wage gains have been won, there has been little or no change at the level of democratic rights. Kellee S. Tsai (2007) counters the analysis of many who argue that democracy must be on the agenda in China given the spread of capitalism, noting that the economy is thriving and the employers are happy: "Remarkably, most entrepreneurs generally think the system works for them" (p. 3).

At a more general level, the history of political and economic development in the **Global South**, sometimes called the **Third World**, does not seem to show a simple connection between democracy and capitalism. As we discuss in Chapter 3, democracy expanded in many places in the Third World through anti-colonial national liberation struggles, often imbued with a distinctly anti-capitalist orientation. The character of these struggles makes sense in light of the fact that capitalism had been introduced by brutal colonial or neocolonial regimes, generally without any trappings of democracy. Gordon (2010) explains that the colonial powers of the nineteenth and early twentieth centuries (such as the United Kingdom, France, Germany, Belgium, and Italy) relied upon "a profound belief in their racial superiority" to justify "the ruthless exploitation of the labour and environment of the Third World" (p. 46). However, he notes that, although contemporary colonial powers "may not be commonly justified through recourse to such explicitly racist or crude formulations as those of the classical age," the people who live in the Third World continue to be portrayed as being "unable to care for themselves, and thus responsible for their own poverty and seemingly endless internecine violence" (Gordon 2010: 47). Sherene Razack argues that this racist world-view helps us understand why Western countries continue to believe in "the need to and the right to dominate others *for their own good,* others who are expected to be grateful" (quoted in Gordon 2010: 47).

The intensification of sharp inequalities within and between nations has been the reality of capitalist expansion in the Global South, and that has often been associated with brutal authoritarian regimes, not liberal democracies. Capitalism has been spread globally through the development of powerful transnational corporations generally headquartered in the Global North, along with a specific world order enforced either directly through military intervention or indirectly through the support of client states beholden through commercial agreements, military treaties, and arms sales. Samir Amin (1993) argues that the lack of democracy in many Third World nations was "neither an accident nor a holdover from their 'traditional culture.' Democracy here is incompatible with the needs of capitalist expansion" (p. 61). Capitalism, in short, impeded rather than nurtured democracy in much of the Global South. McNally (2006) explains how Western governments and financial institutions have used their money-lending power "to compel Third World government[s] to adopt pro-western economic and social policies" (p. 227). In contrast to serving as genuine allies committed to nurturing local control over land and resources, Western governments and businesses have used investment and debt as "weapon[s] with which to systematically discipline the Third World" (McNally 2006: 226).

In the Third World, the pressure for democratization has come largely from below, particularly in the form of national liberation movements. The birth of independent Third World nations was often associated with great hopes for a more just alternative to capitalism. As Vijay Prashad (2007) writes, "The Third World was not a place. It was a project" (p. xv). That project was one of anti-colonial national liberation, which would lead to a new alignment independent of both the imperialist West affiliated with the United States (the "first world") and the so-called "socialist" bloc affiliated with the

Union of Soviet Socialist Republics (the "second world"). This new political and economic arrangement, this new world, would be founded on principles of justice. The aspirations of many of these movements were for "social equality, self determination and internationalism" (Bannerji 2011: 12). Yet the democratic and transformative promise of the Third World project was largely unfulfilled due to two main factors: first, the dominance of the capitalist global economy, fully backed by military power, and, second, the role of specific state-formation strategies pursued by political elites in the Third World (Prashad 2007). These strategies were founded upon pro-capitalist economic policies that often benefited the ruling classes and frequently included an emphasis on ethnic nationalism.

Democracy Domesticated

The idea of democracy has undergone a long voyage since the 1600s, from a scary and subversive idea that haunted those in power to a safe and efficient system of rule embraced by politicians of all stripes, as well as employers and managers. In undergoing this journey, the conception of democracy reflected in the official frame has become much narrower. Whereas democracy was once associated with struggles for genuine people power based on expansive notions of liberty, equality, and comradeship, it now more commonly describes a system of government in which the leadership is elected. Democracy has been tamed, and, in the process, people power has been reduced to consent to being governed.

Adam Prezworski (2010) attributes this trajectory to the narrow conception that animated the revolutionary vision of democracy: "Although democracy in the second part of the eighteenth century was a revolutionary idea, the revolution it offered was strictly political" (p. 85). The project of democratic transformation was "blind to economic inequality, no matter how revolutionary it might have been politically" (Prezworski 2010: 85). However, he believes the non-revolutionary version of democracy that has emerged historically is the best form of self-government we can achieve.

The practice of competitive elections, in which it is actually possible to replace those in charge, is a fundamental accomplishment of liberal democracies. As Prezworski (2010) writes, "That is why, in spite of all the ideological and real transformations, I see contemporary democracies as an implementation of the ideal of self-government of the people" (p. 168). The narrowing parameters of official democracy have "made this ideal more coherent and more honest" (Prezworski 2010: 168).

From this viewpoint, democracy cannot and should not be extended beyond its pragmatic limits. This necessary limitation of democracy is partly due to the character of market economies in which there are "purely technical, perhaps inexorable, limits to economic equality" (Prezworski 2010: 169). It is also due to the limits on the everyday political engagement of citizens. Not all citizens are equally positioned to take part in political processes, and, often, "the calls for increased participation privilege those who have more resources to participate" (Prezworski 2010: 169). Prezworski argues that we do better to recognize the limits of self-government than to bristle against them. Certainly citizens can exhort democracies to do more, but the idea of a fundamental deepening of democracy throughout all areas of life is simply not practical, however attractive the ideal might seem. Indeed, it risks the democracy we have to aspire to drive it deeper. Prezworski (2010) concludes: "We should be aware of the limits because otherwise we become prey to demagogical appeals, which more often than not mask a quest for political power by promises that cannot be fulfilled by anyone anywhere" (p. 171).

Accepting democracy's restricted nature does not mean being uncritical of the limits capitalism might impose on democracy. Advocates of **social democracy**, associated with political parties such as the Labour Party in Britain, the Social Democratic Party in Germany or the New Democratic Party in Canada, have argued that, although a capitalist economy has the potential to enhance democracy, when left unchecked, it actually threatens universal human development. Therefore, although capitalism is compatible with democracy, it must be closely regulated. Responding to the rising human misery brought on by the 1970s deregulation of the postwar economy, Marquand writes,

> Either democracy has to be tamed for the sake of capitalism, or capitalism has to be tamed for the sake of democracy. The capitalist market is a marvelous servant, but for democrats it is an oppressive, even vicious master. The task is to return it to the servitude which the builders of the postwar mixed economy imposed on it, and from which it has now escaped. (Marquand, quoted in Berger 2002: 32)

The goal of social democratic reformers is to seek improvements to workers' lives by working within the capitalist system (Callaghan 2000). The purpose of government would be to "compensate for the defects of even the most responsible market system" (Socialist International Declaration of principles, quoted in Myers 2010: 72). As long as there were mechanisms in place to ensure that public representatives would determine the overall shape of the economy, capitalism and democracy could coexist, even benefit from each other.

Democracy Unleashed

In contrast to Prezworski's argument that we accept the limits of official democracy, there are those who argue for pushing beyond those limits and pursuing new levels of democratization. This argument is founded on the premise that capitalism—no matter what form it takes—will always undermine democracy. From this perspective, which is aligned with the view from below, achieving true democracy requires throwing off the capitalist system and developing an economy based on democratic principles whose purpose is the fulfilment of human needs, not the accumulation of private profit. In the words of Ellen Wood (1995), "the greatest challenge to capitalism would be an extension of democracy beyond its narrowly circumscribed limits" (p. 15).

In a capitalist society, vast areas of social life are outside of public control. The tools, natural resources, and information that go into making all the things societies need to reproduce themselves are privately owned. This private ownership means not only that the rewards of production and innovation are controlled by a small group of people but that decisions about what will be produced and how are made by individual owners whose main interest is their own profitability, not the enhancement of human life. According to Magdoff and Sweezy, "We have the productivity and the resources, in fact, to produce all that would be needed to eliminate poverty and provide everyone with fuller and richer lives" (quoted in Broad 2011: 68). Poverty persists around the world because of the way priorities are developed under capitalism, not because of any lack of productive potential.

Consider the ways in which the natural environment is being destroyed in the process of turning ever-greater profits. There is no great political movement in favour of environmental degradation; no one—not even the oil executives—want to see the planet destroyed. And yet food and other goods come encased in absurdly over-packaged containers, forests are clear-cut, species are destroyed, and poisons are pumped into the sea, all because doing so helps to accumulate profits. It is as though we have no control over the consequences of our own actions. Profit-driven innovation is presumed to have a mind of its own; yet we know that it "will tend to gravitate toward the sectors of an economy with the greatest profit potential. Plastic surgery techniques, for example, have advanced far more quickly than has the development of high-quality, low-cost housing" (Myers 2010: 64).

Wood (1995) argues that this way of organizing society is inherently undemocratic. The fulfilment of the promise of democracy therefore requires that capitalism itself be challenged. One articulate voice arguing that democracy is a promise as yet unfulfilled is that of the Polish/German revolutionary Rosa Luxemburg. She argues that democracy in capitalist societies, which she refers to as "bourgeois democracy," is an incomplete project. Socialists, explains Luxemburg, should not reject democracy, even in its stunted "bourgeois" form, but instead argue for its completion:

> We [socialists] have always distinguished the social kernel from the
> political form of bourgeois democracy; we have always revealed the hard
> kernel of social inequality and lack of freedom hidden under the sweet
> shell of formal equality and freedom—not in order to reject the latter
> but to spur the **working class** into not being satisfied with the shell....
> (Luxemburg 1918: chapter 8, par. 3)

She argues that radicals must take democracy seriously, and she was critical of the ways it was curtailed in the Soviet Union after the Russian Revolution of 1917. She shares the revolutionary **Marxist** convictions of Russian revolutionaries such as Lenin and Trotsky but expresses concern that they were undervaluing the importance of self-government in the transition to **socialism**:

> Socialist democracy is not something which begins only in the promised
> land after the foundations of socialist economy are created; it does not
> come as some sort of Christmas present for the worthy people who, in the
> interim, have loyally supported a handful of socialist dictators. Socialist
> democracy begins simultaneously with the beginnings of the destruction
> of class rule and of the construction of socialism. (Luxemburg 1918: chapter 8, par. 4)

This relationship of capitalism and democracy draws on the idea that capitalism is an economic mode characterized by profound social inequality, rooted in the exploitation of the majority of the population by a small minority. The analysis of capitalism as a system of exploitation is the core task of Karl Marx's book *Capital*. Marx's framework for explaining why true human freedom is impossible under capitalism has inspired generations of activists and scholars, and even his critics have noted that "his works are useful for thinking about [the] ... age-old tension between the power of wealth and 'people power'" (Pitkin 2004: 341). Here we will trace out the core of Marx's argument in *Capital*.

In Marx's analysis, capitalism is distinguished from economic relations in other class societies by the way exploitation takes place, not by its absence. The characteristic of all class societies is that the producing class must not only do enough work to keep itself going but also create a surplus over and above its subsistence—a surplus it hands over to those in power. As described in Chapter 1, in a **tributary mode**, the production of surplus took a few different forms. Sometimes peasants or slaves were given their own land on which to produce the goods they needed to sustain themselves and their families, in exchange for working on the landowner's fields. Other times, peasants or slaves had to hand over a certain amount of their harvest to the landowners and then were allowed to keep some for their own subsistence.

At first glance, it may not be obvious where the surplus comes from in a capitalist society. Indeed, capitalism is distinguished from tributary modes of production in that the worker is free, the owner of his or her own body. The employer and employee are formally equal to one another, and the workers are paid wages to cover the day's work. It is easy to look at this system and see it as one of free and equal exchange rather than exploitation.

But Marx argues we need to push a bit deeper. Workers in capitalist society are in fact "doubly free": on the one hand, they are owners of their own bodies, and, on the other, they are "free" of any ownership of the means of production (i.e., the fundamental resources required to transform nature to produce what people want and need, such as patents, assembly lines, mines, earth movers, or land). Thus, under capitalism, workers are obligated to sell their capacity to work for a wage to someone who owns the means of production.

Marx pushes further to try to figure out how the relationship between workers and employers could look like a free contract between buyers and sellers and, at the same time, have an exploitative character. He traces this disconnect between appearance and reality back to the most basic rules of exchange in a capitalist society. The price of goods in a capitalist market economy is not completely arbitrary, nor is it simply the product of supply and demand. Rather, he argues, all commodities (goods produced for exchange on the market) are evaluated on the basis of the measurement of a single common ingredient present in all human products, a given amount of labour time (minutes or hours of work). Marx refers to the amount of socially necessary labour time present in any commodity as its "value."

If every commodity exchanges at its value, based on the socially necessary labour time it contains, then it is not immediately clear how profits are generated. Marx answers this dilemma by pointing to the one commodity that can be purchased at its value and yet continue to add value to the process of production— labour power, the human capacity to work exchanged on the market for a wage to cover a specific period. The wage represents the value of labour power, the cost of keeping the worker alive. Yet workers add more value during the working day than they receive in wages. The source of profits is this surplus value: the value over and above the wage workers add through their labour. Employees working an eight-hour day, for example, might add value equivalent to their wages over a six-hour period and then continue to work for another two hours, which constitutes a surplus that goes to the employer.

Capitalists have no choice but to use profits as the basis for building up their capital. The competitive system pits them against other capitalists, each attempting to use new technologies and the reorganization of work to drive down the quantity of labour power in their products and therefore to be able to undercut each other in terms of prices. Those who do not reinvest, constantly seeking leading-edge processes, will find themselves marginalized, unprofitable, and ultimately driven out of business. Marx (1976) writes in *Capital*, "Accumulate, accumulate! That is Moses and the prophets!" (p. 742).

Companies that dominate the market, as General Motors did in the North American car market until the 1970s, can suddenly find themselves in a vulnerable position, facing competitors who can sell better products more cheaply. Even worker-owned cooperatives have to keep up in this cycle of

---

EXERCISING YOUR DEMOCRATIC IMAGINATION
The Principle of Equality

A system of government based upon *rule by the people* reflects the modern belief that all humans are equal in some essential manner. "Democracy has been described as a political response to the logic of equality" (Myers 2010: 95). However, the nature of human equality and how it should be nurtured is a point of deep disagreement.

The official view of democracy seeks to achieve equality through citizenship rights and a market-based economy. Equality is achieved through ensuring that all citizens have the same right to participate in the political process (through voting, running for office, or exercising their right to free speech) and the same right to buy and sell goods and services on the market. From this point of view, "the market is simply a field of opportunity in which to search for the necessary resources with which to pursue subjectively held interests" (Myers 2010: 49).

The democracy-from-below perspective also believes in the importance of equal freedom, but it argues that achieving this aim will not happen through the combination of formal political equality through citizenship rights and market mechanisms. It emphasizes that, in reality, *inequality* is the prevailing condition in modern democracies. The existence of these kinds of systematic inequalities suggests that the framework of official democracy has not succeeded in fulfilling its democratic promises. In fact, critics from this perspective argue that people don't even have equal opportunity because wealth and power are so unevenly distributed in reality. Substantive inequality is the norm in modern democracies precisely because of how the market economy favours those with greater wealth and resources.

The Occupy movement of 2011 used the language of "the 1%" to describe the tiny elite that benefits from the existing order, as opposed to "the 99%" whose situation is worsening.

How could the decisive power in a democracy rest with the 1% rather than the 99%?

profit making and reinvestment, essentially exploiting themselves to remain competitive. The goal of profit is not primarily to satisfy the personal greed of employers (albeit, that is not irrelevant) but to reinvest to keep the firm competitive within the terms of the capitalist system.

Thus, capitalism is fundamentally a system of exploitation. It reproduces substantive inequality (such as that between workers and employers) through mechanisms of formal equality that establish the same legal rights for buyers and sellers of labour power. Democracy in a capitalist society is thus limited to preserving a system fundamentally rooted in exploitation and in the endless predation of the natural environment to produce growth. It is only through extending democracy beyond the political realm and into the economic realm that a more just society can develop. Under capitalism, the working class, which includes most people, is excluded from ownership or control of the key productive resources in society. Only when the working class takes over those resources and administers them collectively and democratically in the interests of all can the limits of mere political democracy be transcended.

Genuine democracy, then, requires that the alienation central to capitalist social relations be overcome. In his early works, Marx argues that humans are distinguished as a species by our capacity for conscious action on the world. Humans alone make deliberate choices about transforming nature to meet our wants and needs. Yet, in capitalist society, most people do not control the key productive resources (factories, offices, tools, patents) and thus must sell their capacity to work to those who do, which means being alienated from our human potential to be fulfilled by acting purposefully on the world. The worker in this situation of alienated labour "does not affirm himself but denies himself, does not feel content but unhappy, does not develop freely his physical and mental energy but mortifies his body and ruins his mind" (Marx 1977: 71). Alienation, in this sense, can only be overcome by a robust democracy extending into every area of life, so humans can collectively make choices about how we organize ourselves to meet our wants and needs.

Democracy as a Practice of Everyday Life

DEMOCRACY @ WORK

At first sight, the idea of democracy at work seems almost funny. It is far removed from the actual practices in the workplace, where the bosses rule even if their mode might vary from consultative to autocratic. Yet democratic workers' control has long been an aspiration of socialist and anarchist movements that embrace the idea of democracy from below. Indeed, it is a recurring theme in workers' activism whenever people get confident enough to go beyond relatively narrow trade unionism aimed at developing and defending decent work conditions and wages. As Ken Coates (1964), a long-time advocate of workers' control in Britain, writes,

> Whenever the Labour movement is able to abandon the defensive postures which have regrettably come to seem "normal" during long stretches of its history, and whenever, then, it begins to step over the borders of its allotted prerogatives, one begins to hear again the noise of argument about workers' control. (P. 69)

Standard collective agreements since the 1940s often include clauses specifying management rights and excluding discussion of workers' control from union negotiations. The normalization of collective bargaining after World War II in Canada, for example, legally recognized unions as the bargaining agent for workers but, at the same time, regulated the process so as to outlaw immediate direct action at the shop-floor level as problems arise or secondary strike action in support of other workers on the picket line. The unions, as David Camfield (2011) argues, became legally responsible for restraining workers from action outside of a specific window in which strikes were legal:

> Workers could legally strike only as part of bargaining for their own contract, and not over disputes that arose during a contract, in solidarity with other workers, to support a political demand on the government or to pressure the employer to recognize their union. (P. 70)

Management rights clauses became a core feature of collective agreements, recognizing limits on what could legitimately be negotiated by workers. Coates (1964) provides an example from an agreement in Britain: "The employers have the right to manage their establishments and the trade unions have the right to exercise their functions" (p. 69). A management rights clause, then, is designed to separate the collective organization of workers from democratic control of the workplace. It delimits the realm within which workers and management negotiate, excluding fundamental questions about what is produced and how that takes place.

This delimitation of the realm of trade unionism has been around for a while, and it now seems natural. It was established through a series of battles in which the realm of trade unionism was narrowed through negotiations with management. These negotiations also occasioned serious disputes within unions, between clusters of more militant and more conciliatory workers with contending visions for contract negotiations and union activism (see Dollinger and Dollinger 2000 for one record of some of these struggles in the automotive industry). Yet despite the establishment of "management rights," the use of the collective power of workers to attempt to reshape the workplace democratically has re-emerged in periods when workers gain confidence through increased combativeness. In the 1970s and 1980s, workers in British military plants worked on strategies to redeploy their plants toward other, socially useful, areas of production. They did not succeed, but their efforts raise issues about democracy and the workplace.

At first glance, workers' control might seem like Utopian dreaming of the first order, so far is it from current workplace practices. Yet the idea of workers' control in fact emerges organically from actual workplace experiences under capitalism. Because of the character of labour processes, each worker develops a rich knowledge of her or his specific job, often exceeding that of supervisors and managers. For example, workers on automotive assembly lines often improvise their own tools to make the job easier. And they use their understanding of the immediate labour process to regulate the pace of work, even in an assembly-line situation, for example, by completing tasks faster than required to gain unofficial breaks. In the auto plants of the 1970s, this improvisation took the form of "doubling up": workers took turns doing two jobs at once so another worker could grab some unofficial time off (Glaberman and Faber 1998: 108–11).

To maintain control over the workplace, managements try to harvest the knowledge of workers or to redesign work processes to undercut the skills workers develop doing their jobs. Harry Braverman (1974) argues that an important impetus toward the scientific management methods associated with the rise of mass production and the assembly line was the reduction of workers' discretion to make decisions in performing tasks, which separated the conception of the work process (the task of management and process engineers) from its execution (by workers). This process of deskilling attempts to reassert management control over the workplace in the face of workers' tendencies to take some degree of control over jobs they know better than anybody.

In other words, there is an ongoing struggle over control of the workplace between management and workers, not only in factories but in white-collar sectors too (see Smith, Knights, and Willmott 1991). One of the key features of management power is that managers alone have the big picture, an understanding of the process as a whole, while each worker has ongoing access to only his or her own work and immediate surroundings. The democratic combination of workers, however, offers opportunities to pool knowledge and develop big-picture perspectives. Worker control emerges as a possibility as workers radicalize in large numbers, as they deepen their critiques of the present system and take activism to a new level.

Workers' democratic control has been a recurring theme when workers begin to challenge the power of the employer and the state on a mass level. Workers have taken over production and restarted it under their own collective and democratic control during the Russian Revolution (1917), in mobilizations in Germany and Italy around the same time (1918–1920), in the uprising against Franco's attempt at a Fascist takeover of Spain (1936), and in the mass movements for democratization and against state "socialism" in Hungary (1956) and Poland (1981). As James Rinehart (1987) writes, "At each of these historical moments, working people replaced, or attempted to replace, centralized, authoritarian structures of feudal, party or class power with democratically organized bodies to regulate workplaces and communities" (p. 198).

The collective and democratic control that workers establish has tended to fade when normal times return and mass insurgency de-escalates as a result of either management concessions or harsh defeats. There are, however, examples of sustained workers' control. Workers in Argentina took over factories that management tried to shut down during an economic crisis in the 1990s and ran them successfully. Some continue to operate under workers' control to this day.

In Spain, an early industrial cooperative began in Mondragón in 1956 and has been an important example of a sustained workers' cooperative based on fundamental democratic principles. From its origins, this cooperative has grown to become a corporation that includes a total of 256 companies and bodies, about half of which are themselves cooperatives. Each cooperative is governed by a general assembly of workers in which everyone has one vote, and management functions are delegated to individuals by the assembly, which remains the highest authority. Individual cooperatives also select delegates to send to the MONDRAGON Co-operative Congress.

Transparent access to information on behalf of all workers is a core principle, as control over who knows what is a major basis for management power in the hierarchical workplace (Cheney 2002). There is considerable debate about the sustainability of democratic workers' cooperatives in a predominantly capitalist setting, where competition can force even these organizations to adopt practices that weaken self-government. There seemed, for example, to be a decline in authentic workplace democracy at the MONDRAGON collectives, opening up debate about the sources for this shift (Cheney 2002).

These historical experiences of workplace democracy must, at the very least, open up some sort of discussion about everyday democratic practices and how far these principles can be extended. Those who argue that democracy is not practical outside of the realm of public administration need to recognize the recurrence of workers' democracy as an alternative to employer control of the workplace.

DEMOCRACY @ SCHOOL

The structure of schools and universities would seem to indicate that people are reluctant learners. Formal educational institutions use a combination of incentives and punishments to make people learn specific things in particular ways. At the most basic level, for example, schooling is compulsory and non-attendance for those under a certain age is, in fact, illegal. It is hardwired into these institutions that people must be made to learn, either through compulsion or through such inducements as grades. The forced character of learning in these institutions means that democratic practices are not integrated into their everyday operation. The experience of being a student is primarily one of being subjected to the power of others, not of participation, election, or consent.

Yet all the evidence from human experience would tell us that people are avid learners from the youngest age, deeply committed to exploring the world and developing their capacities. Indeed, people devote incredible effort to learning about those things they are passionate about, and it is actually difficult to keep them from learning. Some will spend hours shooting baskets to improve their accuracy while others will learn new languages to decode the secrets their parents are trying to keep from them by reverting to a mother tongue not used in the household. People channel tremendous energy into their political or spiritual development, and they amass knowledge about gardening, painting, classic car collecting, cooking or other hobbies from every available source.

Children devote incredible energies to learning, often through play with others. The persistent "why" question that can drive adults up the wall demonstrates a desire to make sense of experiences and come to terms with causality at an appropriate level of comprehension. The child development work of Jean Piaget focuses on documenting the ways children develop their own capacities through their work on the world. He argues that teaching denies children the chance to learn for themselves and proposes, instead, that we recognize the importance of their own work on the world:

> Education, for most people, means trying to lead the child to resemble the typical adult of his society. . . . But for me, education means making creators. . . . You have to make inventors, innovators, not conformists. (Piaget, quoted in Bringuier 1980: 27)

Formal education treats avid learners as reluctant ones and, in doing so, drains learning of important democratic elements. The classroom, for example, tends not to have a democratic character in that the key decisions are made by the teacher with no mandate from the students. The character of informal learning reminds us that another kind of education is possible, one that is far more democratic and learner driven.

The idea of democratic schooling tends to appear where radical social movements emerge on a larger scale. The 1960s, for example, saw widespread movements for free schools, student power, and the renewal of curriculum to reflect the experiences and aspirations of the historically excluded, such as indigenous peoples, women, people of colour, workers, and lesbians and gays. The free schools movement was an attempt to bring a democracy-from-below frame focusing on collective self-government and individual freedom to schooling, even of the very young. One of the model free schools was Summerhill in Britain, and its founder A.S. Neill was an articulate advocate for freedom in education:

> At Summerhill we don't try to mold children in any way. I mean, we let them live and govern themselves. It's not so easy when they're four or five years old. We don't get them till they're five or six, and then they gradually sit in the self-government meetings and talk, very often talk sensibly when they are five. Fundamentally, I think, the child must be free from the very beginning to be itself without being told how to live. (Neill, quoted in Montessori and Neill 1966: 9)

Students in Neill's school participated in general assemblies and made democratic decisions about all areas of life. Free schools based on this democratic model were established in many places. Yet there are important questions about the readiness of children to participate fully in self-government. Mario Montessori, a representative of the Montessori educational method, challenges Neill a bit on this front. He argues that children need some structure as they are learning to order reality, though that structure should not be coercive:

> [The child] starts to classify.... During a sensitive period early in life, he is attracted by nature to building such experience. If the child cannot fulfill his natural urges, he escapes into fantasy. The aim is not to stop him from escaping into fantasy, but to try to bring him back—to implement his natural urges toward coordination, self-control, intelligence. (Montessori, quoted in Montessori and Neill 1966: 7)

There are clearly debates to be had about democracy and formal education and about the practices that are appropriate. These debates are not, however, foregrounded in contemporary discussions of education, as self-government is not seen as a core feature of educational policy. In fact, schools, colleges, and universities take the forms they do in part to habituate students to operating in contexts of being ruled over, in contexts such as the workplace. Indeed, the "hidden curriculum" of getting younger people to internalize the fundamental codes of behaviour appropriate to contemporary hierarchical institutions might be more important in determining educational policy than the actual content of the classes. The hidden curriculum consists of the "non-academic but educationally significant consequences of schooling that occur systematically but are not made explicit at any level of the public rationales for education" (Vallance 1983: 11). One simple example of the hidden curriculum is the way young elementary students learn to regulate their bathroom breaks according to the timetable of classes, which prepares them for a life of using facilities only when the rhythm of work permits.

Formal schooling, then, teaches young people to manage their bodies and minds in accordance with external authority. Only secondarily do students learn about literature, math, or science. Democracy as self-government is thus marginalized within schools, even if those institutions of formal learning claim, in part, to be preparing active citizens for a life of participation.

The democratic potential of schooling is also undercut by another form of "hidden curriculum," which naturalizes social hierarchy. The knowledge taught in the classroom disproportionately reflects the viewpoint and experiences of European man, who mistakes himself for all of humanity, so that knowledge that claims to be universal is actually grounded in his position and perspective on the world (Gordon 1995: 3). The experience of indigenous peoples, for example, is presented from the point of view of the European intruders who make others knowable by bringing them into history (Wolf 1982). At the core of the formal educational curriculum is a specific set of cultural and historical tools forged in very specific times by particular groups and used as if they were universal, reflecting the experience of all "men." You might reflect back on your own education, for example, to think about the ways you learned about the "explorers" in the Americas and Africa and about whose point of view shaped the histories and literatures that you read.

When viewed from below, democratic schooling would require, then, not only a change in the practices of education that impede self-direction and collective self-government but also a decolonization of the curriculum to ensure that all have a place in the "community of learning." Inclusive and democratic education means more than adding new materials to bring in the perspectives of those who have largely been marginalized or excluded; rather, it means transforming the "core" curriculum so that it no longer consists of the experiences of one slice of humanity pretending to stand for the whole global community.

DEMOCRACY @ EVERYWHERE

The widespread development of collective self-government would transform work and school, along with a whole range of other relationships. The relationship between authority within the family and democratic participation would certainly provoke rich debates. The meaning of democracy in sexuality and intimate relationships is something that would need to be discussed. Democracy in the realm of sports raises questions about the balance between elite sports in which the best athletes compete (such as the Olympic Games) and mass participation in movement and activity for a healthier and happier population. Democratizing theatre, dance, or music might raise questions about the right of the conductor, choreographer, or director to shape collective activity around her or his own singular vision.

One place the extension of democracy is certainly an ongoing challenge is in labour and social movements to change the world. Many of these movements, though aiming for a more just world, practise democracy in only limited senses as an organizing tool. In some cases, such as trade unionism, bureaucratization can create a leading layer of "representatives" whose conditions of life, perspectives on the world, and interests begin to diverge from those of the membership as they become invested in the maintenance of the organization more than the well-being of participants (see Chapter 5). In other cases, security concerns can be used to create a secretive organizing style that excludes broader participation in decision making, as well as the messy reality of clashing world views. In yet other situations, a group of experienced people rich in knowledge and skills lead the movement without taking the time to develop similar capacities in others. This chosen leadership style can reflect mistrust in people's ability to learn and be transformed, which risks widening the gap between members and the leaders.

Thus, democracy poses challenges even in radical movements for social change. In the end, it is perhaps right that the question of how and where democracy might be practised should be solved democratically in the realm of action rather than theoretically in a book. These questions can be opened up only by challenging the naturalization of the limits of democracy in early twenty-first-century societies, pointing out that it is political settlements not intrinsic barriers that have confined democracy to the realm of government and limited its practice in other realms. That is what we have tried to do in this chapter, not to provide answers (though clearly we are not "neutral" in these debates) but to challenge you to think for yourself about what it might mean to really live in "a democracy."

3 CITIZENSHIP AND INEQUALITY

Each year the Government of Canada hands out a small number of citizenship awards. According to Canada's Minister of Citizenship, Immigration, and Multiculturalism, these awards are given to Canadian citizens "who help to nourish the Canadian story by promoting the value of citizenship to all Canadians and making a real difference in the lives of newcomers to Canada" (Government of Canada 2011a). Similar awards are given out by school and city officials to recognize people's contributions to the health of their communities. Democracies make deliberate efforts to nurture the qualities associated with good citizenship, including many educational initiatives through the school system such as civics education.

In everyday life, the term citizenship is often used in a general sense to evoke community-mindedness and social engagement. For example, university mission statements commit themselves to "supporting and celebrating ... active citizenship" (Princeton University 2011) or challenging "people to become engaged and aware citizens of an increasingly complex world" (Wilfrid Laurier University 2003). Citizenship is there in the title of newspapers such as the *Amherst Citizen* (out of Massachusetts) or simply *The Citizen* (out of South Africa). The phrase "corporate citizenship" has been coined by the business community as a way of arguing that corporations "can thrive, while at the same time make a meaningful contribution to a more sustainable future" (Corporate Citizenship Limited 2011). There is even a brand of wristwatches called "Citizen," a name chosen by the founders of the company "so it would be 'Close to the Hearts of People Everywhere'" (Citizen Watch Co. 2011, par. 1).

In addition to its popular usage, the term "citizenship" has a more technical definition in relation to existing democracy. Indeed, citizenship is the basic unit of democratic government in the official frame. Strictly speaking, being a citizen means being a formal member of a specific political community and thus having the right to participate fully in that community. For this reason citizenship tends to be associated with inclusivity and engagement. However, expanding the democratic imagination means also looking into the ways in which citizenship is about exclusion.

Citizenship draws clear lines around who is entitled to certain rights and privileges and who is prevented from accessing the benefits of membership in the exclusive political club. Border guards make this crystal clear with the first question they ask international travellers: "What citizenship do you hold?" Many activists and scholars working from a democracy-from-below perspective have argued that citizenship in a liberal democracy maintains exclusions even within citizen populations.

This chapter explores the contradictory character of citizenship. It focuses on key moments in the development of citizenship to shed light on different views of what citizenship is, how it came to take its current shape, and what it could become in the future. The views people hold about citizenship are deeply connected to their overall perspectives on democracy and its relationship to popular power. In the official frame, citizenship is an essential tool to governing with the consent of the people. Critics from below, despite often struggling for more expansive citizenship rights within existing democracies, tend also to question whether citizenship and self-government are compatible.

Membership Matters

Citizenship is the foundation of official democracy. Citizens elect governments and hold them accountable. The nation-state is a political community of citizens organized around a specific administrative apparatus. In the words of Charles Tilly (1996), it is useful to think of citizenship as "a continuing series of transactions between persons and agents of a given state in which each has enforceable rights and obligations uniquely by virtue of the person's membership in an exclusive category, a category of native-born or naturalized people" (p. 230). Citizenship status is indicated in official state documents such as birth certificates and passports. It binds citizens to the state by requiring them to adhere to various laws and regulations, and it provides them with specific rights and protections.

The constitution is the core contract of citizenship in this official view. A constitution is the "body of fundamental principles according to which a nation, state, or body politic is constituted and governed" (OED Online 2011); and the rights and duties of citizenship are often clearly laid out in a country's constitution. The American Constitution, for instance, includes the Bill of Rights that guarantees citizens "the freedom of speech ... the right of the people peaceably to assemble ... to be secure in their persons, houses, papers, and effects, against unreasonable searches and seizures," equal protection under the law, and, in the case of criminal prosecutions, "the right to a speedy and public trial, by an impartial jury" (Government of the United States of America 1791). If governments pass legislation that contradicts the basic laws set down in the constitution, courts have the authority to strike down the new laws for being unconstitutional. At the same time, citizenship involves reciprocal obligations to the state. For example, the official study guide for people applying to become Canadian citizens states, "in Canada, rights come with responsibilities. These include: obeying the law ... taking responsibility for oneself and one's family ... serving on a jury ... voting in elections ... helping others in the community ... [and] protecting and enjoying our heritage and environment" (Government of Canada 2011b: 9).

The United Kingdom has no written constitution but has established citizenship rights through a history of case law, acts of parliament, and political conventions or traditions (Turpin and Tomkins 2007). Rights protected through common law, for example, rely on precedents set over centuries of legal decisions. Citizenship rights were not a part of Canada's written constitution until the Charter of Rights and Freedoms was enshrined in Canada's *Constitution Act, 1982*. Proponents of the Charter argued for its adoption by drawing attention to how easily rights had been stripped away from Japanese Canadians during World War II. In 1941, when Canada was at war with Japan, the Canadian government imprisoned more than 20,000 Japanese Canadians and took away their homes and businesses on the grounds of "military necessity" (JapaneseCanadianHistory.net 2011). They were considered enemies of the state, not because of any actions they had committed but because of their Japanese heritage. Civil-liberties advocates argued that such gross violations of citizenship rights would have been less likely if a constitutional bill of rights protecting against unreasonable search and seizure had existed at the time.

From the perspective of official democracy, then, citizenship appears as a formal status—a relationship between citizens with equal rights and "their" state—embedded in a constitutional framework. It is acknowledged that there will be ongoing debate about the precise parameters of citizenship rights and the best method for protecting them, but, through the lens of official

EXERCISING YOUR DEMOCRATIC IMAGINATION
Minority Rights

Alexis de Tocqueville wrote about American democracy in the 1830s, from the perspective of a French visitor fascinated with the system. One of the things that concerned him was the "tyranny of the majority." He argued that a democratic majority that did not respect a minority with a different perspective could be compared to an authoritarian tyrant who assumes absolute power: "If it be admitted that a man possessing absolute power may misuse that power by wronging his adversaries, why should not a majority be liable to the same reproach?" (de Tocqueville 1835).

The question of the tyranny of the majority is made a bit more complicated by the reality that there are different kinds of minorities in capitalist societies. There are minorities defined by their opinions, such as those who find themselves in a district where they are always voting against the grain for losing candidates. Other minorities are defined by social relations of inequality, meaning that they face systemic discrimination. These "minorities" can sometimes even constitute a numerical majority. Finally, there are privileged minorities, like "the 1%" who benefit from the current economic and social relations by harvesting super profits to live with enormous wealth and power. It challenges any simple notion of the tyranny of the majority to begin to think of these different minorities and whether they should have the same rights.

Is it an attack on a minority to think of raising the taxes of the richest 1% of the population?

How can minority rights be protected in democratic situations of majority rule?

democracy, the fundamental character of citizenship is constitutionally established. As noted in Chapter 1, constitutionally protected citizenship rights are in part about ensuring that the principle of majority rule cannot be used to override the basic political entitlements of people from a minority group.

Citizenship is therefore highly valued in the official view of democracy, a great honour not to be taken lightly. It is the marker of membership in the nation, the basis of a whole set of rights and responsibilities. Although citizenship takes slightly different forms in different countries, it is generally portrayed by governments as a core institution for achieving equality, a key democratic principle. It is the institution that provides core democratic rights, including the franchise (right to vote) and freedom of speech or association.

The Limits of Citizenship

The democracy-from-below perspective opens up a more critical perspective on citizenship. To begin with, this approach identifies the limits of citizenship and current democratic practices. Ellen Wood (1995) argues that, although there is real power in citizenship freedoms and protections, that power is highly constrained. In a capitalist society, the political sphere in which citizenship rights carry their greatest force is separated from the economic sphere in which decisions are made by private owners in response to activity on the market. For example, citizenship in a nation guarantees the political right to criticize the government for allowing inequality to spread but not the economic right to equitable living standards. All citizens have the right to vote in elections but not to decide democratically whether a local automobile plant closes its doors.

Understanding the limits of citizenship involves recognizing the fact that modern citizenship has developed in relation to capitalism. As discussed in Chapter 2, a capitalist system is founded upon the principle of private ownership of the key productive resources in society, including workplaces such as factories and offices, raw materials, and technical knowledge. Within capitalism, everyone has the formal right to buy and sell in the marketplace, but the actual access to goods and services depends upon how much money you have. Thus, the logic of the market provides the potential but not the actuality of equal participation. Each participant has the right to buy and sell in the market, but, in reality, most of us have nothing of substance to sell aside from our capacity to work and are in a position to purchase little beyond the necessities of life.

Like market rights, citizenship rights provide formal but not **substantive equality**. If citizenship were to guarantee not simply equal political rights but a more equitable standard of living—the right to affordable housing, for example, or the right to healthy food—this would require narrowing the authority of the market in society (McNally 2006). A capitalist system can thrive alongside a framework of citizenship rights designed to protect individuals against government encroachment on their person and property. But a conception of citizenship based on the principle of ensuring substantive equality would pose serious problems for capitalism.

The fact that citizenship has developed in a way that is compatible with capitalism does not mean that it was designed exclusively by the wealthy to serve their own narrow interests. If that were the case, there would likely be far fewer protections for working people against the demands of capitalist profitability. In fact, as Beetham (2005) writes, citizenship rights are in important ways "the result of struggles of the common people, often at considerable cost to themselves, to limit the power of oligarchic and oppressive regimes, and to make government more publicly accountable and responsive to the whole community" (p. 13). Rights did not emerge and evolve "naturally," and they were not happily passed down to the people from enlightened and generous political leaders. They were obtained through struggle over time. The nature of these struggles has meant that citizenship victories have never been fully complete and have always been contradictory. Citizenship involves both important freedoms and severe restrictions that reflect the history of the struggles through which it was formed.

The Birth of Modern Citizenship

The French Revolution that broke out in Paris in 1789 was a formative moment in the history of modern citizenship. In a matter of only a few years, France's entire political, economic, and social system was overturned and a new one put in place. The new political order included a developed conception of citizenship—one that is worth reflecting upon in light of the fact that "French revolutionaries invented important elements of the citizenship our world knows today" (Tilly 1996: 225). The citizenship that emerged through revolutionary struggles was grounded in radically new democratic principles such as individual liberty and equal political rights; yet this emergent form of citizenship remained restricted when it came to addressing deeper inequalities running through French society. The contra-dictions of citizenship at the start of the twenty-first century have roots in the French Revolution.

Prior to the revolution, a period that has since been called the "Old Regime," the political system placed absolute authority in the hands of the king. He was understood to rule by the will of god (or "Divine Right"), as opposed to by the will of the people. The hierarchy of absolute monarchy extended throughout all of society. The Old Regime presumed that "men were unequal, that inequality was a good thing, and that it conformed to the hierarchical order built into nature by God himself" (Darnton 1990: 11). The feudal system divided society into three "estates" (another word for "ranks"). It gave specific rights and privileges to people depending on the estate to which they belonged.

The first and second estates consisted of the relatively small number of nobility and clergy: "Nobles ... were exempt from most taxes other than royal income tax, received degrees more quickly at universities, had preferred access to offices at court, and were the only legitimate owners of noble estates" (Fahrmeir 2007: 20). The third estate consisted of the remaining masses of the population. It included both French peasants and the growing bourgeois class composed of small business owners and other urban professionals (e.g., bankers, lawyers, and shopkeepers). Although peasants and other poor people in the third estate had little wealth of their own, they were also the ones who were expected to pay the taxes that funded both the luxuries of the upper classes and the French military adventures.

In the years running up to 1789, demands for state revenue grew rapidly, in part due to the costs of warfare in Europe. The tax increases imposed on the third estate and chronic food shortages during this period of economic crisis stoked widespread anger against the king. Facing bankruptcy, King Louis XVI hoped to extract wealth from members of the nobility by calling a rare meeting of representatives from all three estates in the French city of Versailles in May and June of 1789. His aim was to use the anger of the third estate to his advantage by calling for a vote on a plan to impose taxes on the nobility. His plan backfired in spectacular fashion.

Instead of going along with the king's scheme, representatives of the third estate made radical demands of their own. At first they proposed reforms to increase their influence within the estates system, and eventually they began meeting separately from the other estates and calling themselves the "National Assembly." After Louis XVI closed the group's regular meeting place, the Salle des États in Versailles, representatives of the third estate gathered in a nearby tennis court and swore an historic oath. The Tennis Court Oath declared the third estate to be the fundamental source of government power, the true embodiment of France. It reaffirmed France's first National Assembly and promised to develop a new constitution based on the sovereignty of the French people and to never separate until that constitution was on solid foundations, effectively dismissing the authority of the estates system. France was launched into crisis.

Years of revolutionary debates, violence, and changes followed. "It took violence to smash the mental frame of the Old Regime, and violence itself, the ... world-destroying, revolutionary sort of violence" can be difficult to imagine for people who've never experienced it (Darnton 1990: 12). At times during the revolution, street fighting and public executions were so common that, in Paris, people "could not walk through the center of the city without covering their shoes in blood" (12). Indeed, the crowning moment of the revolution—both in terms of symbolism and what it meant legally—was the 1792 beheading of King Louis XVI and his family. The guillotine, a beheading machine with a wooden frame and steel blade designed during the revolution to make executions quicker and easier, severed the king's head from his body and along with it the last vestiges of monarchical government from the new French republic.

The revolution put everything into play and provided an opportunity to lay the foundation for a radically different type of society. Revolutionary violence was not brutality for its own sake but one part of a moment of intense political and cultural activity addressing the most basic of questions:

Who would make law, and how would it be administered? Darnton (1990) has described the French Revolution as a period of "possibilism against the givenness of things" (p. 19).

The revolution did indeed produce government on the basis of popular sovereignty: the radical principle that "all worthy and responsible persons should not only enjoy state protection but also participate directly in governing the nation" (Tilly 1996: 228). It levelled the estates system and established French citizenship: "a class of persons enjoying common rights, bound by common obligations, formally equal before the law" (Rogers Brubaker 1989: 35). The founding documents of the revolution demonstrate that this meant taking seriously the right of individuals to free speech, religion, and assembly. For example, the "Declaration of the Rights of Man and of the Citizen" announced that "Men are born and remain free and equal in rights"; that the law "must be the same for all, whether it protects or punishes"; and that all citizens "are equally eligible to all dignities and to all public positions and occupations, according to their abilities," as opposed to by bloodline. The focus on the rights of men was challenged by revolutionary women's organizations, which produced the first modern conception of women's rights (Rowbotham 1972).

These citizenship rights radically changed the social order in France by ending the rule of the monarchical class, which opened the way to epic struggles within the former third estate. Under the Old Regime, although business owners and traders had a degree of autonomy, their wealth was ultimately the property of the king. The revolutionary demand of the bourgeois or business-owning faction of the third estate was a form of government that would protect private interests against the interference of the state; however, members of the bourgeoisie would also need to protect their property and money from more radical elements within the third estate. Revolutionary peasants, manual labourers, and the urban poor wanted to see collective self-government extended by moving control over society's wealth into the political sphere, where decisions about the production and allocation of resources could be decided democratically.

The democratic vision that ultimately prevailed was that of the wealthy and propertied elements of the third estate. The bourgeois faction fought the Old Regime alongside peasants and other poor revolutionaries to overthrow the king, who was a common enemy. However, the revolution ended up institutionalizing the authority of bosses over workers in the form of a citizenship framework based upon private property rights. Formal political equality and being governed by consent became the basis of the new citizenship regime, but, despite establishing radically new civic rights and freedoms, citizenship did not involve guarantees of social equality among citizens. This general pattern has held, despite being revised in some ways, throughout the key democratic struggles of the past 200 years.

Fights for Rights

Struggles over citizenship in the century and a half following the democratic revolutions in France and other parts of the world centred on the question of who could claim citizenship rights, especially the right to vote. Throughout the 1800s, no democracy in any part of the world granted full political rights to all people. The right to vote and to hold political office in Great Britain, France, Canada, and the United States was denied to women in general and to men who did not own a specific amount of property. In Canada, indigenous people were denied the right to vote unless they renounced their First Nations status. Some jurisdictions prevented poor and uneducated people from voting by making voters pay a poll tax or pass a literacy test before they could cast a ballot. Rules such as these tended to disenfranchise disproportionately people of colour, who were already discriminated against in numerous areas of society.

Paul Foot (2005) argues that, in the United Kingdom, the right to vote was only ever won by new segments of the population through massive demonstrations of popular power. These demonstrations took a variety of forms: strikes, occupations, parades, targeted property damage, and assemblies of alternative political institutions. One protestor, Emily Davison, killed herself to draw attention to the demand for women's suffrage after throwing herself under the king's horse at the Epsom Derby in 1913.

While millions of people took to the streets to demand their rightful place in the political sphere, parliamentarians from all parties tried to stop the expansion of citizenship at every step of the way. Voting rights were indeed expanded numerous times by laws passed in the British Parliament, but this happened despite what politicians and jurists of the period actually wanted. Foot uses the words of politicians themselves to conclude that governments would not have expanded the franchise to include poor and working segments of the population without massive mobilizations that challenged the established powers. For example, in the words of the high-ranking British judge Lord Abinger in 1842, one threat to these powers was "A popular assembly devoted to democratic principles and elected by persons, a vast majority of whom have no property and depend on manual labour ... the first thing such an assembly would do would be to aim at the destruction of property and the putting down of the monarchy" (in Foot 2005: 114).

Foot describes the mobilization of the "Chartist" movement of the 1830s and 1840s as nothing less than an embryonic insurrectionary movement at the heart of the Western world. He estimates that, although, in the end, its revolutionary ambitions were thwarted, Chartism came closer than any other movement before or since to overthrowing capitalist democracy in favour of a genuine workers' government in Britain.

The Chartists (who got their name by demanding a new political charter) argued that all male workers deserved the vote because it was their labour that produced the wealth of the nation. (In another example of the contradictions of democratic politics, although some individual Chartists supported women's suffrage, the movement as a whole focused its demands exclusively on gaining universal *male* suffrage.) They demonstrated for male suffrage by marching in the hundreds of thousands through London and by striking at their workplaces. In 1842, they helped orchestrate a general strike across the country.

The government's ongoing refusal to make any changes made it clear, not only to Chartists but to a broader layer of working people, that parliament and other institutions of official democracy did not represent their interests. A campaign was mounted to organize a "People's Parliament" that would make decisions on behalf of the masses of Great Britain independently from the official government. Parliamentarians realized that, if the Chartists were not appeased or crushed, they might end up using their mass power to tear down the existing system of government and leave the wealthy with nothing. Memories of the French Revolution were still fresh.

Over time, the Chartist movement was both appeased through piecemeal reforms and crushed by police "in the most relentless repression," which took the form of mass arrests and police violence against demonstrators. Still, although minor reforms and intense repression killed the campaign for voting rights in the short term, the Chartist revolt "was not a failure. It branded on to the history of the century an indelible memory as frightening to the rulers as it was exciting to the ruled" (Foot 2005: 114–15). It forced governments to choose between responding to unrest by expanding citizenship rights or by maintaining tight restrictions on who could vote, which risked fanning the flames of protest. Between the 1830s and 1920s, governments in the United Kingdom and other Western democracies gradually removed voting restrictions based on property and gender exclusions.

A different fight for full citizenship, including the right to vote, was the national liberation struggle against Western colonialism. Broadly speaking, the term colonialism refers to "a practice of domination, which involves the subjugation of one people to another" (Kohn 2011, par.1). The term is being used here to refer more specifically to longstanding processes through which Western governments have controlled and exploited peoples of the Global

South and indigenous peoples around the world, often through military conquest and the formation of administrations run from the imperial homeland. Bannerji (2011) describes Western colonial projects as "outgoing, aggressive, occupying ventures which combine a moral mission with an economic object" (p. 7). By nature of this relationship, people living under colonial rule are not free to exercise even the degree of self-determination provided within official democracies. They are not citizens in the sense of being full members of the official political community. For example, under British colonial rule in India, many Indians were prevented from holding government offices, paid lower wages than European labourers doing the same work, and denied access to certain forms of education. In short, they had few political or civil rights.

Resistance to colonialism has been continuous, often starting from the moment that conquest and the subordination of people and appropriation of resources began. It took the form of specific struggles for independence in the 1700s in Haiti, in the 1800s in South America, and in the 1900s throughout the Global South and among indigenous peoples in the Global North. It continues in the twenty-first century among indigenous peoples who have been denied the right to self-determination, from Palestine to Australia to Canada.

Historically, national liberation struggles were struggles for full citizenship and self-rule against the second-class status imposed by colonial rulers. The second-class status of colonial subjects was reflected in every social relation, and it fuelled powerful freedom movements in response. These movements sought to establish different ways of living in contrast to European models, often building upon ways of living that had been in place before colonization. The renowned anti-colonial thinker and activist Frantz Fanon (1963) explains the innovative and oppositional character of these movements: "Let us decide not to imitate Europe; let us combine our muscles and our brains in new directions. Let us try to create the whole man, whom Europe has been incapable of bringing to triumphant birth" (p. 313).

The idea of the whole person living in a society of real freedom is a model of citizenship linked to anti-colonial struggles, and it thus stands in sharp contrast to European democratic traditions. In the 1950s and 1960s, these anti-colonial struggles led to the rise of a broader Third World project: an aspiration for a better way of organizing society, grounded in new forms of freedom and self-rule. In Prashad's (2007) words, "The Third World project included a demand for the redistribution of the world's resources, a more dignified rate of return for the labour power of their people, and a shared acknowledgement of the heritage of science, technology, and culture" (pp. xvi–xvii).

Ultimately, the Third World project did not achieve its goal of full emancipation, and there is a great deal of debate about why (see Berger 2004;

Prashad 2007). There is no question, however, that powerful nations of the world, where transnational corporations were headquartered, strangled aspects of the project with military and economic force (Prashad 2007). Moreover, within the Third World, elite-led projects rooted in narrow ethnicity-based nationalisms obstructed broader visions of emancipation. Prashad criticizes Third World socialist experiments, such as the *ujaama* agricultural reform policy in Tanzania, for attempting to impose social transformation from above, ignoring both the material restrictions and potential insights of the great majority of the population, and excluding people from a sense of ownership of the policy. Himani Bannerji (2011) argues that the rise of an ethnic conception of citizenship in India not only displaced broader visions of freedom from the anti-colonial struggle but also increased the subordination of women, who were positioned as reproducers of the ethnicity or race and rewarded or brutalized for their success or failure in fulfilling that role: "women's chastity and maternity are particularly important for their reproductive capacity as vessels for nurturing the hindu race and its purity" (Bannerji 2011: 67).

Clearly the parameters of citizenship have expanded because of struggles from below. Yet the history of the expansion of the right to vote and of national liberation illustrates that citizenship is a contradictory category. On the one hand, the extension of voting rights, which means the extension of citizenship, is an important democratic victory by any definition. Historically, it involved tremendous self-organization and action on the part of masses of people and forced Western governments to represent their populations more effectively. However, the extension of voting rights did not end up overturning power relations in a more fundamental sense. Citizenship continues to be a mechanism for achieving government by consent, as opposed to self-government. Moreover, social inequality remains deeply embedded in Western democracies, even after all citizens won the right to vote, and in countries in the Global South, even after the victories of national liberation struggles and the achievement of full citizenship. As the next section explains, one response to this contradictory development was the struggle to expand the bounds of citizenship to include social rights such as programs and services that might challenge economic inequity.

Social Citizenship

World War II began in 1939 and ended in 1945. During the war, governments took on greater responsibility for ensuring that citizens were achieving at least a minimum standard of living. If men and women are going to consent to be sent off to fight and die in the name of their nation, they need to believe that they are part of a nation worth fighting for. It is in the state's interests, then, to prepare its people for battle by building up a sense of shared national identity, as well as by ensuring the physical well-being of the population of potential soldiers.

World War II saw the state taking a deeper role in people's lives, sending citizen-soldiers to war but also caring for them and their families in new ways. These trends that developed during the war years would be extended throughout society in the following decades. As Cowan (2008) writes, "The soldier is not a figure associated with democracy or political rights. . . . And yet, paradoxically, it was through the mass sacrifice of the population in service to the nation during the Second World War that post-war citizenship was assembled. Welfare was a reward for the serving citizen, and a means to harness the labour and allegiance of a divided population for the nation" (p. 255). Citizenship expanded during the war years and the decades after because of both the material needs of warring states and the sense of entitlement growing among newly mobilized populations.

The war against Hitler's Germany, Mussolini's Italy, and Japan's Emperor Hirohito was portrayed by the United Kingdom, the United States, Canada, France, and their allies as a war for democracy. Citizens of the democratic countries were called upon to fight both for their national dignity and for the survival of democratic principles such as liberty and civic rights. In his presidential address to Congress in 1941, Franklin D. Roosevelt reported that "the democratic way of life is at this moment being directly assailed in every part of the world." Western leaders portrayed the war as a decisive showdown between the forces of fascism spreading throughout Europe and the forces of freedom charged with resisting them.

Deborah Cowan (2008) argues that the experience of collective armed struggle in World War II forged a stronger sense of national identity among people in the Western countries. "One particularly powerful legacy of war," she writes, "is that people become *a people*. Mass war provided a singular project and demanded a unified polity organized around the cause of national work" (p. 26). British propaganda posters announced: "*YOUR* courage; *YOUR* cheerfulness; *YOUR* resolution WILL BRING US VICTORY" (Morgan and Evans 1993: 17). The state used poster campaigns, radio addresses, civic education, and other media to emphasize the idea that winning the war and defending democracy demanded the active participation of every citizen.

Yet this vision of the war ran up against brutal social exclusions in the self-proclaimed democracies. African Americans faced segregation in the armed forces, leading to a mobilization for rights that began to reshape military and civilian life, including bus boycotts in the South before the civil rights movement. As Robin D.G. Kelley (1994) writes, "Black Americans were expected to support a war against Hitler—whose plan for Aryan supremacy was treated as a threat to Western democracy—while white supremacy and segregation continued to be a way of life in the Deep South" (pp. 55–56). In the United States and Canada, as previously mentioned, citizens of Japanese origin were rounded up and shipped off to camps exclusively on the basis of their ethnicity. The idea of national identity included both new solidarities and new exclusions.

The war became a time of massive protests by African Americans for human rights and by workers in factories facing speed-up policies, wage controls, and a refusal by management to recognize unions, even as corporate profits skyrocketed while producing materials for the war machine. As Tilly (1996) points out, war has a tendency to force rulers "to bargain with their civilian populations for the essential [person] power and means of war" (p. 235). And World War II exemplifies this observation: the state called citizens into action, and citizens reshaped the state through both their contribution to the war effort and their expectations about what they deserved in return. In 1958, the British researcher and teacher Richard Titmuss reflected on how the war changed the role of the British state. His comments shed light on the reasons that government responses to the demands of war eventually expanded throughout society:

> Comprehensive systems of medical care and rehabilitation, for example, had to be organized by the state for those who were injured or disabled. They could not be exclusively reserved for soldiers and sailors, as in the past, but had to be extended to include civilians as well—to those injured in the factories as well as the victims of bombing. The Emergency Medical Service, initially designed to cater for a special section of the population, became in the end the prototype for a medical service of the whole population. (Quoted in Cowan 2008: 35)

On the last day of World War II in Europe, millions of Americans listened to Norman Corwin's broadcast "On a Note of Triumph." Corwin's poem celebrated the victory of "the Allies" as a win for the "little guy" at the root of Western democracy. He declared that the enemy had

> given up! / They're finally done in and the rat is dead in an alley back of Wilhemstrasse / Take a bow G.I. / Take a bow Little Guy / The superman of tomorrow lies at the feet / Of you common men of this afternoon." (Corwin 1945)

The poem suggests that this democratic spirit should go forward into the postwar world. He urged the collective "little guy" to

> Appear now among the parliaments of conquerors and give instruction
> to their schemes: / Measure out new liberties so none shall suffer for his
> father's color or the credo of his choice … / Sit at the treaty table and
> convoy the hopes of the little peoples through expected straits / [… so]
> That man unto his fellow man shall be a friend forever. (Corwin 1945)

The meaning of citizenship was expanding on both emotional and legis-lative levels. At the conclusion of the war, this broadening and more inter-ventionist state turned its attention to rebuilding the economies around the world. Within the context of the postwar economic boom and in the face of pressure to maintain broad consent among populations who had sacrificed so much during wartime, Western governments became more involved than ever before with providing support for their citizens. In the language of Sears (1999), the era of the broad **welfare state** that emerged in the postwar years "was marked by a broadening of the conception of citizenship and the standardization of the population through policies which established social minima (using programmes and benefits to provide at least a specified mini-mum level of income, housing, health and education) and enforced norms" (p. 92). A new form of social citizenship was emerging in response to trends that had developed during the war for democracy.

According to T.H. Marshall (1964), social citizenship includes "the right to a modicum of economic welfare and … to live the life of a civilized being according to the standards prevailing in the society" (p. 79). In other words, the state assumes a greater role in providing the basic necessities of life to all citizens. For example, Britain established its publicly funded, universally accessible health care program in 1946. In 1954, the United States government extended social security benefits to government employees, hotel workers, agricultural workers, some domestic labourers, and self-employed people. France introduced a minimum income for the aged in 1956.

Social citizenship, then, is partially rooted in egalitarian political principles, a commitment to moving society toward "meaningful social equality" (Myers 2010: 33). But despite the egalitarian advances of social citizenship after the war, not everyone benefitted equally from the increasingly interventionist state. As Fahrmeir (2007) notes, although citizenship entitlements grew substantially, non-citizens were still prevented from accessing them. In postwar Europe, the legacy of wartime migration and displacement meant that large segments of the population in so-called welfare state democracies were not citizens of their new home and therefore were excluded from the full benefits of social citizenship. Moreover, people of colour and women continued to be discriminated against in workplaces and at home: "One of the major themes of political struggles during the welfare state era was the demand of various excluded groups for full social citizenship rights" (Sears 1999: 93).

From the perspective of official democracy, the welfare state grew out of the national pride, generosity, and technical expertise of Western democratic leaders in response to the Great Depression and World War II. In this view, presidents Roosevelt and Truman in the United States are seen as visionary rulers who forged a new state strategy for stability and social inclusion. The broad welfare state is therefore understood as the logical extension of a democratic history founded upon principles of equality, freedom, and justice.

By contrast, the democracy-from-below perspective views the expansion of the welfare state as a much more contradictory development. Far from being simply the outcome of generous politicians and visionary leaders, the welfare state, argue proponents of democracy from below, is in fact the result of a largely defensive manoeuvre on the part of ruling elites to guard against challenges to their authority. The upsurge of labour militancy and other forms of social unrest in the 1930s and 1940s seriously threatened the official democratic order of the time. Workers were organizing in growing numbers in increasingly powerful unions, and their thousands of strikes for better wages and working conditions made economic expansion intermittent and unpredictable. Recognizing serious and growing tensions within the basic relationship that makes labourers subservient to their employers, governments introduced welfare state policies as a way of firming up popular support for the established order, concomitantly subsuming the growing social conflict within the framework of the state (Finkel 1979: 2). For example, as discussed in Chapter 2, the state's recognition of collective bargaining rights is seen by democracy-from-below theorists as a victory for labour won through strikes and solidarity actions. However, once collective bargaining rights were brought into the orbit of state administration, they were integrated into a whole legal framework that regulated unions and limited their capacities for action (Camfield 2011; Palmer 1983). The development of social citizenship, therefore, was simultaneously an extension of popular power and a mechanism for ensuring that it grew within a democratic framework based upon popular consent to being governed. During the militant struggles of the 1960s and 1970s, this framework was at times pushed close to the breaking point.

"The Times They Are a-Changin'"

During the 1960s, the push for a more inclusive and robust form of citizenship was strengthened by new developments in forces from below. While labour unions continued their push to expand workers' rights, new political organizations and networks of activists stepped up struggles for women's rights, aboriginal self-determination, nuclear disarmament, student empowerment, equal rights for gay and lesbian people, and an end to racism, importantly inspired by anti-colonial struggles. People of colour, queer communities, and other segments of the population that had been excluded from full citizenship rights demanded full inclusion in the official political community.

In one popular pamphlet of the time, student activists welcomed "signs of a new period of struggle, with youth as the new carriers of revolutionary infection" (Situationist International 1966). Under the slogan "All power to the people!" the Black Panther Party in Oakland, California, organized local breakfast programs and built up community-based security forces to protect the neighbourhoods of people of colour against the state's racist police system. Aboriginal groups in Canada mounted militant opposition to proposals to narrow their citizenship status. A second wave of the feminist movement demanded not only greater political and economic rights for women but also reproductive freedom and an end to all forms of male domination. Anti-colonial movements in the Third World grew stronger and successfully tore down formal colonial relationships in various parts of the world. In the words of sociologist Suzanne Staggenborg, "the world was experiencing a major wave of protest that would have aftershocks for decades to come" (Staggenborg 2008: 43).

Tariq Ali was a Pakistani student activist living in London during the late 1960s. In a recent interview, he said that 1968 was "a pivotal year" for movements from below around the world. Within the span of a few months, 1968 saw mass student and worker revolts in France, major advances of the Vietnamese liberation army against aggression by the US government, and democratic breakthroughs against the **Stalinist regime** in Czechoslovakia. Ali's words about May 1968 in France give a sense of what monumental shifts were taking place:

> You had a general strike in France, involving ten million workers, which was the largest general strike in the history of capitalism. You had French workers occupying their factories and saying they wanted to run the factories. You had other French workers and their student allies saying they wanted to run France in the interest of the majority of the people.

At that point, for about a week, it looked as if the French system might collapse. (Ali 2011: 213)

The slogans of May 1968 that activists scrawled across banners, barricades, university walls, and any other surface they could reach reflect the expansiveness of the democratic imagination in that moment: *It is forbidden to forbid; Boredom is a counter-revolutionary act; Barricades shut down the street but open the way; Under the cobble-stones, the beach!* For many people, envisioning new ways of doing democracy did not seem like hopeless optimism. In France, London, Chicago, Prague, and other cities around the world, millions of people were collectively acting up to make their democratic dreams into reality. Civil rights demonstrations, anti-war protests, and innovative forms of collective action among different segments of the working class "were all evidence of new democratic forces flexing their muscles outside the ruling parliaments, congresses and bureaucracies" (Foot 2005: 361). The sense that the boundaries of the possible were being pushed back was vividly expressed in Bob Dylan's 1964 song "The Times They Are a-Changin'"—which was also the title of his third studio album (Dylan 1964/2011).

The militant struggles of the 1960s and early 1970s were at least somewhat successful in transforming the character of democratic citizenship and extending full citizenship rights to new segments of the population. In the United States, for example, full political rights were granted to people of colour after years of militant actions by civil rights movements. These movements employed a range of tactics: letter-writing campaigns; massive political rallies, such as the 1963 March on Washington (where Dr. Martin Luther King, Jr. delivered his famous "I have a dream" speech); civil disobedience; and armed rebellion. Michael Schudson (1998) argues not only that "the legacy of the civil rights movement was the widening of the reach of the idea of citizenship itself" but that it also "helped inspire a new generation of young activists trained in and willing to use direct action methods" (pp. 257–58).

Staggenborg (2008) writes that "the protest cycle of the sixties had an enduring influence, both in spawning new social movements that survived beyond that period and in challenging the dominant culture" (p. 51). Today, looking back on the 1960s, this challenge to authority is often represented in images of feminist rallies, anti-war marches, and street barricades, but its influence went far beyond any one of these single moments. The 1960s protest movements signalled popular mobilization on a massive level to win greater freedom and economic security. The central role in these struggles played by women, people of colour, queer people, First Nations activists, and other marginalized groups forced the expansion of citizenship both in law and in broader democratic cultures.

The Tide Turns: Citizenship in Neo-liberal Times

Since the mid-1970s, social citizenship has been challenged by a new model of lean citizenship associated with the ideology of **neo-liberalism**. The term neo-liberalism refers to an approach to government that seeks to push people onto the market to meet all their wants and needs, eliminating alternatives including social programs and benefits. Examples of neo-liberal policies include government cuts to public pensions and unemployment insurance programs, attacks on collective bargaining rights, and hikes in user fees in the fields of education and transportation. In contrast to the principle of universal access to state entitlements, a principle connected to social citizenship, the lean citizenship promoted in the neo-liberal era is about reducing citizens' rights and entitlements in the name of greater freedom through market choice.

Neo-liberalism emerged during the global economic crisis of the 1970s when corporate profitability fell due to the development of too much production capacity during the postwar economic boom (see McNally 2011a: Chapter 2). Economies around the world went into a tailspin. Businesses and governments began searching for ways out of the crisis and a return to profitability.

In the context of this economic crisis, the broad welfare state system came under attack from corporate advocates and state policymakers. The welfare state was blamed for causing the economic crisis and was said to be blocking a return to economic prosperity because it "contributed to the development of labour market rigidities in the form of high wages, limited wage differentials, [and] entitlements through social programmes and labour market regulations" (Sears 1999: 99). In other words, critics claimed that the welfare state provided too many benefits and too much protection to working people. This "overabundance" was seen as costing too much money and denying employers the flexibility required to run successful businesses.

Neo-liberal governments like those of Margaret Thatcher (in the United Kingdom), Ronald Reagan (in the United States), Tony Blair (in the United Kingdom), and Stephen Harper (in Canada) have associated their demands for lower taxes, less government regulation, free trade agreements, and support for private industry with ideals of liberty, freedom, and individual choice. In this sense, neo-liberalism sets itself up as the democratic dream of a world in which innovation is freed from the shackles of the state.

In the neo-liberal era, citizenship, or the relationship between people and governments, has been increasingly modelled upon that between consumers and businesses. The citizen-taxpayer-consumer seeks services offered by a government-business. In this relationship, the citizen-taxpayer-consumer should be given as much freedom and choice as possible in determining the services he or she wishes to receive, and people should expect a strong return on their investment (tax dollars) from the service provider (government): "Recent policy changes have concentrated on introducing an element of 'consumer choice' by charging at least a symbolic amount for most public services at the point of access" (Fahrmeir 2007: 225). The proliferation of user fees "has turned users into customers and state agencies into service providers" (Fahrmeir 2007: 225). This is a significant change from a form of citizenship based upon the non-market principle of universal access: "The extension of user-pay in Canada has included a dramatic increase in post-secondary tuition frees, the introduction of user fees for such programmes as drug benefits, and increases in transit fares and park administration" (Sears 1999: 103–4).

Since the 1970s, neo-liberal governments have scaled back citizenship entitlements. They have moved closer to the dream of neo-liberal visionaries such as Friedrich von Hayek, who wrote a book in 1944 advocating a minimalist state whose only role would be "to safeguard individual and commercial liberty, and strong private property rights" (MacLeavy 2010: 136). In fact, neo-liberal governments have cut welfare payments and made social assistance more difficult to attain. Some have eliminated welfare altogether and replaced it with "workfare," a system that requires recipients of public services to labour in some way as a condition of receiving government assistance. These policies are in addition to the privatization of industries that previously were publicly owned and the introduction of user fees for services that used to be free. Neo-liberal governments have cut programs and agencies dedicated to achieving more equitable social standing for groups marginalized on the basis of gender, race, ethnic background, sexual orientation, age, and ability. They argue both that these divisions are no longer the basis for inequalities and that people should navigate their social identities in their private lives.

Yet, although citizenship entitlements have been scaled back in recent decades, the neo-liberal state remains highly interventionist in certain areas. For example, the world's foremost neo-liberal governments ensured that trillions of public dollars were pumped into private banks and corporations to bail them out during the economic crisis of 2008 (McNally 2011a). Moreover, the most committed neo-liberal governments favour massive government spending on policing, prisons, and the military. This seeming dichotomy should not be surprising considering that, as "neoliberal policies take effect, social divisions and inequities tend to proliferate, increasing the need for a well armoured state" to protect dominant interests (Carroll 2005: 12).

Citizenship has not been abandoned under neo-liberalism, but it is changing dramatically and becoming much thinner than it used to be. Birch and Mykhnenko (2010) argue that this trend is dangerous because it shifts responsibility for social issues to individuals who lack the means to address them: "What we end up with are ... strategies in which responsibility for the delivery of political priorities is shifted further and further downwards until what results is a new model of citizenship in which societal rights and responsibilities transform 'deficiencies' (such as unemployment) into 'failures' of the individual rather than society" (p. 7). From the perspective of neo-liberalism, substantive inequality is expected to exist alongside formal political equality, and it is not the government's responsibility to change that.

No One Is Illegal

Despite the hollowing out of citizenship under neo-liberalism, struggles from below for greater rights and freedoms have by no means disappeared. As Sasha Lilley (2011) notes, the state's attack on workers, poor people, and public services "has spurred combativeness of all sorts" (p. 11). In the wake of the most recent economic crisis, these attacks provoked resistance that "brought down Iceland's government; generated civil unrest and recurring general strikes in Greece and France, as well as country-wide strikes in India, Spain, and Portugal; and led to pan-European trade union actions, mass student walkouts and protests in the UK, and significant labor militancy in China" (Lilley 2011: 11). Struggles over citizenship remain heated.

These struggles are significantly shaped by the sharp rise in international migration since the 1970s: "During the last three decades of the twentieth century alone, seventy-five million people moved across borders to settle elsewhere" (Benhabib and Resnik 2009: 1). Advances in communication and transportation technologies have facilitated these transnational flows of people, but the main driver of migration continues to be the dislocation, whether economic or political due to war or oppression, that pushes people from their homes. It is no coincidence that human migration has increased alongside the increasingly transnational flows of capital: people have been forced to follow and flee the ever-shifting grounds of capital investment. In the words of Tanya Golash-Boza and Douglas A. Parker, two sociologists working with the group Sociologists Without Borders: "The current flows of immigration into the United States are a result of the actions of the US government and US-based corporations" in other parts of the world (Golash-Boza and Parker 2006: par. 5).

This transnational migration has created new supplies of non-status, vulnerable workers who have been integrated into the economy in precarious positions. Western governments are using new techniques to prevent non-citizens from attaining full citizenship rights while, at the same time, temporarily allowing them to live in the country as labourers whose work is essential to economic growth. For example, Canada has recently stepped up its use of the Temporary Foreign Worker Program, in which foreign workers are granted the ability to work for wages in Canada for a set period without gaining the right to permanent residency or the opportunity to apply for full citizenship. Introduced in 1973, the program was revised in 2002 to make it easier to access temporary work permits across a wider range of industries. Between 2003 and 2008, the use of those permits nearly doubled.

In addition to doing "jobs few Canadians want—for example, dismembering pigs on 'disassembly lines' in meat plants" (Contenta and Monsebraaten 2009: A1)—temporary foreign workers also lack any form of job security. If their factory closes down or their employer refuses to hand over the wages promised, these workers can do little without risking deportation. They are clearly a lower-tier type of worker than people with citizenship status. In 2009, facing questions over whether the Alberta economy would be able to absorb the temporary foreign workers it had admitted before the bottom fell out of the economy, the minister of employment said in the legislature: "we need to recognize that the word temporary is exactly what it says and if it is impossible for [temporary foreign workers] to move into other occupation[s], then there is an expectation that they should go home" (quoted in Fudge and MacPhail 2009: 44).

The minister's words give weight to Fudge and MacPhail's interpretation of the program as "an extreme version of labor flexibility" whose primary aim is not to provide people with rights but to provide "employers with a pool of unfree workers who are disposable" (Fudge and MacPhail 2009: 43). Workers who stay beyond the time allotted on their permits or who enter the country without the necessary papers end up living as "undocumented people" who, although often continuing to provide a vital source of labour to the economy, are considered illegal aliens in the eyes of the state.

Many groups have criticized the Temporary Foreign Worker Program and other government restrictions on the free flow of people across borders, as well as its crackdown on **undocumented workers**. One group fighting for migrant justice does its work under the provocative slogan "No One Is Illegal." The very name of the organization—*No One Is Illegal* (NOII)—is a fundamental challenge to citizenship as it has been conceived and practised up to this point in Western democracies. In addition to helping specific people address a variety of immigration issues (work that often puts the group in direct conflict with the Canadian state), NOII also helps people mobilize in their communities against the exclusionary aspects of citizenship. Among NOII's political demands are calls for "an end to all deportations and detentions ... the implementation of a full and inclusive regularization program for all non-status people ... access without fear to essential services for all undocumented people ... [and] an end to the exploitation of temporary workers" (No One Is Illegal—Toronto 2011a).

The term "regularization program" refers to a process that "allows non-status immigrants to apply for legal status" without risk of being penalized for their undocumented position in society (Khandor et al. 2004: 7). Proponents of such programs note that hundreds of thousands of people are already living and working without status in Western democracies. They argue that, rather than being forced to live on the margins of society, often in poverty, fear, and poor health, "all the while being the most exploited in the workplace," undocumented people deserve the chance to become full citizens (No One Is Illegal—Toronto 2011b). The bold argument that *no one is illegal*—that people by virtue of being human have certain inalienable rights wherever in the world they might be—challenges the taken-for-grantedness of systemic social inequality masked by relations of citizenship. It highlights the fact that, for most people, the privileges that come along with citizenship represent an unearned set of advantages attained merely by the fortune (or misfortune) of where they happened to be born.

The Shifting Borders of Citizenship

The political scientist Kalu N. Kalu (2009) writes about "the paradoxical nature of citizenship" (p. 20). He calls it paradoxical because citizenship creates "both equality (in terms of rights) and inequality (in terms of differences in socioeconomic status)." Citizenship is also paradoxical in the sense that it is "oriented toward both the singular actors who constitute a political community and the collective body politic" (Cowan and Gilbert 2008: 10). Citizenship is both a tool for achieving popular consent to being governed and a field upon which activists from below have struggled for richer forms of popular power. Citizenship is inclusive in the sense that it provides the same basic formal protections and guarantees for everyone who enjoys citizenship status; however, the core of citizenship is exclusion. Contemporary citizenship excludes non-citizens from the most basic rights, and it excludes strategies for achieving genuine social equity from the realm of citizenship rights and obligations. In other words, it excludes problems of gross social and economic inequalities from the jurisdiction of citizenship. Modern citizenship is focused on protecting individual rights to private property not on ensuring a more equitable standard of living for all.

This chapter has demonstrated that the meaning and practice of citizenship has changed over time. At times the concept has expanded, both in terms of who is considered a citizen and in terms of the entitlements that citizenship entails. At times citizenship has narrowed. Although some aspects of social citizenship remain intact in most Western democracies, others have been eroded, if they have not disappeared altogether. Neo-liberal governments continue to privatize what used to be public services, impose user fees on services that used to be universally accessible, and frame citizenship in terms of customer service, as opposed to civic entitlement. Yet neo-liberal trends are not uncontested: "Every time neo-liberalism tears another hole in the fabric of people's lives, rebellion ensues" (McNally 2006: 267). The recent popular uprisings in North Africa, West Asia, Europe, and other parts of the world demonstrate powerful resistance to neo-liberal conceptions of citizenship. They hold out the possibility of democratic engagement being founded upon more inclusive terms. It is not clear what these struggles will lead to, but, at this moment, debates about what citizenship will mean in the twenty-first century remain at least partially open.

Kakabadse and Kakabadse (2009) are right to exclaim that "citizenship is a dynamic concept!" (p. 24). The democratic imagination draws on this dynamism, asking basic questions about who ought to qualify for citizenship and what being a citizen means. Is it fair that some people have citizenship and others do not merely because of where they were born? Should citizenship expand to include the right to postsecondary education? Should citizens be guaranteed access to clean air and drinking water, or should these resources, too, require user fees or be moved onto the market? Why should some entitlements be included within citizenship and others excluded? Discussion of these pressing everyday questions will fuel the democratic imagination. It may push people not only to work out their own views but also to act on the world to try to influence events.

4 THERE AND NOT THERE: REPRESENTATION AND PARTICIPATION

At the start of the twenty-first century, the most significant act of democratic participation for most people living under democratic governments is voting to elect representatives to office, such as a president, representative, member of parliament, or mayor. A visit to the polling booth is often portrayed as a sacred act, and voting tends to be a highly ritualized process. The moment of voting is governed by a code of rules that creates a particular setting, one that may or may not contribute to participants feeling powerful and engaged. To some, democracy is protected by the individualized privacy of the voting booth and the high seriousness of the procedures that ensure only eligible voters participate and elections take place in an environment free of influence and coercion. To others, these same electoral procedures serve as a reminder of both who is excluded from active democratic participation and the individualized passivity of the act of marking an "x" or pulling a lever to select among narrowly constrained choices.

Representation is central to the operation of democracies today. Voters elect representatives to make decisions on their behalf, and democratic governments claim to represent the people as a whole. Indeed, the election of representatives seems to be the basic mechanism of democratic organization at every level of society, from the student council to the trade union to the political representative in government. In this chapter, we will look at the complex relationship between representation and democratic power. Some people claim that the election of representatives is the most effective form of democratic power in a large-scale, complex modern society, while others argue it is the negation of popular power, marking consent to the domination of a ruling layer.

Iris Young (2002) argues that representation is necessary in contemporary democracies "because the web of modern social life often ties the action of some people and institutions in one place to consequences in many other places and institutions" (p. 124). It is impossible for everyone to be in the same place at the same time, making decisions collectively. This idea has led Young and others to conclude that the sprawling size, diversity, and interconnectedness of twenty-first-century democracies make political representation inevitable.

Yet representation complicates the basic idea of democracy. Andrew Rehfeld (2005) calls this complication "the central paradox of modern democratic government: Political representation excludes almost all of a nation from the institutions that 'democratically' govern it" (p. 5). The nature of representation itself imposes a layer between the elector and the decision-making process, creating indirect forms of democracy that threaten to undercut popular power. At the same time, advocates of representative democracy argue that this separation allows for the development of a sense of what is good for the people as a whole through processes of deliberation and informed decision making at some distance from the immediate self-interest of voters. New highways, for example, might never be built if residents in the affected areas could make the decision democratically.

Representation therefore poses challenges for both the official and the from-below perspectives on democracy. As we will discuss, advocates of official democracy generally favour "representative democracy," though they are often concerned about problems in existing systems of elected government. For example, many states in the United States introduce plebiscites, special ballots that allow all voters to decide specific issues, as a complement to the broader framework of representative democracy. It is suggested that plebiscites create a measure of accountability in the face of the potential corruption of elected officials, some of whom have shown a tendency for pursuing their own self-interests rather than following the will of the voters.

The focus on self-government in democracy-from-below perspectives aligns with more critical approaches to representative democracy. Yet given both the problem of scale and the real need to deliberate as part of decision making, many have attempted to realize democracy from below through systems that involve election and representation. Although, for some, representation cannot be reconciled with genuine popular power, for others—even some critics of representative democracy—it is a crucial tool in the development of systems of self-government.

This chapter examines the tensions between representation and democracy, and asks you to reflect upon the opportunities and limitations of one person standing in for others during key decision-making processes. It critically examines systems of representative democracy and alternative forms of popular participation. It also raises broader questions about the cultural impact of representation on the democratic imagination.

Representative Democracy

Arblaster (2002) has written that "virtually everywhere today, democracy is taken to be synonymous with some kind of representative system" (p. 79). The crucial idea in a representative democracy is that "people have power because they choose representatives and those representatives are regularly accountable to the voters for the decisions that they make for the collectivity" (Catt 1999: 95). Popular power is exercised not in the day-to-day activities of government but through the periodic activity of voting in elections for public office. This is why political scientists talk about elections being the "democratic linchpin of the regime" (Malcolmson and Myers 2005: 159). In choosing representatives through elections, voters provide rulers with the authority to govern, "a mandate." From the view of official democracy, the actions of representatives cannot be separated from the people's own choices because the authority of representatives is rooted in popular support.

The question of a mandate becomes particularly complicated given that public opinion is generally cross-cut with a wide variety of perspectives, and decisions are seldom unanimous except in the most coercive and authoritarian circumstances. The majority principle is often associated with democratic decision making, the idea being that winning ideas or candidates for public office are the ones that enjoy the support of the majority of the population. Yet, in most contemporary democratic systems, there is no rule requiring representatives to receive more than 50% of the votes, and when more than two candidates run against each other, the winning candidate is often elected with far less than half the votes. The plurality principle is what determines victory in these cases: the fact that one candidate received more votes than any other, though not necessarily a majority.

Dyck (2008) writes that the advantages of an election system based on the plurality principle include "its simplicity for the voter, its quick calculation of results, and its provision of a clear-cut representative for each constituency" (p. 306). Election systems that demand winning candidates receive the majority of the ballots cast tend to require more complex systems for ranking voter preferences, as well as multiple rounds of voting, which can span months.

Yet, regardless of whether elections are decided on the principle of majority or plurality support, no political representative enjoys the support of every single citizen. Even when representatives enjoy the support of 80% of their constituents (which is extremely rare), there is still a considerable minority that feels differently.

The question of plurality is further complicated by the role of political parties in electoral systems. The presence of political parties might seem to interfere in the mechanisms of accountability between an elected official and her or his constituents. Parties are sometimes presented as an institutional constraint on wise and informed decision making by elected politicians in dialogue with their constituents. A column by Frank Bruni (2012) in *The New York Times* laments the evolution of Maine Senator Olympia Snowe toward a party-line voting record and away from her more independent history. He describes her former independence, noting that, for Snowe, party affiliation did not mean "signing on automatically to everything it championed, to each plank in its sprawling (and often suffocating) platform" (p. 3).

Political scientist Maurice Duverger (1954) in his influential analysis expresses serious concerns about the impact of political parties on the practice of democracy. Rather than reflecting the popular will, parties tend to shape it, he argues: "Parties create opinion as much as they represent it; they form it by propaganda; they impose a prefabricated mould upon it" (Duverger 1954: 422).

Yet political parties also create a kind of accountability. Rather than voting for an individual and relying on his or her good judgment, electors, through the party system, vote for a program with some commitment for follow-through. If you vote for someone who runs with a party that supports same-sex marriage or opposes tax increases, you know what to expect if she or he gets elected. Should this representative diverge from the election platform that garnered support, voters can hold him or her accountable.

Duverger (1954) concludes that a non-party electoral system "is further removed from democracy than the party regime" (p. 426). Party-based systems might constrain democracy in certain ways, but non-party elections are even more of an impediment. Political parties are particularly important for those who want to change the world, as they provide a vehicle to amass forces to challenge the existing order and work together to clarify thoughts and mobilize for change. Non-party systems are therefore more likely to be conservative, to support the current social and economic arrangements (Duverger 1954: 426). It is often limits in the range of political parties (for example in the United States with its fairly rigid two-party system) and the bureaucratic form of existing party organizations that limits democracy, rather than the existence of parties in general.

Who's In, Who's Out?

If you've ever watched the television show *American Idol*, you'll know that each week one of the contestants is eliminated from the singing competition. As the host Ryan Seacrest announces the name of the losing contestant—the one who received the lowest number of viewers' votes that week—he looks earnestly into the camera and declares: "Ladies and gentlemen, America has spoken." The logic of the show is clear and seems fair. Millions of individual Americans have voted for their favourite singer, and the one with the most votes on the final night wins. The process is similar to the one that decides elections for political office.

So, if America has spoken, why are the winners generally bland middle-of-the-road singers? Considering the narrow range of musical options *American Idol* offers, it's not surprising that so many potential viewers tune out. Despite minor differences among contestants' tones and hairstyles, most fall within a fairly narrow range when it comes to musical genre. Hip-hop, operatic singing, and serious heavy metal, for example, have no place on the show. The majority of the finalists are pop or country singers, most are white, and virtually all speak English as their first language. The judges often reinforce very traditional notions of gender in their criticisms of contestants. Despite the show's claim to represent America's musical taste by inviting all TV-watchers to vote, its form goes some distance to ensuring that certain tastes are reproduced and others are hidden. Certain people will see themselves reflected in the bodies and tastes of contestants; others will find it difficult to feel that they are being represented on the screen.

American Idol immediately tunes out a segment of the population, yet the show claims that the winner of the competition represents popular taste. Pannekoek (1948/2003) suggests that representative democracy does something similar: "Though parliamentary theory considers the man elected as the representative of the constituency, it is clear that all these voters do not belong together as a group that sends him as its delegate to represent its wishes" (p. 47). This paradox leads to vexing questions: How can a representative genuinely represent the interests of both wealthy landlords and homeless people, both of whom live in that representative's constituency? Who represents homeless people in democratically elected national assemblies? People without a fixed address are not allowed to vote, and we've yet to see a story about a homeless member of parliament. Just as the United States is home to a much richer set of musical tastes than the ones on offer during *American Idol*, voters reflect a much more diverse set of experiences and perspectives than their elected representatives do.

Pannekoek's concern is that being required to choose among the candidates on offer produces a false impression of unity among populations with contradictory interests. A system based on political representation unifies the people being represented in ways that ignore significant differences among them. Territorial constituencies, ridings or districts organized within specific geographic boundaries, do the work of creating this imaginary unity of a population that is diverse in terms of gender, race, ethnicity, class, and political perspective.

The system of electing representatives based on territorial constituencies is so widespread that it tends to shape our image of what democracy looks like. As Andrew Rehfeld (2005) argues, "Territorial constituencies have become such a habit of mind that it may seem 'natural' for political representation to be defined by where people live" (p. 8). Yet, in practice, territorial constituencies leave many voters substantially unrepresented, particularly those who are members of minorities in the area, whether in terms of political opinion or ethnic background. Further, the very scale of the constituencies generally used in representative democracies means that they do not represent any form of active community engaged in ongoing processes of discussion and debate. These constituencies are much too large to encourage genuine interchange and deliberation among voters (Rehfeld 2005: 171).

Research on the composition of electoral bodies such as parliaments and congresses shows that representative democracy has systematically excluded certain kinds of people from positions of political power. Schouls (2009) writes that, although the situation in Canada has seen some improvement over time, "it is undeniably the case that the composition of the House of Commons is only a very pale reflection of the diverse social characteristics of the Canadian population" (p. 342). Specifically, although women make up half the population, they typically hold around 20% of the seats in the House of Commons. In the 2006 election, visible minorities, while making up more than 13% of the Canadian population, won less than 8% of legislative seats. In the categories used by the government of the United States, the 112th Congress (2011–2013) included 44 black representatives out of a total of 435 seats in the House of Representatives (Office of History and Preservation 2011). Thus, although African Americans make up 12.6% of the US population, they hold only 9.8% of House seats. In the same session, not 1 of the 100 US Senate seats was held by an African American. While roughly 16.3% of the US population is Hispanic, Hispanic representatives hold only 6% of House seats and 2% of Senate seats (Congressional Hispanic Caucus Institute 2011). In the United Kingdom, Muslims make up 2.7% of the population but hold only 1.2% (8 of 650) seats in the House of Commons.

Representative institutions have a long history of exclusion. As Chapter 3 discussed, throughout most of the 1800s, exclusion was achieved by placing narrow limits around who was allowed to participate in official democracy in the first place. Women were not allowed to vote in most Western countries until around 1920, and aboriginal peoples in Canada did not win the right to vote until the 1960s. Paul Foot (2005) demonstrates that property qualifications prevented well over half of British men from voting until the 1860s, and universal male enfranchisement was won only through mass militant struggle against strong resistance from members of parliament at Westminster. But, as the numbers show, even after winning formal political equality, women, people of colour, and poor people have continued to be grossly underrepresented in positions of political power.

This raises important questions around what political theorist Hanna Pitkin (1967: 60) calls "descriptive representation," that is, the question of whether "a representative body is ... an accurate correspondence or resemblance to what it represents" (p. 60). Jane Mansbridge (1999) argues that there are good reasons "disadvantaged groups may want to be represented by ... individuals who in their own backgrounds mirror some of the more frequent experiences and outward manifestations of belonging to the group" (p. 628). Suzanne Dovi (2002) also supports the principle of descriptive representation, but she makes the more provocative argument that some "descriptive" candidates are more preferable than others. She answers "no" to the provocative question in the title of her article: "Will just any woman, black, or Latino do?" In Dovi's words, "preferable descriptive representatives have strong *mutual* relationships with *dispossessed* subgroups" (p. 729). Dovi's suggestion is that descriptive representation is important to ensure not just that representative bodies look like the populations they rule over but also that the experiences of dispossessed people are genuinely represented there.

Olson (2002) writes that the problem of exclusion is in one respect a product of a system based on the majority/plurality rule. The majority principle, writes Olson, "turns politics into a zero-sum competition for power rather than a means of including everyone in the processes of governance" (p. 403). However, Olson points out that this problem is exacerbated by the legacy of racism in contemporary democracies. Focusing on the case of the United States, Olson explains that the majority principle is especially harmful in political systems

in which the majority is racially prejudiced against the minority to such an extent that the minority is consistently excluded from representation and policy making. When this happens, majority rule perpetuates racial inequality, as the combination of a winner-take-all system and white prejudice turns African Americans into permanent political minorities. Permanent minority status prevents African Americans from participating meaningfully in politics, even when their political rights are guaranteed by the Voting Rights Act. (Olson 2002: 403)

Dovi (2009) argues that the ways in which representative institutions systematically uphold forms of **privilege** and work against more inclusive forms of representation mean that strengthening representative bodies will require the strategic use of *exclusion* for democratic ends:

> This perspective recognizes that power and influence must be taken away from privileged groups who are overrepresented within democratic institutions if the representation of historically disadvantaged groups is to be improved. Not only do some voices need to be brought in, some voices need to be muted. (Dovi 2009: 1172)

The preponderance of wealthier white men is a challenge that will need to be overcome to create genuinely representative legislative bodies. Laurel Weldon (2011) takes a somewhat different approach to the underrepresentation of disadvantaged groups in established legislative bodies, arguing that social movements can, under certain circumstances, be the most effective means for representing the interests of groups that have faced discrimination and exclusion. Simply electing members of those groups to parliament may do more to transform the life of the individual representative than to raise the condition of the group as a whole: "For example, electing working-class people to legislative office literally transforms their class position" (Weldon 2011: 150). Rather than tampering with legislative systems, Weldon (2011) argues for the development of social movements, including demands on the state to foster such movements actively: "In fact, social movements offer a solution to the deepest, most persistent problems of representation" (p. 170).

Even if representative bodies became more reflective of the diverse populations over which they rule, this would not change the fact that some of the most revered representative democracies—Canada, the United States, and Australia, for example—are European settlements on indigenous land that many aboriginal peoples claim was never willingly surrendered to the colonizers. These countries, which often talk about their long history of democracy, are the result of centuries of massacres, exclusion, racism, and denial. The language and laws of representative democracy tend to hide this bloody history and ongoing indigenous resistance. Representative democracies legitimize themselves through the majority principle, equal citizenship rights, and institutionalized opposition parties. However, many aboriginal people and their allies view the whole European model of representative democracy as illegitimate: incapable of truly representing the lives and legacy of all people living under its rule.

EXERCISING YOUR DEMOCRATIC IMAGINATION
Money Talks

The two main contenders running for US president in 2008 (Barack Obama and John McCain) together spent over $1 billion on their election campaigns. Electoral contests at all levels of government are extremely expensive. How might the cost of running a successful campaign shape the make-up of representative assemblies? Explain why you do or don't view these trends as contributing to the health of democracy.

Representation and Participation

Given the previous discussion, it is not surprising that questions of representation are topics of heated debate. These debates do not align simply with official or from-below views of democracy but rather raise important challenges within each perspective. In the official perspective, the role of democracy is to accomplish government with consent of the people, leading to debates about the selection of representatives to ensure a genuine mandate, their ongoing accountability to electors, and the need for complementary forms of popular participation, ranging from forums to citizens' assemblies to plebiscites. In contrast, the role of democracy in the from-below perspective is to achieve self-government, leading to debates on whether representation constitutes an obstacle to genuine popular power or a tool to help accomplish it.

Official-democracy perspectives tend to favour representative democracy, not merely as a practical solution to the problems of popular power in large-scale societies but also as an effective way of governing with consent. Representative democracy is understood to be a suitable form of government because the elected representatives make decisions based not only on the specific interests of their constituents but also on the general interests of the nation (or the state, province, or municipality) as understood through debate and decision making in legislative institutions.

Supporters of the official view of democracy thus tend to believe that representatives ought to have a degree of independence from the opinions of their electors. The character of existing democratic government is that those selected to make decisions must ultimately have the capacity to overrule the populace. This view is known as the "trustee model" of representation, in contrast with the "delegate model." In the delegate model, the role of the representative is to advocate for the views of the electors. Trustees, in contrast, "are more flexible because they do not act under direct instruction from the individuals whose interests they are upholding. Instead, they are empowered to do what they think best" (Brito Vieira and Runciman 2008: 75). The argument in favour of a trustee model is partially a practical matter. It is virtually impossible to imagine how someone representing thousands of constituents could possibly be a mouthpiece for every one of their interests. No less important is the principled argument that being a political representative means being a special kind of independent thinker who is able to choose what is best for the people as a whole, even if that choice is not always the most popular one.

This view was clearly articulated by Edmund Burke, who was a member of parliament in Great Britain during the late eighteenth century. In his famous "Speech to the Electors of Bristol," which was delivered on election day in 1774, Burke argued that a representative's "unbiased opinion, his mature judgment, his enlightened conscience" should never be sacrificed to the whims and personal desires of individual electors. The job of a representative, argued Burke, was to represent "*one* nation, with *one* interest, that of the whole." As he explained, "Your representative owes you, not his industry only, but his judgment; and he betrays, instead of serving you, if he sacrifices it to your opinion" (Burke 1774/1987: par. 3). Burke was a conservative, but his conception of representation has been practised by conservatives and progressives alike. For example, when the majority of Canadian legislators voted against a proposal to bring back the death penalty in 1987, public opinion polls showed that most Canadians favoured the return of capital punishment. The independence shown by representatives voting for what was not the most popular decision is closer to a trustee model than a delegate one.

There is a fairly widespread consensus among supporters of official democracy in favour of the election of representatives with some independence from the immediate views of their electors. At the same time, representation does pose challenges for official-democracy perspectives. Government with consent of the people requires appropriate mechanisms to ensure that at least most of the people are able to see their own views authentically and effectively reflected in the debates and decisions of legislative bodies.

In some places, official democracy takes the form of proportional representation, a system designed to ensure that minority currents of opinion have at least some presence in elected legislatures. In proportional representation, seats in the legislature are allocated on the basis of the proportion of the overall popular vote each party captures, as opposed to the results of individual constituency battles. A legislature based on individual constituency battles can see a party win an overall majority of the seats with a minority of the vote, for example in Canada where the Conservative government won a majority of the seats (54%) in the 2011 election with a minority of the votes (40%). Electoral systems based on proportional representation are used in Brazil, Germany, Italy, and South Africa, among other places. This system can be justified in terms of liberal equality as the best way to assume that every individual voter has the same weight in deciding the final result and that no political parties are disadvantaged in competition (Van Der Hout and McGann 2009).

Particularly in an era of declining voter participation, advocates of official democracy may also favour complementing representation with other forms of citizen participation, ranging from consultative forums to full plebiscites. For example, Rebick (2000, 2009) has repeatedly praised the "participatory budgeting" process used in the Brazilian city of Porto Alegre. The process includes an annual series of open meetings about budget priorities, and thousands of residents have participated in them. "What is so exciting about this participatory budget is the interaction of active citizens, elected politicians, and career officials. Instead of playing an advisory role, as do many citizen bodies in our political system, the regional and sectoral assemblies actually discuss and debate budget priorities" and have a strong track record of shaping final government decisions (Rebick 2000: 29). Other governments have used the power of the Internet to hold "electric town meetings" that pull together so-called *citizen assemblies*: "hundreds, sometimes even thousands, of citizens ... to deliberate on an issue of public importance" (Ginsborg 2008: 66). In general, these mechanisms are seen not as alternatives to representative democracy but as ways of improving its accountability and inclusiveness.

Democracy-from-below perspectives tend not to favour trustee models of representation, as independence from electors tends to be associated with governing over them rather than enhancing self-government. And many within this perspective are suspicious of all forms of representation. One of the sharpest critics of representative democracy was the French writer Jean-Jacques Rousseau (1712–1778). He condemned not merely a particular model of representation but the whole idea of one person representing another in the exercise of self-rule. In Rousseau's words,

> Sovereignty cannot be represented. . . . Any law which the people has not ratified in person is void; it is not law at all. The English people [who live under representative democracy] believes itself to be free; it is gravely mistaken; it is free only during the election of Members of Parliament; as soon as the Members are elected, the people is enslaved; it is nothing. (Rousseau 1762/1968: 141)

The essay from which this quotation is drawn begins with the powerful statement that "Man was born free, and he is everywhere in chains." Systems of political representation were among the fetters created over the course of history that Rousseau believed kept people from living freely and to their full potential as human beings.

From the view of democracy from below, even if the act of voting in an election is meaningful, it is fleeting and rare, and therefore incapable of serving as the basis of a democratic society. Hannah Arendt, for example, argues that "those activities of 'expressing, discussing, and deciding' ... are the activities of freedom" (quoted in Sitton 1987: 82). The fact that representative democracy "restricts the broad mass of the citizenry to private concerns" (as opposed to public affairs) means that most of its citizens are not truly free. Self-rule is a process, not a destination. It exists only when people are regularly participating in making decisions about the issues that affect their lives.

For Marx, democracy is the only form of society that allows for the flourishing of our unique capacities as humans because it is the only one in which all of humanity, as a collective, has full control over the productive powers of our species (Le Blanc 2010). To make decision-making power the job of an elite group is problematic, not merely because specific rulers might end up abusing this privilege (although clearly that is also a risk), but because doing so means depriving most people of the chance to take part in the activities that make us human.

Ironically, these critiques are backed up by the writings of some of the earliest proponents of representative democracy. As Wood (1995) explains, the Founding Fathers of the United States saw representation not as "a way of implementing but of *avoiding* or at least partially circumventing democracy" (pp. 122–23). In 1776, the American colonies declared independence from their British rulers, and a new Constitution (or set of founding principles and laws) based upon representative democracy was proposed. In a series of famous newspaper articles now known as *The Federalist Papers,* three prominent public figures urged Americans to adopt the proposed Constitution. One of their main arguments in favour of the new system was that "representative democracy avoided the dangers clearly inherent in 'simple democracy,'" by which they meant mass participation in government (Arblaster 2002: 39).

A special danger identified by the Federalists was allowing poor and other marginalized people to gain control of the levers of power. In the words of Alexander Hamilton, a Federalist who would go on to become US president, if you are to have participatory democracy on a mass scale, "you must expect error, confusion and instability" (quoted in Arblaster 2002: 39). More to the point, you must also expect the large number of poor and marginalized people to demand a share in the wealth of society (Pitkin 2004: 338). An attack on the privileges of the rich is what Hamilton, himself a wealthy property owner, feared more than anything. Protecting property and wealth explains his argument for creating a Senate that would "give 'the rich and well-born' a 'distinct, permanent share in the government' through which they could 'check the imprudence of democracy'" (Arblaster 2002: 39). James Madison, another Federalist and future US president, argued that representative government was uniquely equipped to provide popular rule over a large territory "while ensuring 'the total exclusion of the people, in their collective capacity, from any share [in the government]'" (Brito Vieira and Runciman 2008: 38). In Madison's eyes, representative government would enhance "the public views by passing them through the medium of a chosen body of citizens, whose wisdom may best discern the true interest of their country" (quoted in Zeitlin 1997: 187).

According to these pioneers of representative democracy, the purpose of the system was to prevent non-experts and people without great wealth from meddling in policy matters. John Stuart Mill, a British member of parliament and political theorist who championed representative government, wrote that he "felt passionately that the working classes, men and women, were not ready or sufficiently educated for democracy" (Ginsborg 2008: 6). Mill believed that while all people should have a right to express their views, representative government should be built in ways that ensured that only economically and socially privileged people would lead.

Historical patterns in representative democracies suggest that Mill's wish has largely come true. Certainly, people from marginalized groups have broken down formal barriers to electoral participation and have won elections. However, as discussed earlier in the chapter, the overall trends in representative institutions reveal the systematic exclusion of poor people, women, people of colour, disabled people, and other marginalized groups. To understand the processes through which these contemporary patterns have developed, we should think about them in light of the exclusionary aims of the original architects of representative institutions.

The existing system of representative democracy, with its trustee method of representation, is thus incompatible with the self-government that is the goal of democracy from below. Yet there are sharp debates within democracy-from-below circles about the extent to which representation and self-government are compatible. Although some favour delegate models and see representation as a valuable tool in effective self-government, others see a loss in popular power as the necessary consequence of any system of representation.

The delegate model holds that the job of the political representative is to act as closely as possible to how the people being represented would act if they were involved in the same situation: "The representative must do what her principal would do, must act as if the principal herself were acting" (Pitkin 1967: 144). The strength of the delegate model is its commitment to the principle of self-governance through keeping the interests of the electors (as opposed to the personal motivations of the elected) at the forefront of public affairs. Delegate systems often include very active accountability processes, for example making recall easy if the representative ceases to represent her or his electors and ensuring that elected positions come with no special privileges to create separate interests from those of the people.

The Paris Commune of 1871 was an example of the delegate system in action, developed in the heat of struggle. The Commune refers to a popular uprising in which thousands of working people in Paris rejected the authority of the national government and kicked out the French army from the city (Tombs 1999). In an effort to establish a system of genuine collective self-rule, the Commune declared that all government positions were to be paid at a workers' wage, all representatives could be recalled and replaced by their electors at any point, and the only legitimate physical force in the area would be the National Guard, which, unlike the official police and army under the old regime, would be a genuine people's army, consisting of all able-bodied men.

Carolyn Eichner (2004) has argued that the Parisian revolt "temporarily overthrew hierarchies of gender, class, and religion" (p. 18). Although male privilege and other forms of discrimination did not stop all at once, Eichner notes that "women played integral roles in myriad ways throughout the Commune. They formed political clubs ... re-established vigilance committees ... created a citywide labor and defense association, wrote and published newspapers and political tracts, demonstrated in the streets, and fought and nursed on the battlefield" (p. 26). Her research suggests that there is something about the outbreak of participatory democracy on a mass scale that tends to open up "a field of opportunity, both real and imagined, for the reshaping of hierarchies and power relations, and for the potential cessation of privilege and oppression" (p. 208).

Labour unions with a vibrant shop steward system are another example of the delegate model of representation. Camfield (2011) writes that, over the history of the labour movement, "shop stewards—shop floor workers elected to represent their fellow union members in dealings with management and who often organized work stoppages and other forms of direct action when conflicts arose—were often central in enforcing workers' rights" (p. 10). A strong steward system is based on regular interaction among stewards and rank-and-file workers. Stewards are effective delegates to the extent that their representative role is informed by the collective will of the broader union membership, as formulated and expressed in formal mass meetings, membership surveys, and informal conversations. Of course, as unions become more bureaucratic, the stewards can become far more distanced from the rank-and-file activists, tied instead to the leadership and buried in formal procedures specified in collective agreements and labour law.

Delegate systems can contribute to self-government by making structured deliberation an important part of decision making, even in large-scale societies. One of the great challenges of self-government is ensuring informed decision making—developing methods of interchange to ensure that people hear a variety of perspectives and learn from each other's, even when they disagree. Murray Bookchin (1999) argues that dissensus, a diversity of perspectives, is "a most vital aspect of all dialogue" (p. 149). Delegate systems create forums to ensure that a variety of views are engaged in discussion and debate leading up to decision making. Examples of such delegate systems have emerged in forms of council democracy, which see mass meetings at the level of the workplace, school, or neighbourhood elect delegates to local councils, which then elect delegates to regional councils, and so on through a series of steps up to the highest level. The revolutionary upsurge at the end of World War I led to the development of delegated soldiers, sailors, and workers councils along these lines in Austria, Germany, Russia, and elsewhere (Gluckstein 2011).

In contrast, other proponents of democracy from below see representation as incompatible with popular power. They tend to favour decentralized systems of assembly-style democracy in which all present are full participants and no decision making is delegated. Such systems require serious decentralization, as assembly-style meetings can accommodate only a finite number of people. At the core of this model is the ideal that genuine self-government can be accomplished only when the people themselves give over none of their powers to representatives, even those with limited mandates as representatives. The Occupy movement has certainly seen an intense focus on the general assembly as the core decision-making process, preferring the presence and participation of all in open meetings to any form of delegation. As David Graeber (2002) argues, "It is about creating and enacting horizontal networks instead of top-down structures like states, parties or corporations; networks based on principles of decentralized, non-hierarchical consensus democracy" (p. 70).

Terry Eagleton (2011) argues that no one can know for sure what genuine self-governing democracy will actually look like: "if the new social order is to be genuinely transformative, it follows that there is a strict limit on how much you can say about it right now. We can, after all, describe the future only in terms drawn from the past or present; and a future which broke radically with the present would have us straining at the limits of our language" (p. 73). A new system based on democratic self-government would have to begin from where we are now; and the road between here and there could only be mapped fully as it was travelled. In the meantime, advocates of democratic self-government have drawn lessons and hope from important historical examples.

The Haudenosaunee Confederacy, which is an indigenous government on lands that European settler governments call Canada and the United States of America, created "one of the first and longest lasting participatory democracies in the world" (Haudenosaunee Confederacy). Haudenosaunee government is based upon "consensual decision-making, and a participatory political process" (Alfred 1995: 78). The Haudenosaunee Great Law of Peace makes it clear that politics is not something that can be separated out from society and left to an elite group of representatives. Politics is, rather, deeply rooted in a holistic understanding of human life and the natural world, and therefore the domain and responsibility of all members of the community. In spite of being subjected to centuries of violent and legalistic attacks from European colonizers, this traditional system of democracy continues to govern members of the Six Nations reservation outside of Brantford, Ontario. However, traditional governance now exists alongside—and in

---

EXERCISING YOUR DEMOCRATIC IMAGINATION
Too Much Democracy?

The Economist magazine ran an editorial in April 2011 entitled "The Perils of Extreme Democracy." It talked about California, where limits on taxation resulting from decisions made through referendums have put the state in a position where it cannot afford basic services such as education. Voter initiatives or referendums, forms of democracy allowing citizens to set government policy directly by voting on specific ballot initiatives at election time, are shaping the political terrain in the state in important ways. This began in 1978, with Proposition 13, a referendum that permanently lowered property tax rates.

State services, such as education and social assistance, are in very serious decline in California. Tuition fees for post-secondary education are rising rapidly. It is becoming increasingly difficult for elected governments to make sensible decisions about economic and social policy, as they lack the policy tools in areas such as taxation to fulfil their basic mandates. In the words of *The Economist*, "This citizen legislature has caused chaos" ("The perils" 2011: 11). Further, referendums are being used to attack human rights. In November 2008, a California referendum overturned the right of people in same-sex relationships to get married. The right of a majority to vote away minority rights is certainly a problematic feature of the referendum system. The case of California raises important questions about how far democracy should go.

Is there such a thing as too much democracy?

What would need to be involved in practices of deeper democracy to avoid the kind of trouble California is facing?

tension with—forms of representative democracy imposed by the settler Canadian government. Part of the tension between these two systems is explained by their contending visions of the role and character of democratic representation and participation.

A belief in the virtue of mass participation was also embedded in elements of democracy in the ancient Greek city of Athens. Although more than half of the population (including women, slaves, and foreign-born individuals) were prevented from becoming citizens of Athens, the citizen population was deeply involved in government. Participation in the Athenian assembly, the main policy-making body, was open to all citizens, and higher political offices were filled on a rotating basis or by lottery. In Arblaster's view,

> The system of the citizens filling offices by random rotation, and of having the right to take part in the assembly, meant that Athens between, say, 462 and 322 BC came as near as any community every has to achieving the democratic ideal of government by the people themselves, through citizen participation, rather than the modern substitutes of representation or even delegation. (Arblaster 2002: 21)

The Paradox of Representation

The word representation traditionally refers to "the action of standing for, or in the place of, a person, group, or thing" (OED Online 2011). Because the concept is so familiar, it can easily seem straightforward. However, according to the political theorist Hannah Pitkin (1967), representation is a complex process that always involves a paradox; for "in representation something not literally present is considered as present in a nonliteral sense" (p. 9). Something that is absent is made present. A familiar example in the context of democracy is the notion that, although my body does not literally stand in parliament when laws are being debated, supposedly I *am* there, in a non-literal sense, in the form of my elected representative.

Pitkin (1967) explains that there is more than one type of representation. She has developed specialized terminology to distinguish between the different forms and consequences of one thing representing another. For example, she explains that some cases more heavily involve "symbolic representation": the process through which a person or object evokes ideas of some other thing. A heart calls forth ideas of love; a map is a stripped down sketch of the city; the bald eagle symbolizes the United States. There is no negotiation between the two objects. No instructions are delivered that allow the represented to indicate how they wish to be depicted. Symbolic representation concerns the ability of an image to conjure some other thought.

In contrast to symbolic representation, "substantive representation" refers to activities carried out by a representative on behalf of some other individual or group. An example would be a lawyer representing a client: one speaks on behalf of the other, but the client is likely an active participant in the process. There is a rational and deliberate element in this relationship that doesn't exist in mere symbolism. Subsequently, substantive representation involves a responsibility on the part of the representative to carry out the wishes of the people being represented.

The history of democracy is filled with both of these types of representation identified by Pitkin. Often the same situation involves elements of both. For example, if you've ever seen pictures of the US presidential inauguration, the ceremony that puts a new president in charge, you'll know that symbolic representation continues to be central to political power. There are flags everywhere (which symbolize the nation); row upon row of military, political, and judicial dignitaries (which symbolize the power and legitimacy of the state); and the ceremony unfolds according to a series of traditional procedures (which symbolize the continuity of today's system with the long history of the United States). In the case of Barack Obama's inauguration in 2009, many people also saw the president as a symbol of success in the ongoing struggles of people of colour. Yet, at the same time as Obama symbolized the American people and their history, he was also their representative in a substantive sense. Obama was there because the American people elected him to lead their country, and his inauguration speech described in broad strokes what he viewed as being the instructions given to him by the people he now represented.

What traditional notions of representation share is the assumption that the person or symbol doing the representing is standing in for an authentic object, feeling, or person—some thing that actually exists. As Terry Eagleton playfully puts it, "one reason why a photograph of a chipmunk represents a chipmunk is because it is not the actual animal" (Eagleton 2007: 213). From this point of view, the crown on the king's head is not itself the authority of the king, but it represents the king's authority, which is real indeed. A novel about World War I may be written long after the guns have stopped shooting, but it represents battles that actually took place. According to traditional notions of representation, although the political values and choices of one person or group may be represented by someone else, the original values and choices exist in reality, independently of processes of representation.

In contrast to this traditional perspective, one influential trend in recent scholarly research takes the extreme position that nothing real exists outside of representation. This view of representation has important political implications. Broadly speaking, **postmodern (or "signifactory") perspectives** "argue that signs do not refer to external entities but only to other signs" (Ebert 1986: 895). By viewing language and culture as the foundational elements of human existence, postmodern thinkers tend to erase "the distinctions between signs (representations) and reality: everything is signification and signification is all we know about reality" (Ebert 1986: 895). The real world exists "not through presence but through *difference*"—through the interrelationships among words, symbols, and other elements of culture (Sears and Cairns 2010: 104). Thus, from this point of view, there are no coherent, stable objects, identities, and truths that exist independently of signification; rather, there are only our representations of how we understand the world. Postmodernists assume that "there is nothing, no thing-in-itself, that can escape representation by signs. There is, in short, nothing we might access behind signs or outside of representation" (McNally 2001: 58).

This radical assumption of postmodern thinkers such as Michel Foucault challenges taken-for-granted "truths" about human nature, as well as the legitimacy of governmental power and social institutions. Foucault is particularly interested in the power of what he calls "discourse" to represent a historically particular and partial configuration of ideas and practices as though it is the eternal, universal Truth. In Stuart Hall's words, discourse is "a group of statements which provide a language for talking about—a way of representing the knowledge about—a particular topic at a particular historical moment. [...] Discourse is about the production of knowledge through language" (Hall 1992: 291). Foucault points out that the power of some groups over others is embedded in prevailing systems of representation, but he also argues that dominant discourses can and do change over time. For example, his research shows that the definition and approach to "madness," the discourse of mental illness, was very different in the seventeenth century than it is today. Many activists and writers have drawn on Foucault's insights to denaturalize and call into question the legitimacy of contemporary social norms and institutions.

Critics of Foucault argue that his work has had "the effect of encouraging his followers to neglect the influence of the material, economic, and structural factors" involved in reproducing unequal **relations of power** (Hall 1997: 51). For one thing, the assumption that there is no reality outside of representation weakens our critical capacity to analyze the embodied forces responsible for creating and maintaining experiences of hunger, occupation, and sickness. A postmodern perspective that begins with the belief that there is no reality outside of representation will find it difficult to accept that hunger, occupation, sickness, and poverty are *real*—that they exist in an authentic material sense, irrespective of how they are represented or made meaningful by discourse.

Similarly, postmodern perspectives have trouble articulating how injustice should be resisted. Sanbonmatsu (2011) writes that postmodern thinkers believe that "the human being is best seen as an effect of power, as something almost wholly produced by power and discourse" (p. 220). People's language, ideals, and practices are products of the dominant discourse in which they live. Yet, if there are no authentic, actually existing stable points of view outside of discourse from which social transformation can be formulated and enacted, how do movements of resistance develop, and how can people be expected to support and deliberately strengthen them? Sanbonmatsu notes that postmodernism in general "avoid[s] making arguments for particular moral and social norms or universal ideals" (p. 221), and he says that Foucault, especially, "was very skeptical that we could talk meaningfully about one system versus another as being more free than another" (p. 225). Sanbonmatsu concludes that postmodern theories of representation tend to diminish the potential of democracy; for if humans are without agency and merely reflect the powers of discourse bearing upon them and if ethical arguments are inadmissible because there is no eternal truth outside of representation, then it is not at all clear on what grounds dreams of a better world could be imagined—or who might be expected to build movements on their behalf. The tension between human agency and representation runs throughout this chapter.

Making Your Voice Heard

Ginsborg (2008) argues that, at the start of the twenty-first century, the central task of people who believe in democracy is "to invent new forms and practices which *combine* representative with participatory democracy, in order to improve the quality of the first through the contribution of the second" (p. 12). It may indeed be appealing to integrate these two democratic models, but it makes sense to reflect upon the basic tensions between representation and participation before designing new mechanisms meant to merge the two.

One of the main themes of this chapter is that current representative institutions tend to over-represent certain social groups and under-represent others, in terms of both embodiment and political interests. It is arguable, therefore, that making representative democracy more inclusive must involve not only engaging larger numbers of people in deliberation but also responding to the demands of marginalized groups struggling to make their voices count in decision-making processes.

There is also the recurring question of what role representation can legitimately play in a democracy, and general views concerning representation's role vary depending on whether you see democracy as a system of government or as a central element of self-government. Pitkin (2004) has written that "the arrangements we call 'representative democracy' have become a substitute for popular self-government, not its enactment" (p. 340). Reopening the democratic imagination involves asking what adjustments would need to be made within the existing system to make it more democratic, as well as whether a more fundamental shift in the balance between representation and participation is necessary for popular power to flourish.

5 RED TAPE: BUREAUCRACY, DEMOCRACY, AND THE STATE

Everyone reading this book can probably testify to at least one painful experience with bureaucracy. It is pretty hard to avoid dealing with sprawling administrative structures in one part of your life or another. Bureaucracy is usually at its worst when it is most important to you. You get to the front of the line after a long wait, and bureaucrats tell you they cannot help you. Maybe they point to the even longer line you are really supposed to be in, tell you about some form you neglected to complete, or read out an obscure policy that makes your request impossible. Bureaucratic processes tend to be dismissive of what makes your case unique, and those applying these processes can appear to make decisions on the basis of what can seem like arbitrary reasons. Nevertheless, these decisions can mean your livelihood or relationships when they affect desperately needed social assistance, student loan cheques, a travel visa, or immigration status.

The list could go on. These are situations governed by procedures that are never made clear to you, so you never feel in control. The key is the feeling of powerlessness in the face of a machine—you simply cannot get to the people who actually have the authority to make a difference.

People often associate bureaucracy in this negative sense with government. In fact, conservative politicians have a history of making hay attacking government bureaucracy, as in the case of Mayor Rob Ford of Toronto, elected in 2010 in part for his attacks on the "gravy train" of the city's bureaucracy. We sometimes forget that corporations such as banks and insurance companies can match governments for mind-numbing, machine-like procedures and for impersonality. The exception, in the case of corporations, is generally when they are trying to sell you something.

Because the bureaucratic method of administration values standardized, hierarchical decision-making processes, it exists in some tension with democracy. However, in government, bureaucracy and democracy have become so codependent that we do not think very much about the complex relationship between them. The view from official democracy sees bureaucracy as a natural part of government. By contrast, the democracy-from-below perspective argues that collective self-government is an uncomfortable fit with impersonal and unresponsive bureaucratic administration. This chapter examines the reasoning behind these contrasting perspectives and explains why the function of bureaucracy will look different depending upon the basic assumptions held about the role of bureaucracy within the modern state. Most political commentators portray bureaucracy as necessary because of its neutrality and expertise in administrating government policy, yet many also describe it as being out of touch, impenetrable, and alienating. The difficulty the public feels in simply entering government buildings layered with security procedures and other barriers should raise some questions about whether "we the people" are really in charge.

Bureaucracy and Efficiency

As discussed in Chapter 1, democracy means rule by the people. Bureaucracy, in contrast, is defined in the dictionary as rule by offices or "government by bureau" (OED Online 2011). A "bureau," in this sense, is "an office or business with a specified function; an agency for the coordination of related activities, the distribution of information, etc." An office, in other words, is a unit with a defined area of responsibility and specific procedures, which are to be followed regardless of the individual who fills the position.

In modern democracies, these specialized bureaucratic departments regulate all areas of human life. Government bureaucracy divides up the world not simply in a metaphorical sense; rather, it actually sorts every component of human experience into rigidly defined administrative departments, each one with responsibility for regulating affairs within that realm. Different names are used for these bureaucratic units ("departments" or "ministries" are most common), but, generally speaking, the administration of relationships between, for example, workers and bosses, falls under the jurisdiction of bureaucrats in the department of labour. Tax law is regulated by officials in the finance ministry. Bureaucrats (who are sometimes called "civil servants" or "public sector workers") in the ministry of the environment are responsible for administering environmental policy. No aspect of human existence lies outside the sprawling reach of bureaucratic regulation.

Roles and responsibilities within departments are organized around rigid hierarchical systems. "The civil servants in each department are divided into various ranks. At the top of the ladder in each department is an official known [in many systems] as the deputy minister, a career civil servant who usually has advanced technical training and a good deal of civil service experience" (Malcolmson and Myers 2005: 118–19). Civil servants lower down the ladder are mostly responsible for implementing decisions made by their superiors. Bureaucracy is often associated with impersonality because the job of public sector workers is to fill very clearly defined roles within a very clearly defined hierarchy. If you search for images of "bureaucracy" in an Internet database, you will find pages of pyramid-shaped organizational charts detailing who reports to whom on the basis of bureaucratic rank.

Personal discretion is highly controlled in bureaucracy. It is conceivable that an individual who is a passionate supporter of migrant rights might get a job in the immigration bureau (though that person could easily get screened out at the job interview stage). But if that civil servant had a higher rate of admitting immigrants to the country than other bureaucrats in the same position, there is a very good chance he or she would be disciplined. Modern bureaucratic administration aims to remove the human influence in decision making and to rule uniformly through strict rules.

In tributary societies ruled by the nobility, government authority was personal and not highly dependent on the administrative procedures of the office (see Chapter 1). The French king Louis XIV is famously quoted as saying, "*L'état c'est moi*," meaning, "I am the state." He was claiming quite literally that his person was the French state, and so he had remarkable decision-making discretion. In contrast, bureaucratic office holders, wherever they may be located in the hierarchy, are bound by the very specific practices and regulations that limit decision making based on personal views.

One of the foremost social theorists of bureaucracy was Max Weber (1958: 196–98), who identified the core characteristics of bureaucracy in his work in the early twentieth century. According to Weber, bureaucracy is constructed as a clear hierarchy of offices, each with its own specific jurisdiction, including reporting and supervisory relationships, as well as clearly identified avenues for appeal. The request, for example, to speak to the supervisor of someone who has just told you that you were not eligible for a student loan might or might not constitute a legitimate channel for appeal, depending on the rules that apply in that particular area. Two of the key markers of bureaucracy are the maintenance of written records and the use of files to establish a history for each case or situation. The effort to build up precedent and institutional memory through constant documentation is part of the overall strategy of embedding impersonality into bureaucratic administration, thereby diminishing the autonomy of individual bureaucrats.

Bureaucratic officials are appointed on the basis of training and qualification, not elected. The problem with election is that the most qualified person does not necessarily get the job. Further, the elected person has a certain authority as a result of the way he or she obtained the office, a mandate from constituents: "In principle, an official who is so elected has an autonomous position opposite the superordinate official. The elected official does not derive his position 'from above' but 'from below'" (Weber 1958: 201). By contrast, bureaucrats are directly accountable to their superiors, not to the citizens at large. There is no opportunity for citizens to vote civil servants out of office. Consequently, according to Weber, it is easier for bureaucrats to make rational decisions that are not clouded by personal feelings or loyalties or by political pressure. The public, then, should be able to count on bureaucrats to make fair and consistent decisions, meaning that any given individual in line for service should be judged by exactly the same criteria as the person behind, whether the line ends at "Desk 1" or "Desk 15."

This conception of bureaucratic fairness, however, often matches poorly with the needs and expectations of people who require services. Toronto dub poet Lillian Allen (1993) powerfully describes the interaction between a social worker and a person trying to access services. The social worker voice says, "You see, my job is to explain our / policy / i don't make them / I just apply them / ... we don't have a policy to deal with your er ... r / request." The client's voice says, "whose side are you on" and later "fit et et et in / a little square / a computer printout page / fit" (Allen 1993: 67).

Bureaucracy often leaves service users with the feeling that their large and complex problem has not been understood and that the help they receive (if any) is inadequate. Anthropologist Elliott Leyton (1978) did a powerful study of the interaction of the officials from the Workmen's Compensation Board in Newfoundland with miners in Newfoundland suffering from health conditions such as cancer and lung disease. The miners themselves tended to classify their condition as "mine disease," attributing their illness and disability to years working in the mines and expecting fair compensation for their lost earning power and poor physical state. The officials, on the other hand, used precise medical criteria to diagnose each individual. They identified a variety of possible causes for the illness, not only working in the mine, and had a complex calculus of disability. This calculation meant that individuals were compensated very differently depending on how their inability to function was assessed. The end result was conflict: miners felt they did not get what they deserved and officials felt disrespected and manipulated.

Leyton (1978) provides a powerful quotation from an interview in which a miner describes some of his experiences with the board. The miner outlines what he sees as the board's refusal to hand over benefits that are rightly deserved: "They don't want to give it to you *any* way. They just try to keep it. And they'll try every way, in every shape and form, to keep it away from you." Specifically, he reports frustration with the medical specialists who seemed to misidentify his occupational disease. "You start to fight, trying to get your compensation, then, and you got every doctor down there against you. They try to tell you you got T.B., you got pneumonia, and you got this and you got something else. They knows goddam well what you got!" (Leyton 1978: 81).

The bureaucrats of the board were shocked by this kind of response from miners. Leyton (1978) argues they saw themselves as "professionals and public servants, dispassionately administering government regulations on behalf of injured workmen," carrying on deliberations that were "not only dispassionate in quality, but humanitarian in consequence" (p. 82–83). This situation comes down to a basic clash in world views: the officials see themselves as treating everyone by the same formal and impersonal standards while the community members experience this treatment as irrational, unfair, and arbitrary. As a result, bureaucrats judge the community members as ignorant of the regulations, focused on material gain, and insensitive to impartiality because guided by their own interests (Leyton 1978: 89).

The bureaucratic world view that miners found so vexing is carefully sustained by specific laws or regulations that frame every decision, as well as by a hierarchy that carefully monitors consistency with that legalistic frame in every decision extending from highest officials down to front-line officers. Most often, the regulations and legislation are designed with the assumption that a key job of officials will be to filter out the false claims of those who have no legitimate right to specific benefits or services. Someone training to be an immigration officer once caused great hilarity when she answered the question "What is the job of an immigration officer?" by saying, "To make people feel welcome in Canada." Anyone who has ever crossed a controlled international border is aware that the officials there are not greeters and that their harsh scrutiny is disproportionately targeted at certain populations.

Bureaucracy, Red Tape, and Democracy

In everyday usage, we tend to associate bureaucracy with red tape, meaning inefficiency, slowness, and incompetence. The term "red tape" derives from the "woven red or pink tape used to secure legal documents and official papers" (OED Online 2011). It is hard to hear "bureaucracy" and not think of red tape, glacial pace, and numbing impersonality. Tim Hudak, the leader of the Progressive Conservative Party in Ontario, is typical of politicians who claim they will attack bureaucracy if elected to office. He describes one government agency as "a needless layer of bureaucracy that is getting fatter and fatter every year" (CP24 2011: par. 2). We discuss issues of bureaucracy and body image in Chapter 7.

Weber has a very different view of the operation of bureaucracy. He argues not only that bureaucracy is highly efficient but also that there is no sound alternative in a large-scale, modern industrial society:

> The fully developed bureaucratic apparatus compares to other organizations exactly as the machine does with the non-mechanical modes of production. Precision, speed, unambiguity, knowledge of files, discretion, unity, strict subordination, reduction of friction and of material and personal costs—these are raised to the optimum point in the strictly bureaucratic organization. (Weber 1958: 215)

In fact, Weber believes that the efficiency of bureaucracy is so great that it tends to override other administrative systems, including democracy:

> Under normal conditions, the power position of a fully developed bureaucracy is always overtowering. The "political master" finds himself in the position of the "dilettante" who stands opposite the "expert," facing the trained official who stands within the management of administration. (Weber 1958: 232)

This is not to say that government bureaucracy functions completely independently from elected officials. "In theory, the permanent executive [or bureaucratic arm of government] carries out the orders of the [elected] political executive" and is therefore ultimately responsible to the people (Ellis and MacIvor 2008: 269). The small group of officials in charge of setting priorities and overseeing the work of bureaucratic departments is called the cabinet. And though different types of democratic systems have different methods for selecting members of the cabinet, in all cases the cabinet is by some mechanism responsible to the electorate. Thus, the line of accountability runs from lower-level bureaucrats, who answer to higher-ranking managers in each department, and from there up to senior civil servants, who, in turn, answer directly to the elected political executive (who, again, in theory, answers to the people).

In the United States, the political executive is the elected president and the cabinet he or she appoints. In parliamentary systems, the political executive is made up of the prime minister and cabinet, all of whom tend to be elected members of parliament. However, as Malcolmson and Myers (2005) point out, the relationship between cabinet ministers (or "departmental secretaries") and high-ranking bureaucrats in their department is not always as straightforward as bureaucratic organizational charts suggest: "In theory, the deputy minister [who is a member of the civil service] is merely the minister's chief advisor; in practice, however, the deputy's superiority in knowledge can lead to a situation where he or she is really the one who runs the department" (p. 119).

The elected representative, from whatever field of life, faces experienced bureaucrats who have been at their posts for a long time. Those civil servants have developed tools to limit democratic oversight, including the characterization of huge swaths of knowledge known as "official secrets" (Weber 1958: 233). Even elected politicians are excluded from knowing many things about the functioning of the government that is supposed to be accountable to them in the name of the people: "Career civil servants possess a mastery of the complex and often challenging details of policy and governance, a mastery that most temporary cabinet ministers cannot hope to match" (Ellis and MacIvor 2008: 269).

This situation, the hapless elected representative contending with the wily bureaucrats, is the source of the comedy in the old British television show *Yes Minister,* dating back to the 1980s. The first episode of the series shows a first-time cabinet minister struggling with the smooth and experienced civil servants in the "Department for Administrative Affairs" (Jay and Lynn 1980). The bureaucrats always get the minister to do what they want him to, while, at the same time, convincing him that they are doing what he wants them to do. In their first meeting, the minister announces his plan to implement his party's platform favouring greater transparency or open government. Sir Humphrey, the bureaucrat in charge, hands him a file that maps the route to implement "open government."

The minister, not expecting such compliance from the bureaucrats, says, "I must say I'm rather surprised. I expected to have to fight you all the way along the line on this."

Sir Humphrey, the seasoned senior bureaucrat, replies, "People do have funny ideas about the civil service. We're just here to help you formulate and implement your policies."

But of course they are not. Among other things, the minister is taken aback by the fact that they already have a full appointment book or diary for him. "My diary? You didn't know I was coming."

Bernard, the other bureaucrat present, replies, "We knew there would be a minister, Minister." And, a bit later, Sir Humphrey adds, "Her Majesty does like the business of government to continue even when there are no politicians around."

Later, three civil servants are having a conversation among themselves in some sort of gentlemen's club. Sir Humphrey says of his new minister, "We'll have him housetrained in no time .... As long as we can head him off this 'open government' nonsense."

Bernard, the more junior bureaucrat, asks, "But what's wrong with open government? I mean, why shouldn't the public know more about what's going on?"

The most senior bureaucrat present, Sir Arnold, soon answers him: "My dear boy, it is a contradiction in terms: you can be open or you can have government."

Bernard challenges him, "But surely the citizens of a democracy have a right to know."

"No," replies his boss Sir Humphrey, "they have a right to be ignorant. Knowledge only means complicity and guilt. Ignorance has a certain dignity."

Yes Minister is a humorous portrayal of the tension between democracy and bureaucracy as it works out in government offices. One person who theorizes this tension is Robert Michels, a German theorist who explores the reasons why even the most radical democratic movements seem to yield bureaucratic regimes. Indeed, even the internal life of radical movements, such as labour movements and social democratic parties, tend to become bureaucratized, let alone the state administrations they are sometimes elected to govern. Michels (1962) describes this process as the "iron law of oligarchy," meaning that he thinks it is inevitable for all organizations to transform eventually into bureaucratic decision-making structures: "The formation of oligarchies within the various forms of democracy is the outcome of organic necessity, and consequently affects every organization, be it socialist or even anarchist" (pp. 365–66).

Michels believes it to be a scientific fact that genuine democratic self-government is impossible. He argues that "social wealth cannot be administered in any other manner than by the creation of an extensive bureaucracy" (Michels 1962: 347). For him, both the necessity of administration in large complex societies and the impossibility of genuinely collective self-rule make bureaucracy and hierarchy inevitable. Self-rule he describes as impractical because of the very character of human collectivity, which learns very slowly, creating the "objective immaturity of the mass." This immaturity cannot be overcome, as "it derives from the very nature of mass as mass, for this, even when organized, suffers from an incurable incompetence." The mass does not, according to Michels, benefit from the knowledge of all involved but rather has its own quite limited capacities as a collective. When someone shouts fire, the mass does not deliberate, and individuals do not make their own assessment; instead, everyone runs, even to the extent of trampling children or elderly people. The reason is clear: "the mass *per se* is amorphous, and therefore needs division of labor, specialization, and guidance" (Michels 1962: 367).

Despite all that, Michels (1962) argues that it is still worth striving for democracy, as that struggle might somewhat temper the oligarchical tendencies in human life:

Democracy is a treasure which no one will ever discover by deliberate search. But in continuing our search, in laboring indefatigably to discover the undiscoverable, we shall perform a work which will have fertile results in the democratic sense. (Michels 1962: 368)

Michels points to a fascinating contradiction— even in our movements for change that are critical of the existing bureaucratic forms of rule, bureaucratization creeps in and undercuts effective democratic functioning. Many critics challenge his fundamental explanation that there is an iron law making democracy unviable because the people are unready and unable to rule themselves. Richard Hyman (1971) argues that Michels ignores many countervailing tendencies to his so-called "iron law" and therefore misses key possibilities for democratic practices in unions and radical movements. Hyman, for example, points out the role that shop stewards have played in mobilizing shop-floor democracy, in contexts that are vibrantly democratic, challenging employer power to control production in important ways.

In large factories and mines, the position of the shop steward was crucial as trade unions developed. The stewards were the front line of union organization, elected members who coordinated union activism in a particular shop or area. They took up issues with management on behalf of workers and called direct actions at the shop-floor level when that was necessary and possible. Ralph Darlington (2002) argues that effective shop stewards can play a significant role "in translating shopfloor discontent into a sense of injustice and in mobilising workers for collective action" (p. 98). For example, when an immediate threat to the health and safety of workers is brought to the attention of the stewards, they might call for people to halt production immediately and walk out until the problem is addressed. Indeed, historically, many worker grievances were worked out directly through immediate action on the shop floor, whether that related to the pace of work, the decisions of a supervisor, or something as simple as access to a washroom break. The role of shop stewards has been declining over a long period, due to a combination of work reorganization and the development of bureaucratic procedures that orient stewards toward the filing of formal grievances rather than shop-floor direct action (Darlington 2010).

The history of shop stewards, then, shows that the democratic accountability of worker leaders in the workplace varies considerably depending on the organization of work and the impact of laws and collective agreements. Rather than an "iron law" that applies in all cases, the bureaucratizing tendency might be more accurately considered as the result of how movements and institutions are situated within society as it now exists or within the dominant social relations. After all, social movements and institutions do not emerge in the idealized mountain breeze of freedom but in the actual places where we live, work, and play. They are influenced by the existing cultural, legal, and social relationships that already shape the space. David Camfield (2011) argues that bureaucracy exists in workers' movements because "people are subjected to formal rules that limit their ability to determine what they do and how they do it, rules they cannot easily change" (pp. 58–59). He argues that the overall context of labour law, the specific language of collective agreements with particular employers, and the character of union constitutions all produce a bureaucratizing effect that undercuts the democratic functioning of unions.

It is not uncommon, for example, to see a strike shut down by the union leadership just as it is gaining momentum and popularity. In 1997, teachers in Ontario went out on a province-wide general strike to protest new legislation that would change the curriculum, weaken democratic control of school boards, and affect teachers' bargaining rights. The provincial government sought an injunction ruling the strike illegal, but the courts did not grant it. The lack of an injunction seemed to inject new energy into the strike, yet, at that crucial moment, the leaders of the teachers' unions declared the strike was over, without any consultation with the membership (Sears 2003: 240–41).

This is not a unique situation. Union leaders also shut down a growing wave of strikes in British Columbia in 1983, strikes protesting against a new government that introduced legislation cutting social programs and attacking worker rights (Palmer 1987). Union leaders settled for deep concessions in a 2004 strike by health care workers in British Columbia, despite growing solidarity action (Camfield 2006). Finally, workers in Wisconsin who walked out of work to join massive protests against Governor Scott Walker's attacks on union rights in 2011 were sent back to work by union leaders who accepted sharp concessions and wanted to end the protests to focus on change through legislation and elections. Kim Moody (2011) describes what happened in Wisconsin in terms that could also apply to the other events outlined here: "the union officialdom had called into being a movement that exceeded its expectation or intentions" (p. 15). As the movement builds, the horizons of activists expand beyond narrow collective bargaining to questions of who should rule and whether genuinely democratic decisions should be made. Union officials in those situations tend to see it as their job to channel this energy back toward normal routines of bargaining, protesting, and electing. The basic form of bureaucratic administration appears to exert its own pressure.

We do not claim that the role of union leaders and paid staffers is always conservative. Indeed, at a time when movements are at a fairly low ebb, such as the moment in which we are writing this book, leaders and officials are often more oriented toward union activism than their members. Their vision of activism, however, tends to be shaped by the assumption that the goal of unions is to win agreements within the dominant framework, not to challenge capitalism.

This kind of bureaucratic orientation is not limited to unions, though the importance of unions as social institutions makes that process very significant. Franzway, Court, and Connell (1989: 143) discuss the "bureaucratization of feminism," which took place as feminists were hired by the state and began to adopt its policy framework for advocacy work. Anti-racist and lesbian-gay movements have undergone similar transformations. For example, when a government decides to address a problem such as the perception of police bias against people of colour by hiring more **racialized** officers, there is an important question about whether the institution will be transformed or those new officers will themselves be changed, picking up the dominant attitudes even if that was not the initial intent of the policy.

Marc Burke (1993) interviewed lesbian, gay, and bisexual police officers in Britain about their experiences. Certainly, some felt they could do useful work, improving policing and the lives of lesbians, gays, and bisexuals. One officer said, "I'm potentially a much more useful asset to the police than they realize, and a useful asset to the gay community as well" (Burke 1993: 184). Yet things did not always work out as these officers might have hoped. Indeed, one officer expressed concern about being called upon to use insider knowledge of gay venues to enforce unpopular laws:

> I'm concerned about the possibility of police using gay officers to go into gay pubs to find offences simply because they know that those officers will feel comfortable in those venues and not stand out so much. If that happens then those officers will find themselves involved in controversial legislation involving their own community and that will eventually destroy all the bridges that are being built to bring the two closer together. (Burke 1993: 190)

Indeed, lesbian and gay officers could feel stuck in a difficult place between two very different views of the world. An officer told Burke (1993) about the pitfalls of liaison work with the lesbian and gay community: "I think that anyone who tried to liaise between the two would just end up taking shit from both sides, and in the end their heads would blow" (p. 189).

The bureaucratization of movements is complex. It is a result of very real successes, of a movement actually winning new prominence within the portals of power. This achievement can lead to meaningful changes, while, at the same time, redefining movements and the role of activism. Such a shift often leaves the conditions of the most disadvantaged virtually untouched. Sivanandan (1985) tracks the trajectory of anti-racist movements in Britain, noting the way concerted government action after riots in 1981 created a new emphasis on racism awareness education as an alternative to militant black power activism. The impact of racism awareness programs on the lives of the most vulnerable people of colour in Britain was negligible: "And yet, in terms of the **material conditions** of the workless, homeless, school-less, welfare-less blacks of the slum city, all this paroxysm of activity has not made the blindest bit of difference" (Sivanandan 1985: 22).

Theories of State and Bureaucracy

The line-ups and endless procedures that make people feel so powerless in the face of bureaucracy can be understood as a horrible error, produced by some confluence of factors such as organizational size, history, employment relations, and mandates. Conservative politicians often represent red tape as the product of self-serving public employees, fat cats who lazily feast on the taxpayer's dime. But imagine, for a second, that bureaucratic inertia is not an accident but a deliberate system in which our sense of powerlessness is the intended outcome.

At first sight, it seems contradictory that the people who supposedly control the state by electing governments also feel completely powerless when dealing with it. The answer to this contradiction depends on the overall theoretical framework you use to interpret the state, how it works and in whose interests it operates. This topic stimulates important theoretical debates, reflecting very different perspectives on democracy and bureaucracy.

Beetham (1996: 87) argues that there are two very different frameworks for understanding bureaucracy as an impediment to democracy. In the first, democracy is associated with maximizing individual freedom of choice, and bureaucracy is seen as a limit, an intrusion into the private realm and in marked contrast to the market, where individual consumers are in a position to select among competing products. In the second, democracy is associated with collective self-rule, and bureaucracy is cast as an imposed authority that impedes collective decision making and interferes with democracy in key areas of social life. These different perspectives on the character of bureaucracy draw on very different theoretical approaches to understanding the role of the state in contemporary society and through history.

Not every form of human society has had a state. In the forager societies of the past, for example, when people survived on the harvest of nature around them, they lived in relatively small bands and managed their affairs together, with no dedicated rulers. Basically, everyone played some role in the core productive work of society (hunting, gathering, herding, raising children), though that role varied given the division of labour between women and men. The band or village was governed collectively, and governance involved a great deal of open discussion in which people might be accorded different levels of authority based on their life experiences. These societies tended to be characterized by a strong anti-authoritarianism, an emphasis on cooperation paired with respect for individuality, and the resolution of conflict through social means, such as talking it out at great length, teasing, and engaging in specific rituals to work through antagonism (Leacock and Lee 1982: 7–8).

State forms of government, then, arise in specific conditions to play a particular role in society. Of course, there is tremendous debate about the role of the state at every level, from pitched debates about bureaucracy, services, and deficits in election campaigns to the more abstract theorization in academic research. Often in these debates, people simply talk past one another, repeating their own views again and again and assuming anyone who does not understand or agree is an idiot. The different positions articulated, however, often derive from specific founding assumptions about such things as nature, human experience, and the role of government.

The official view of democracy tends to be premised on the idea that the role of government is to preserve social order and prevent humanity from falling into chaos. The role of the state is "to serve and protect," in the words of the motto printed on the side of Toronto police cars. The state serves the interests of all to prevent the chaos that always threatens to bubble up, particularly in a large and complex society.

The defeat of the home team Canucks led to a riot on the evening of June 15, 2011, in an area of Vancouver. Riots after sporting events, whether victories or defeats, are commonplace. In the official view, the threat of disorder is a feature of modern society, particularly where crowds congregate. The state serves everyone when it controls this kind of outbreak; it prevents the spread of chaos and restores order.

EXERCISING YOUR DEMOCRATIC IMAGINATION
On Not Being Governed

Bureaucracy is a mode of administration, a way of governing. In the official view of democracy, bureaucratic governance can be seen as an overall contribution to society, bringing people together and organizing their interactions in a sensible way. In the view from below, this form of governance can be seen as way of subjugating people, establishing control to permit exploitation.

The anthropologist and political theorist James C. Scott (2009) is in the second of these schools. He argues that it was not so long ago that "self-governing peoples were the great majority of humankind" (p. ix). Now most of these people have been incorporated into nation-states. But that process of incorporation was keenly contested because it went along with new relations of inequality and exploitation.

Scott argues that the hill people in the highlands of southern Asia constitute the last remaining large-scale holdouts from this process of state building. These peoples have actively resisted incorporation. "Hill peoples," writes Scott, "are best understood as runaway, fugitive, maroon communities who have, over the course of two millennia, been fleeing the oppressions of state-making projects in the valleys—slavery, conscription, taxes, corvée labor, epidemics and warfare" (p. ix).

These self-governing people were seen as less civilized. Indeed, in China the non-governed people were referred to as "raw" as opposed to the "cooked" and civilized Han Chinese (Scott 2009: 120). Yet these hill peoples were not simply leftover, old-fashioned cultures waiting to be "modernized" but rather the descendants of people who had consciously fled from state power. Scott argues that "a view of hills peoples' state-repelling societies—or even anti-state societies—makes far more sense of their agricultural practices, cultural values and social structure in the hills" (Scott 2009: 128).

Is bureaucracy the necessary outcome of human progress toward more complex and larger-scale societies?

In this view, the state serves us all by preserving order. The state stands above society as a referee who steps in to enforce the rules that keep the game fair and clean. In this sense, the state is neutral, not aligned with any of the interest groups that contend to influence the shape of society (such as employers, unions, ethnic associations, neighbourhood groups, professional organizations, and voluntary associations or clubs); rather, it regulates the conflicts between these groups and governs on the basis of fair compromise. The official view of democracy is therefore associated with a liberal pluralist state theory that understands the contention between interest groups as a good thing that makes the state democratic, providing that disputation is effectively refereed by a state acting in the interests of all (Carnoy 1984).

Political power in this perspective is dispersed among a variety of interest groups. Politics is therefore a series of adjustments between competing interest groups, regulated through a specific set of institutions that sit above society, autonomous from the rest of life (Callinicos 2004). Legitimate grievances (such as those of women and people of colour seeking equity) can be accommodated within the system if groups play interest politics correctly. The pluralist state is seen as the most effective mode of administration for a modern capitalist regime, and therefore the tendency toward liberal democracy in industrial societies is largely inevitable in the long run. The alternatives are seen as illusory and less effective, as government that is informed by a plurality of voices and that has the consent of the people is bound to work better than authoritarian regimes, and the notion of collective self-government in all areas of life is said to be unrealistic.

The liberal pluralist model associated with the official view of democracy tends to presume that the ends in politics are largely given, consisting primarily of nurturing economic growth, enhancing equity, and maintaining social order. This perspective leads to what Brian Fay (1975) describes as a technological politics, in which debate is largely about the best means to attain those given ends. One candidate might argue dramatic cost cutting is the best means while another might argue for stimulus expenditures to encourage greater employment. The ends, however, are largely seen as given and not subject to debate.

In sharp contrast, the democracy-from-below approach tends to associate the state not with pluralism but with domination. The state is not preserving order against chaos but rather is protecting a particular social order in which members of the dominant group benefit while others are subordinated. The state cannot truly be neutral or act in the interest of all when it is limited to operating within the existing set of social and economic relations that serve the interests of the dominant group.

In this view, official democracy comes down to a series of debates about how to keep the system going. Opposition voices tend to be heard within this system primarily when they confine themselves to the terms of the official debate. Broader questions are seen as fringe issues, so it is outside the parameters of discussion to introduce matters such as the justice of capitalism, the persistence of male dominance and violence, the brutality of racism, the destruction of the environment, the colonization of indigenous peoples, and the marginalization of people with disabilities.

The role of the state is to keep the system operating smoothly. Whatever the political program of the party elected, once in office, that party becomes responsible for a capitalist economy and its associated relations of domination, unless the system as a whole is overthrown. Social democratic parties like the

New Democratic Party in Canada and the Labour Party in Britain originally included specific anti-capitalist commitments in their core documents. Once elected, however, they found themselves bound to rule within the parameters of the system, even if they did not like it.

Just imagine, for example, a government that resolved to pay everyone a living wage immediately and to end the rights of corporations to lay people off at will, thereby eliminating hunger and a whole range of social problems. That government would raise the minimum wage to a rate that would allow people to obtain the food, shelter, and other needs that they had. Right now, many people earning minimum wage often need to make use of food banks to survive or live in substandard housing conditions. Government would raise social assistance rates so people could actually survive on their cheques, in contrast to the current situation where it is simply not enough for the most basic subsistence.

Try to imagine how corporations would react to these changes. There can be little doubt that they would shift investments out of the country and argue that their ability to make profits was severely compromised by these laws. Indeed, companies could possibly go out of business in these conditions. If the economy began to tank, this new government would risk losing its popularity.

The state that undercuts capitalist profitability definitively can provoke a crisis but cannot create an alternative (Clarke 1983). That alternative must come from below through struggles. Just imagine, for example, a huge wave of protests and strikes that ground society to a halt. In this situation, it might be possible for the state to grant concessions that seem to threaten profitability in the short term to quiet down movements and preserve the dominant order. Indeed, democracy-from-below advocates would argue that the historical record demonstrates that the dominant groups have often resisted reforms such as the eight-hour day, unemployment insurance, human rights codes, and socialized health care until the state was pushed into action by militant mobilizations.

The state, then, is not neutral but is aligned with the powerful in the perpetuation of the system. Still, the existing official institutions of democracy are not irrelevant from this perspective. Liberal democracy is seen as an historic gain by the working class and others who were excluded from the state, rather than as an entitlement granted from above. Workers, women, people of colour, indigenous peoples, and lesbians and gays have fought for the right to vote and to participate through winning certain social and civil liberties. Yet this democracy is very partial, as the state itself is purpose-built to sustain the existing social order. C.B. Macpherson (1965) argues that the state was first liberalized and then democratized. The prior liberalization of the state set parameters on its democratization. The distinction between public and private, discussed in Chapter 2, is just one important example of the way the limits on the state mean that it can never fully address the inequities of corporate power, which are cast primarily as issues of private property.

The question of bureaucracy, then, looks very different from the official view than from the perspective of democracy from below. In the official view, bureaucracy is an attempt to administer the public realm neutrally in the interests of all. The democracy-from-below view, in contrast, would cast the bureaucracy as part of the machine of domination that rules over the population, an obstacle between people and much-needed resources they cannot access. The problem of bureaucracy is defined very differently depending on what assumptions you first make about the role of the state. The next time you are standing in line waiting for service at a student loan office or a bank, think about how your broad assumptions about what government is shapes your interpretation of the experience.

Bureaucracy and Inequality

Perhaps the defining feature of bureaucracy in Weber's description is neutrality. The focus on process and procedures, rising above personal feelings and biases, would seem to provide great standards of universal fairness, even at the cost of increasing impersonality and inflexibility. But sometimes, the very procedures that seem to guarantee fairness can, in fact, reinforce the dominant inequalities in society.

Suzanne Franzway, Dianne Court, and R.W. Connell (1989) write that Weber's definition of bureaucracy was officially gender neutral: "But the ideas that went into Weber's ideal type of bureaucratic authority—rationality, impersonality, ordered hierarchy, now sound with a suspiciously patriarchal ring" (p. 30). In other words, the core patterns that Weber attaches to the concept of bureaucracy are associated with masculinity in important ways. Masculinity often gets associated with aggression and violence, but there are many dimensions to masculinities that operate in a variety of ways (see Connell 1995).

The whole realm of impersonal rationality, where every decision is based on general laws without any consideration of an individual's specific situation, is associated with masculinity. The masculinity displayed by accountants and corporate executives might be different from that displayed by pro hockey players or rock stars, but all exhibit behaviour patterns grounded in gender. The ability, for example, to shut down a plant simply on the basis of a cost-benefit analysis, without thinking about the individuals who will be displaced and often thrown into poverty, involves a kind of abstraction that distances the decision maker from the personal and emotional elements of this kind of decision.

Dorothy Smith (1990) argues that this method of basing decisions on what she describes as the "conceptual mode" of abstract reasoning rather than on human considerations is typical of masculinity in Western culture: "It has been a condition of a man's being able to enter and become absorbed in the conceptual mode, and to forget the dependence of his being in that mode upon his bodily existence" (p. 18). In contrast, women "have been anchored in the local and particular." Women's work, both paid and unpaid, inside and outside of the home, tends to be more focused on sustaining life and giving care, which tends to lead to a different world view and way of approaching problems.

These patterns are grounded in specific divisions of labour in society and are not inherent traits associated with being a woman or a man. There are ways of life grounded in the kinds of work we do, and both the dominant division of labour and specific gender ideologies mean that, in the prevailing pattern, women's work is often distinct from men's. There are certainly important exceptions, but there are also real patterns grounded in work and life.

This impersonal mode of bureaucratic reasoning can easily turn into a bullying form of domination, more powerful because of its apparent universality and fairness. Certainly the experience of people with limited incomes who need access to social services for survival and well-being shows the ways that bureaucratic administration can be soul destroying and gut wrenching. Lillian Allen's poem quoted previously reflects the frustration of a person dealing with a social worker, a professional whose job it is to help but who can neither grasp the situation of an individual trying to access social services nor offer the needed remedies.

This bureaucratic power is also racialized. Molefi Kete Asante (2005) argues that being administered by bureaucracies is one of the defining experiences of many African Americans. "As an African American in the twenty-first century, I am one of the most institutionalized human beings in the world. My history is the history of institutions" (Asante 2005: 81). These institutions are governed by a bureaucratic mode of administration, which is marked by elements of "designation, force, power, and above all efficiency" (Asante 2005: 83).

This bureaucratic power does not have to be explicitly racist to have racializing dynamics. Indeed, it is sometimes the apparently universalistic approach of treating everyone the same that can most destructively reflect the dynamics of inequality along lines of race, gender, sexuality, class, or disability, for example. Universalistic reasoning—treating everyone in exactly the same way—can, in fact, reflect an unwillingness to deal with issues. Theo David

Goldberg (2002) argues that the post–World War II policies of "racelessness," which replaced overt discrimination, often deny the impact of racism:

> In all these variations, racelessness was at once as much a refusal
> to address, let alone redress, deeply etched historical inequities and
> inequalities racially fashioned as it was an expressed embrace of principles
> of race-ignoring fairness and equal opportunity. (Goldberg 2002: 212)

In contrast to the narrative of equality in citizenship rights, racializing dynamics have been among the central features of the formation of modern states:

> State apparatuses sew the variety of modern social exclusions into the
> seams of the social fabric, normalizing them through their naturalization.
> So social exclusions in terms of race (complexly knotted with class and
> gender, not to wax too mantric about the principal forms of the modern
> mode) become the mark of social belonging, the measure of standing in
> the nation-state, the badge of social subjection and citizenship. (Goldberg
> 2002: 10)

Modern bureaucratic methods have created more nuanced forms of inequality, soaked in apparent fairness and universality:

> As much as the modern state has been about anything—about increasing
> bureaucratization and rationalization, about sophisticated forms of
> democratization and social control, about law and the control of capital—
> it has been about increasingly sophisticated forms and techniques of racial
> formation, power, and exclusion. (Goldberg 2002: 49)

Bureaucracy, then, can reinforce inequality by treating everybody the same and not paying attention to the different situations people are in or to their different needs. Yet dealing with every case simply on its own terms, without any consistency, can undercut fairness. The ability of bureaucratic methods to accommodate the complex balance between the recognition of difference and the principles of universality is certainly in question.

Bureaucracy and Austerity

As we write this book, there are heated political debates around the world about deficits and the costs of public services. Governments of many political stripes are arguing that it is necessary to cut public services and the wages and benefits of civil servants substantially. These cuts are often advanced in language that draws on the frustrating experiences we have all had with bureaucracy. Yet the civil service provides elements of expertise, clarity, and institutional knowledge to political life. Critics of bureaucracy from the democracy-from-below perspective also have to contend with the tension between their critique of bureaucratic administration within a capitalist state and their support for the health and job security of public sector workers. The goal of this chapter has been to demonstrate that the relationship of bureaucracy and democracy is complex. Many issues are at stake when a politician claims to be going after the "gravy train" or "cutting the fat."

6 THE POWER OF KNOWING

In November 2011, the prime minister of Greece announced plans to hold a national referendum. His government would ask Greek voters to approve the austerity measures required to receive a bailout package designed by European governments and banks. The package was meant to prevent Greece from going bankrupt. On the assumption that a Greek bankruptcy would severely damage the euro currency, the leaders of Germany and France threatened to kick Greece out of the shared euro currency zone and withdraw the massive bailout package if the referendum was allowed to go ahead. In the words of one German official, "We respect their democratic traditions, but a referendum, or even the delay caused by holding a referendum, would unleash hell on the markets" (Saunders 2011: A17). A columnist in the British *Daily Mail* called resistance to the referendum "sheer contempt for the principles of democracy" (Sandbrook 2011: par. 39).

In response to this crisis, the Greek opposition leader proposed "a transitional national-unity government, with a cabinet largely composed of non-partisan 'technocrats,' to manage the restructuring of the country's government and economy" ("Greek politics" 2011: A18). Replacing democratic rule with **technocratic** administration by experts not affiliated with political parties would seem to be a serious setback for the idea of democracy. It might also be understood as a temporary expedient to convince the people of what is good for them. An editorial in *The Globe and Mail* agreed that "painful economic restructurings need broad democratic support," arguing that the crisis in Greece and withdrawal of the referendum idea might win that support: "The prospect of economic shock therapy, to paraphrase Samuel Johnson, concentrates the mind wonderfully. Greece may yet co-operate" ("Greek politics" 2011: A18).

This crisis raised the important issue of whether, as democracy assumes, the people actually know what is good for them and possess the capacity to rule themselves. In authoritarian systems of government, whether the people are knowledgeable matters very little, as the rulers have the power to make their own decisions without any need for popular consultation or formal accountability. By contrast, democracy depends a great deal upon people's intelligence and know-how. Whether through their own actions in labour unions and community organizations or through selecting representatives during elections, the people in a democracy are supposed to be the ultimate decision makers. It follows that, in order for a society to be governed by the people, the people must be trusted to know.

Politicians often express trust in the knowledge and power of the people. For example, in 2009, the head of President Obama's Open Government Directive announced that the White House would be making more and more previously secret information available to the public because "the American people know best what their government should do for them. It's fitting that our open government directive has been significantly shaped by the collective wisdom of the American people" (The White House 2009: par. 7). Shortly after being elected in 2006, a senior member of Canada's Conservative government said in a speech that "we trust in the Canadian people" to lead the way to a prosperous economy (Government of Canada 2006). In both of these cases, the underlying suggestion is that the knowledge of the people is the primary force shaping the direction of government.

Yet the Greek case in 2011 shows that this trust in the expertise of the people is rather shallower than these statements might indicate. When the will of the Greek people seemed to impede measures viewed as necessary to preserving the economic system, there was a call for the technocratic rule of experts who could respond rationally and disinterestedly.

In this chapter, we will investigate the complex and contradictory relationship of democracy and expertise. The basic question posed by the case of the previously mentioned Greek crisis is whether the people can be trusted to know what is good for them. Often, the knowledge of experts is cast as a superior basis for determining what is good for people than their own knowledge of their immediate situation. This judgment raises important issues about expertise and who really knows what is best for people. Answering these questions means investigating the state of popular knowledge and considering whether the people actually know enough to rule, and how they might figure out what they need to know. At the same time, we must investigate the social relations that name certain people as powerful experts and imply that the public is, in fact, rather ignorant.

Democracy for Dummies

The issue of popular expertise and democratic participation seems contentious in the early twenty-first century. On the one hand, people have more schooling and easier access to information than ever before. On the other, there is deep concern about the quality of information and the character of public debate. Ivo Mosley (2000), in his blunt book *Dumbing Down: Culture, Politics and the Mass Media,* argues there is growing evidence that our society is not a democracy but a "dumbocracy ... the rule of cleverness without wisdom" (p. 1). He says that the sizzle and pop of commercial culture has lured people away from the pursuit of higher thinking and focused their minds on selfish, short-term interests. As political parties dumb down political debate by tightening their grip over what elected representatives are allowed to say and do, "true democracy recedes into a dim and hazy distance," and voters lose interest in politics (p. 3). People's minds are numbed and dumbed further "by the constant stream of pandering which pours into our brains from TV screens, newspapers and magazines" (p. 5). Mosley's concerns are not without precedent. In 1972, Dye and Zeigler wrote that "the masses of America are apathetic and ill-informed about politics and public policy" (quoted in Svensson 1995: 216).

This fits with research that raises questions about how much people actually know. In Canada, the Dominion Institute regularly polls the population to test the public's knowledge of history and politics. It is generally dismayed by the results. "Most Canadians Fail Canada Day History Quiz" was the headline of the 2005 report on poll results (Dominion Institute 2005). Although there is certainly room to quibble about the value of these tests as assessments of democratic preparedness, there is widespread concern about the knowledge of the people.

Nelson Wiseman, a political scientist at the University of Toronto, suggests society is probably better off if people who don't know much about politics refrain from voting in elections. A young co-worker once explained to Wiseman his intention not to vote because

> he felt it irresponsible to do so as he had little interest in or knowledge of politics, public policy, and politicians. He felt that, by voting, he would be engaging in an uninformed, empty gesture. He felt it more responsible to

leave voting to those who knew more about the issues and parties than he did. (Wiseman 2006: 22)

Wiseman concludes that "this is a wise and thoughtful response" to doubts about one's political knowledge. It would seem as though heady statements about the wisdom of the people in democracies do not always match up with practice. There is a contradiction between democracy's fundamental need for and trust in informed and engaged citizens, and the view that citizens are, in fact, ill-informed and disengaged.

A special concern is that the institutions supposedly preparing people for democratic participation do not do so. Specifically, some wonder whether the media and schools are doing their job in preparing the people for democracy. Media critics maintain that the role of mass media in democracies should be "to help citizens achieve ... 'adequate understanding' of political issues" (Schudson 1996: 212). This line of thinking assumes that the media in a democracy "have an obligation to serve the public interest" by publicizing thorough and accurate information about political affairs because "power rests with the people" (Taras 2001: 29, 2). The philosopher Mark Kingwell argues that schooling has an especially important democratic responsibility because "democracy depends on a population of engaged, critical thinkers who have general humane knowledge of history, politics, culture, economics, and science" (Kingwell 2011: 11).

Some critics, including Mosley, whose views have been discussed already, believe that neither the media nor the schools are doing their jobs properly, particularly given the information-laden character of contemporary societies in the Global North. Indeed, some argue that this is an era of "truthiness"—a word that Stephen Colbert made popular on his fake TV news show (Zimmer 2010)—where there is so much information coming at people from so many sources that many people have given up on discerning the actual validity of specific claims and instead opt for those that sound most plausible. The difficulty in assessing competing facts with various claims to validity leads to a situation in which people simply construct a reality to support their positions. Indeed, Farhad Manjoo (2008) argues that the proliferation of digital media and deep ideological cleavages have meant "it is more convenient than ever before for some of us to live in a world built out of our own facts" (p. 2). Nico Stehr (2008) writes that "modern citizens live in societies that not only contain more knowledge, but that also require much more knowledge. As a result, questions about the relationship between democracy and knowledge become more urgent questions" (p. 4).

The belief that most people lack the capacity to understand and address the complex problems of society may have contemporary resonance, but it is in fact a very old one. Some political theorists argue that government is best left to the wisdom of experts. Plato's dialogue *Protagoras* (written more than 2000 years ago) depicts the philosopher Protagoras debating the role of expert knowledge with Plato's mentor Socrates, another famous Greek philosopher. Protagoras argues that, because governing involves nothing more or less than administering the affairs of the people, it should be run by the people themselves. We all understand the experience of being governed, and government touches all of our lives. It's only logical, then, that all of us should be permitted to take part in government. The knowledge required to do so is the knowledge we acquire through our everyday experience in the world.

Socrates disagrees. He argues that government is, like other occupations, a specialized task requiring specialized knowledge. To paraphrase his argument: when you want a ship built, you go to the ship builder; when you have a legal dispute, you seek help from a lawyer; and when you're sick, you see a doctor. Why would it be any different when it comes to government? It is no less foolish to think that all people are capable of governing than that all of us could be expected to build ships, argue court cases, or perform surgery. In fact, argues Socrates, not all of us can do those things, and we shouldn't expect to. Governing requires specific skills, training, and temperament, and relatively few people possess these things in the right combination. To open up the process of governing to any and all is to invite confusion, poor decision making, and a weak society.

In the view of Joseph Schumpeter, one of the leading political scientists of the last century and a champion of official democracy, "the participation of the broad population need not be more extensive than what is necessary to keep an electoral system running" (Svensson 1995: 211). In other words, people can be expected to possess no more than the knowledge necessary to choose which experts will rule. Like Plato, Schumpeter believes that the complex task of governing ought to be left to political experts. Schumpeter's contemporary Lester W. Milbrath writes that "high levels of political interest and participation may not be beneficial to constitutional democracy.... A special burden of responsibility for the maintenance of the system rests on the shoulders of the political elites" (quoted in Svensson 1995: 210).

Of course, certain decisions do require substantial expertise. Elections might make sense, for example, as a way to choose the mayor but not when it comes to selecting the local brain surgeon. Some highly specialized, complex tasks require types of knowledge and technical skill that are held by a very small group. This is not to suggest that most people are not smart enough to become brain surgeons, if they receive the support and years of specialized training required to master complex occupations. But, in order for everyone to develop

EXERCISING YOUR DEMOCRATIC IMAGINATION
Who Knows?

There are people who would argue that democracy took a large leap forward on 4 October 2006. That was the day that the name "wikileaks.org" was registered for use on the World Wide Web. Since posting its first leaked government document in December of that year, WikiLeaks has published hundreds of thousands of secret government memos, documents related to the United States–led wars in Iraq and Afghanistan, election campaign files, telephone recordings, and other confidential official sources.

WikiLeaks and its supporters argue that the work of the website is done in the name of democracy. They base this argument on the notion that people have a right to know about the decisions being carried out in their name. From this perspective, by publishing restricted documents, WikiLeaks is merely providing access to information that the public ought to be able to see in the first place. Anything public officials say in private, they ought to be able to say in public. The fact that officials try to hide the details of important international business deals, wars, court cases, and other political issues is exactly why organizations like WikiLeaks are necessary. Journalists have been trying to uncover hidden political stories for centuries; and it is nothing new to see political insiders leaking confidential government information to the public. The development of information technologies—the Internet, specifically—has certainly made it easier to collect and circulate this kind of information. But shining light on the dark hallways of power has always been a democratic exercise. WikiLeaks is simply a much larger and more powerful spotlight than we've had access to in the past.

Conversely, critics of WikiLeaks argue that the website is a threat to democracy. For example, numerous representatives of Western governments have said that publishing secret documents about the Iraq and Afghan wars provides enemy combatants with strategic information, thereby exposing Western soldiers to heightened risks. In fact, one Canadian professor and advisor to the Conservative government caused a stir when he publicly suggested that a Western government might be justified in assassinating WikiLeaks spokesperson Julian Assange in order to neutralize the WikiLeaks threat (Collins 2010). Less provocatively, others argue that WikiLeaks destroys the long-standing and legitimate culture of privacy surrounding the relationship between officials working in foreign countries and their home governments. From this perspective, when foreign diplomats send memos back to their governments, they need to be able to speak freely without feeling as though their interpretations are going to be read as official government statements. Thus, secrecy, argue WikiLeaks' critics, is foundational to democracy.

Thinking about where you might stand in this debate will help to strengthen your democratic imagination.

Is WikiLeaks performing a democratic service, or is it a threat to people power?

Should citizens be able to access all government information, or are there cases in which government secrecy is justified?

Who should decide where this line gets drawn?

expertise in one profession, whole other aspects of life would be neglected. A society in which everyone was an expert brain surgeon would very likely be a society without expert farmers, architects, artists, teachers, and so on.

Expert knowledge certainly can be put to democratic ends. Experts working in various fields have fulfilled democratic mandates to produce water filtration systems, architectural wonders, communication technologies, breathtaking art, and medical discoveries that have cured millions of people. The question is whether expertise in itself qualifies some for power over others. Is the job of doctors to tell patients what needs to be done, or to lay out the choices in clear language so that patients can make informed decisions? And asking whether or not some decisions should be left to experts immediately raises the question of defining who is actually an expert, which opens up complex issues and contentious debates.

Expertise tends to be associated with knowing more, and knowledge is often thought to be connected to objectivity and neutrality. In fact, knowledge is always related to systems of power. Experts are not only people who know a great deal but also those who occupy specific positions in power structures. This relationship is so important that one influential French theorist, Michel Foucault, developed the term *power/knowledge* to describe it. In Foucault's (1980) work, the term power/knowledge is used to highlight the fact that forms of social control (for example, the authority of government, or doctors, or university professors) are inseparable from access to information and the ability to shape what people take for granted as the truth.

Foucault's (1965) book *Madness and Civilization* examines how definitions of "madness" have changed since the 1600s. Foucault argues that the behaviour commonly defined as madness today was once understood to be an acceptable, if unique, part of social life. Only in the past few hundred years have people who today would be called "mentally unstable" been diagnosed as having something "wrong" with them and confined to an institution.

What interests Foucault is how the behaviour hasn't changed, but the interpretation of it has. And, as madness came to be associated with criminality and understood to be a disease requiring medical treatment or institutionalization, a whole configuration of laws and institutions grew up to support the new knowledge regime around madness. Experts with specialized medical and political knowledge were granted increasingly specialized powers to diagnose madness, to treat mental illness, and to pass laws that criminalized certain forms of behaviour. The point is that the capacity to define the "truth" of what madness "is" is inseparable from the power to control people in particular ways.

Terry Wrigley (2003) argues that, at the start of the twenty-first century, the relationship between expert knowledge and democratic control has taken an unhealthy turn. He believes that people in democracies today are more subject to the rule of experts than they are stewards of expert knowledge. Wrigley is especially concerned about trends in public schooling. He argues that decisions made by a small group of people defined as education experts has diminished the power of students, parents, educators, and communities to shape the kinds of learning that go on inside the classroom.

For example, standardized testing has been proposed and developed by education policy experts who say that the intention of evaluating all students on the basis of a standard test is to ensure greater consistency in teaching and learning, as well as to provide more accurate assessments of what students know. However, in Wrigley's view, the push to quantify learning by turning it into a number on a standardized test makes it less likely that students will develop the capacity to figure things out for themselves (see also Wrigley 2004). The need for students to memorize a rigid set of facts or to focus on learning specific skills and content (and to spend considerable time honing test-taking abilities) restricts the teacher's capacity to respond to the particular needs of the classroom and discourages students from pursuing interests that take them outside the narrow focus of what will be on the standardized test. Wrigley concludes that technical tools developed by experts in education policy have been implemented at the expense of local democratic decision making.

The case of standardized testing exemplifies the importance of what kind of knowledge gets defined as expertise. Clearly, policy analysts and political figures in ministries of education are presumed to understand learning in a way that teachers, parents, and students do not. These divergent understandings tend to have particular cultural and class implications, as those in power tend to mistake their own culturally specific knowledge and experiences for universal perspectives embracing all of humankind. Standardized test questions assume a set of shared cultural reference points that privilege some students on the basis of their background and experiences and disadvantage others, who grew up with very different experiences and perspectives.

A standardized system designed by bureaucrats at the centre is indicative of an official form of government by experts that goes against the democracy-from-below assumption that local knowledge uniquely situates those at the grass roots to make decisions about what is best for the people. Grundmann (2008) writes that, in the eyes of one prominent model of public decision making, bureaucrats and other policy experts "are seen as having superior knowledge compared to lay people and therefore they could not be on equal footing." Public consultation on contentious issues is really "an educational process in which the experts educate the lay public in order that it can understand and support the experts' views, recommendations, and decisions" (Grundmann 2008: 86). It follows that, in such a system, what the experts define as useful and important knowledge will have tremendous influence over the kinds of thinking that are valued most in society.

In the early twenty-first century, for example, policymakers tend to define knowledge as useful when it contributes directly to the economic success of the individual and the nation. Mark Kingwell (2011) argues that a growing number of students, parents, and university administrators believe that "university education must be judged according to its ultimate usefulness. [And] that usefulness will be understood as career success of one sort or another, especially as measured by wealth" (p. 9). In the words of the premier of Ontario in 2005, "in today's economy, knowledge plus skills equals prosperity" (Bartleman 2005, par. 95). From this perspective, useful knowledge and expertise are conceived of more in terms of how they can be used to generate money than how they can strengthen popular power or personal insight.

This view has led to considerable efforts to redesign postsecondary education to orient it more toward the creation of marketable knowledge, and particularly toward the leading-edge knowledge required in a competitive market economy. As Jacob (2003) writes, "Although universities have always been in the business of producing knowledge, it is now argued that innovation and not mere knowledge creation should be a first priority" (p. 126).

In short, the knowledge that experts deem essential is shifting in the early twenty-first century, away from preparing students for democratic citizenship and toward making them market ready in the contemporary economy. We might want to be a bit more sceptical than some of these writers about the extent to which bureaucratic and hierarchical education systems ever really prepared people for full democratic participation. But there is no doubt that any knowledge that is not deemed economically essential is being marginalized throughout the educational system, whether that means cutting art classes or funding for music programs or physical education resources.

One of the insidious features of expert knowledge, then, is that experts themselves define what counts as really knowing. Yet, in practice, many forms of expertise are important in daily life. Brain surgeons who are brilliant in their particular field might also be totally ignorant about the most basic elements of human interaction and cause immense pain to patients through their insensitivity. The democratic imagination raises the challenging question of who really knows best what is good for a person—or, indeed, for a whole population. Is it the people themselves, drawing on the resources of information built up from below through expert inquiry and practice? Or is it the experts and officials who know best?

Educating the Educators

In the nineteenth century, Karl Marx advocated the idea that the people knew what was best for themselves. He challenged those who sought to make society better by educating the masses and developing new socialization processes to re-engineer the people in new ways. He was critical of his peers who laid out plans for social change in which a few (the educators) were the active agents while the others (the masses) were passively educated to become better people. As Marx (1976) writes, "the educator ... must be educated" (p. 619). Genuine democracy, according to Marx, is not produced by a small cadre of experts working on the people to make them worthy of participation but through a process in which the population is active in shaping the world that includes them.

Expertise, then, can be antithetical to democracy, producing a narrow elite of knowers who teach the people how to live. Yet growing up in a hierarchical society in which people are disciplined to obey those in charge does not necessarily prepare them for full participation. John Lennon's song "Working class hero" begins, "As soon as you are born, they make you feel small" (Lennon 1970). The song examines the various ways that experiences of family, school, and work lead people to "feel small," so they defer to others and don't think for themselves. The combination of life experience and formal education, then, prepares people to follow rules and respect direction. The capacities for free thinking and collective action tend to be underdeveloped in a society requiring people to obey the expert or authority—the employer, the teacher, the police officer, and the parent. And any process of change that focuses mainly on changing who is in command rather than on genuine popular power will tend to continue the subordination.

Also, even if democracies are not overly influenced by authorities, the challenge remains concerning how the people can develop their own capacities to rule without being reformed from the outside by a new elite of experts in some form. One answer comes through the work of the Italian theorist and activist Antonio Gramsci (1971), who describes the everyday thinking people develop in a capitalist society as "common sense." "Its most fundamental characteristic," he writes, "is that it is a conception which, even in the brain of one individual, is fragmentary, incoherent and inconsequential" (p. 419). Through their lives, people develop views on things drawing on their own experiences and on what they learn from others. These common sense ideas tend not to be worked over consciously; they survive as a bunch of separate bits of knowledge. For example, someone might believe that unemployment insurance simply helps lazy people avoid work and, at the same time, be upset when a friend faces bureaucratic hoops getting benefits after being laid off because of corporate downsizing. Compassion for the individual might not loop back to change this person's overall political attitude.

The fact that common sense is fragmentary and incoherent does not mean it is to be casually dismissed. In fact, common sense is the starting point for knowledge constructed from below. In 1776, Thomas Paine called his revolutionary call for democracy in America *Common Sense*. He intentionally wrote the book in plain language, appealing to readers to reflect seriously on the ideas it contained:

> In the following pages I offer nothing more than simple facts, plain arguments, and common sense: and have no other preliminaries to settle with the reader, than that he will divest himself of prejudice and prepossession, and suffer his reason and his feelings to determine for themselves that he will put on, or rather that he will not put off, the true character of a man, and generously enlarge his views beyond the present day. (Paine 1776: par. 55)

After all, people are experts in their own life condition, even if the knowledge is not consciously honed. A study of workplace health and safety activists, for example, showed that some of them who were motivated to seek change got launched by the recognition that something was affecting their own well-being or that of people around them. They held on to the view that something was wrong, even when experts (employers, inspectors, medical personnel, union officials) reassured them that everything was normal. They then felt a responsibility to learn more about what was causing the ailments that concerned them, so as to be more effective advocates for a healthier workplace. This learning took place through consulting other experts, doing research online, getting more involved in the union, or doing courses (Hall et al. 2006).

The starting point, then, was trusting their own common sense and believing their own bodies, even in the face of experts. Trusting in their own experiences was necessary, but not sufficient. They needed to go beyond common sense to begin to develop their own expertise, seeking systematic understandings in order to begin making real changes. This meant going beyond the realm of their own experiences to seek big-picture explanations, for example, learning about the actual causes of particular ailments. These activists, then, were not passively educated by experts, nor did they rely only on what they already knew. They sought to inform themselves in order to act on the world more effectively, in part by seeking the input of experts.

This kind of self-education does not rely primarily on being taught but rather on being stimulated to inquire. The plays of German writer Bertolt

Brecht are designed to provoke audience members into thinking for them-selves. Rather than providing answers, theatre, according to Brecht, should disturb the understandings that audience members arrive with, so viewers can begin to challenge what they think they already know. Brecht's work goes as far as to challenge even the audience's basic understanding of what a play is supposed to be. The audience in a play is usually encouraged to identify with the characters and to feel: "Yes, I have felt like that too ... It's only natural ... I weep when they weep, I laugh when they laugh" (Brecht 1964: 71). Brecht sought a different response, wanting his audience to respond: "I'd never have thought that ... That's extraordinary, hardly believable ... I laugh when they weep, I weep when they laugh" (p. 71). In traditional theatre, argues Brecht, the audience is treated as "the passive consumer of a finished, unchangeable art-object offered to them as 'real'" (Eagleton 1976: 64). Traditional plays present the audience with a fixed, coherent representation of the world as it is, giving viewers little chance "to think constructively of *how* it is presenting its characters and events, or how they might have been different." In contrast to traditional theatre, Brecht's plays aim to be "discontinuous, open-ended, internally contradictory, encourag-ing in the audience a 'complex seeing' which is alert to several conflicting possibilities at any particular point" (p. 65). To accomplish this, Brecht has his characters speak and gesture in ways that draw attention to the fact that they are not real people but actors playing a part. They might talk directly to the audience or burst into song. Brecht has new scenes introduced by actors carrying placards, which reminds everyone this is a play. This presentation is the opposite of the naturalism audiences had come to expect from the theatre, where the great accomplishment of the actor was to make those watching believe they were viewing a real character.

All of this sounds as though attending a Brecht play would be a rather alienating experience, not at all like the comfortable act of watching a favou-rite television show unfold over the course of an hour or two. In fact, deeply committed to the craft of theatre, Brecht sought to combine troubling effects with powerful theatrical experiences. Indeed, according to Brecht (1964), the experience of going to the theatre should be joyful as well as challenging: "Theatre remains theatre even when it is instructive theatre, and in so far as it is good theatre it will amuse" (p. 73).

At the same time, alienating the audience was exactly Brecht's intention—not because he wanted people to feel stupid for not understanding the point of his plays but because he wanted "to prevent [the audience] from emotionally identifying with the play in a way which paralyses its powers of critical judgement" (Eagleton 1976: 66). His plays aim to challenge common sense ideas about the form and purpose of the theatre, as well as ideas about the broader world. They were to be like an alarm clock to wake people out of the dream-like state induced by the familiar and by taken-for-granted assumptions about the way the world works.

Brecht believed that traditional theatre reinforced dominant representations of the world that take for granted its relative unchangeability. Thus, the purpose of Brecht's "alienation effects" is to cast "familiar experience in an unfamiliar light, forcing the audience to question attitudes and behaviour which it has taken as 'natural'" (Brecht 1964: 66). Brechtian theatre rejects the seemingly fixed nature of the social world and encourages people to think about the world as a place in which fundamental social change is possible. It encourages people to develop new ways of understanding society in the hopes that new methods of inquiry will produce new, more democratic forms of knowledge.

Brecht's theatre is part of a long tradition of thinkers and activists who encourage the development of active knowledge formation through inquiry. From this perspective, an essential part of strengthening the democratic imagination is helping people become more confident, self-directed learners and producers of knowledge. The process of stimulating people to become more active and systematic inquirers, drawing on and moving beyond their own common sense, is more complex than merely revealing a previously hidden body of knowledge to the unenlightened masses. Being this learning catalyst is what Brecht had in mind for his plays. He could not know for sure how they would be interpreted, nor did he want to control exactly what the audience would think. His hope was that, by being jarred out of familiar patterns of experience, people would think for themselves in ways better aligned with the principles of democracy.

A similar effort has been made more recently by educators who have adopted techniques of "problem-based learning" in their classrooms. In contrast to traditional methods of schooling, in which the teacher is positioned as the expert knower who imparts knowledge to students, problem-based learning assumes that students learn best when they are provided the chance to figure things out for themselves. "The PBL method requires students to become responsible for their own learning" (Hmelo-Silver and Barrows 2006: 24). Instead of listening to their teacher spew facts from the front of the room in the hopes of capturing the most important ones (or at least the ones most likely needed for regurgitation onto a test), students in problem-based learning environments are presented with a scenario that requires group-based, self-directed inquiry. They are given enough information to understand that a problem exists, but the exact nature of the problem and the way it ought to be addressed is for them to decide.

The role of the teacher (or facilitator) is not to tell students when they're doing something right or wrong or to reveal the one correct answer at the end but to help students work through the process of figuring out for themselves what they know about the problem based on the information they have, what they don't know, and what they need to find out. Getting better at the process of finding things out is the primary objective, not merely hitting a single "right" final answer.

At first, this method of learning can sound too open ended to be taken seriously, something that might work for dreaming up wild new ideas about abstract art but not relevant to helping students know the real world. In fact, problem-based learning was developed in the field of medicine. It is now used in a variety of disciplines, including ones in both the social and natural sciences. The reason that medical schools first embraced problem-based learning is that this way of knowing reflects very well the fact that the acquisition of knowledge is grounded in experience. Problem-based learning assumes that people learn best through doing, not through being lectured at. And nowhere is this method more clearly relevant than in the work of doctors, whose job often involves assessing unknown problems and making decisions based on the best information available (despite this information always being incomplete). Of course, doctors also do a great deal of learning from reading textbooks and listening to experts lecture, but there is no substitute for the kind of learning they do through the practice of identifying and addressing problems for themselves.

The virtues of problem-based learning help to understand the argument that democracy goes together with an unleashing of learning powers. Dominant knowledge about democracy today consists of restricted bodies of already-known facts about history and systems of government, as discussed previously in the description of official democracy (see Chapter 1). In typical classrooms, newspapers, legislatures, and popular films, democracy tends to be depicted as a system of representative government that includes an electoral component and a large bureaucracy. There are variations among official democracies when it comes to how electoral systems and legislatures function, what the heads of state are called, how constitutions operate, and so on, but the overall model itself is fairly rigid. Either your country meets these standards and is a democracy, or it does not meet them and therefore is not one.

By contrast, an approach linked to the ideas of democracy from below is deliberately open ended and self-reflexive about what rule by the people involves and how it can be put into practice. It never stops asking what is known, what is not known, and what needs to be found out in order for the *doing* of democracy to be strengthened. It actively challenges common sense notions that democracy works only through particular institutions (such as parliaments and bureaucracies) and draws upon the everyday knowledge of people to assess current democratic processes and develop more inclusive and vibrant ones. From this perspective, people not traditionally conceived of as experts are often the bearers of expert knowledge, and expertise is defined as knowledge that serves the flourishing of humans in general rather than narrow, technical knowledge that benefits certain groups of humans at the expense of others. This approach emphasizes the emergent, unfinished character of democracy and argues that democratic government needs to evolve in ways that better reflect people's knowledge about their lives and the world around them.

Knowing What's Good for You

Discussion of democracy and expertise, then, leads to complex arguments about the politics of knowledge and the social relations of expertise. Our consideration of the Greek crisis at the beginning of this chapter, for example, raised the question of whether the people can be trusted to know what is good for them. This complex, recurring question in democracies can lead to a great deal of **moral regulation** by experts who presume to be capable of telling people what is good for them. These are the "educators" that Marx describes.

Perhaps we need to consider the possibility that people with self-determination might not always choose to do what is good for themselves. Terry Eagleton (2007) argues that political observers and activists who want to strengthen democracy need to think seriously about "the ways in which people may come to invest in their own unhappiness" (p. xxii). Self-determination is the keystone of democracy, so to suggest that people do not always know what's good for them or make the best choices for themselves risks being moralistic and condescending.

Yet we all know of situations in which we or others who ought to "know better" have made bad choices. If you know someone who struggles with substance abuse, or have that experience yourself, you are probably familiar with how self-destructive that "choice" can be. Chronic abusers have a habit of feeling lousy when they are not high and destroying relationships after saying and doing things they would never have said or done while sober. Lives can be lost tragically. Sometimes, the person struggling refuses to admit to having a problem, but, other times, people know full well the harm their behaviours are causing. They might even express the desire to stop using but feel they don't have what it takes to put things on a different course. At the same time, unless the person with the problems is resolved to change, there is very little someone else can do to save that person from his or her own choices. Is the democratic solution, then, to deprive people of their autonomy by outlawing dangerous substances and practices, or is it to provide safe circumstances to reduce the likelihood of harm while providing people with the resources and power to make changes when they themselves are ready?

Questions about what constitutes an act of genuine self-determination are no less vexing when directed at the level of society as a whole. Just as we might ask about whether steady heroin use is in the best interests of someone who would like to live a long and meaningful life, it makes sense to ask why so many people appear to willingly, often enthusiastically, go along with trends in social life that contradict their own interests. Why do television news shows that repeatedly attack working people have such high ratings? Why do people accept being fired when losing their job causes such suffering? Why do people go on voting for and obeying governments that continually implement policies that make their lives worse?

One school of thought on these types of questions suggests that people make self-abusive choices because they are plagued by "false consciousness." Commercial advertising and government propaganda have brainwashed people, telling them that, despite its rough patches, this is the best possible world. And they hear this message so often that they are now blind to the real injustices of their lives. From this perspective, official knowledge and common sense are little more than false ideas intended to keep the masses in line, and most people have bought into the "Big Lie." Proponents of the false consciousness thesis use the word "ideology" to refer to the false ideas imposed by society's ruling classes on the miserable many with the purpose of keeping them contained, if not content, within their own limited standard of living. People make choices that go against their own interests because they have been tricked into believing lies.

Eagleton (2007) offers a more complex answer, which involves a more complex conception of ideology. He does not dispute that false ideas are perpetuated by forces friendly to people in positions of power. Contrary to what is suggested in chewing gum advertisements, even the tastiest stick of spearmint gum does not have the ability to make you an extreme skier or win you a herd of beautiful friends. There are lies, too, in government rhetoric about bringing freedom to foreign countries, when, in fact, Western democracies mostly drop bombs and sweatshops on faraway lands. There *are* such things as dominant ideologies, and they "quite often contain important propositions which are absolutely false: that Jews are inferior beings, that women are less rational than men, that fornicators will be condemned to perpetual torment" (Eagleton 2007: 15). Yet notwithstanding his recognition of the falseness embedded in ideologies that maintain inequality, Eagleton differs from the false consciousness thesis in crucial respects.

For starters, Eagleton emphasizes that, although people may indeed consume a great deal of ruling class ideology in the form of advertisements, government propaganda, official histories, and so on, they do not necessarily interpret dominant messages exactly as they were intended by the people who made them. The only thing more unlikely than chewing gum turning you into a better skier is you believing that it will. Yes, some ads are more persuasive than others, government propaganda can be subtly convincing, and it is easy to allow heart-warming fictions to cover up brutal facts when thinking about history. However, Eagleton (2007) makes a crucial point when he writes, "it is surely hard to credit that whole masses of human beings would hold over some extensive historical period ideas and beliefs which were simply nonsensical" (p. 12).

In fact, Eagleton argues, the history of humanity provides an extended case for the existence of something he calls "the moderate rationality of human beings in general" (p. 12). Certainly people are capable of making mistakes, being duped, deluding themselves, and miscommunicating, and vast parts of our existence remain beyond human understanding, but, generally speaking, "our practical knowledge must be mostly accurate, since otherwise our world would fall apart" (p. 13). The human ability to communicate not only within cultures but across cultural and linguistic divides is indicative of a basic ability to interpret reality accurately.

So how are people convinced to act against their own experiences and according to a version of reality propagated by authorities? In Eagleton's view, the reason that dominant ideologies are so powerful is that they are not totally false but tend to contain partial truths that resonate with our lived experience. "Deeply persistent beliefs have to be supported to some extent, however meagerly, by the world our practical activity discloses to us" (p. 12). Thus, the power of dominant ideologies to shape social life lies not in their falsities but in the fact that they draw upon and "encode, in however mystified a way, genuine needs and desires" (p. 12). The myth of the American dream that those who work hard will be rewarded by upward mobility is not totally untrue, as some people do manifest incredible will and discipline in escaping difficult circumstances. However, the actual opportunities for such upward mobility are not unlimited (as the "dream" might suggest); rather, they are highly restricted by a hierarchical social structure with only a limited number of elite spaces. These restrictions operate in such a way that they tend to screen out disadvantaged social groups disproportionately, so that the elite is comprised mainly of the children of privilege.

Thus, Eagleton's conception of ideology makes it easier to understand why people, not just individuals but whole social groups, sometimes act in ways that go against their personal and class interests. They do so not out of weakness of mind or lack of ambition but because the way knowledge is organized by powerful institutions (such as the media, politicians, and the educational system) resonates with particular aspects of their lived existence in a hierarchical society. People are not simply being duped by the big lie. In Nancy Hartsock's words, "The vision of the ruling class (or gender) structures the material relations in which all parties are forced to participate, and therefore cannot be dismissed as simply false" (Hartsock 1998: 107). It is only as people begin to engage in processes of social change that they are compelled to rethink what they thought they knew, generating new ways of thinking and searching out new resources to seek out a richer understanding of reality.

Knowledge Is Located

As people begin to rethink what they thought they knew, one thing they will tend to encounter is the idea that knowledge is located. The dominant view of knowledge in contemporary Western societies is that it is free floating, best attained by setting aside the world and engaging fully in the realm of thought and contemplation. In contrast, critical approaches argue that knowledge is grounded in our practices and interchanges with nature. Knowledge is therefore located in our social relations and can only be understood as such. Material forces such as the environment, the technologies at our disposal, and a variety of economic factors influence what can realistically be considered and accomplished at any particular point in history. This situatedness does not mean that nothing ever changes but that change emerges out of the constant back and forth between material conditions and human responses to them.

The experience of rapid travel and instant connection through Skype and email, for example, make the experience of distance from friends and family different than it is without those resources. The way we think about distance, then, is inseparable from material changes in the human capacity to travel and communicate. But our thinking also depends on where we fit in the system of unequal social relations, as those with money can negotiate distance with far greater ease than those without.

Knowledge, then, is located in specific social relations and draws on our experiences and capacities as they develop in particular circumstances. Further, where people are located within these social relations will frame their knowledge very differently. The workplace looks different through the eyes of a shareholder, a CEO, a supervisor, or a worker. A walk home at night might feel very different for women than men. A "joke" about "foreign" food smells might sound very different to a person of colour than to a white person. The wedding between a man and a woman might seem very different for a gay or lesbian person who does not fit in with the dominant values that are often expressed on these occasions. The elegant stairway at the entrance to a building will seem very different to someone with mobility challenges. Finally, the apparently simple choice between two washrooms, one labelled men and one labelled women, could stymie and anger a transgender person.

Expertise is not a question of knowing more or less but of seeing differently. Indeed, the perspective of those with less social power, the view from below, will provide important insights that are often virtually invisible from the perspective of the dominant. Nonetheless, these insights require work. Hartsock (1998) argues that a standpoint is "achieved rather than obvious" (p. 110). People from less powerful groups need to process their experiences and attempt to understand the big picture of social relations in order to develop maps that can guide freedom struggles. As discussed, though it must start with common sense, transformative knowledge that can lead to social change also requires conscious inquiry that involves engagement with others.

The way things actually are, then, is not always easy to see. Knowledge requires work, to get beyond appearances. In this work of figuring out, it is not necessarily the highly educated and socially powerful expert or official who offers the richest resources. As Dorothy Smith (1987) argues, academics and policymakers have much to learn from women's everyday experiences of their own lives. This process of figuring out pushes us to dig deeper, to try to understand, for example, why the inequality between men and women persists, despite the formal equality guaranteed by official government policies (Smith 1987). As discussed in Chapter 2, Marx (1976) makes a similar argument about how working for a wage is actually a form of exploitation, even though, on the surface, it appears to be a mutually agreed upon contract between the worker and the employer acting as free and equal parties. Himani Bannerji (2000) has written about how official multicultural policies tend to reproduce the marginalization of certain ethnic groups and racialized people, despite their claims about producing a more inclusive society.

This work of seeing beyond what seems to be obvious does not happen automatically but "represents an achievement both of ... analysis ... and of political struggle on the basis of which this analysis can be conducted" (Hartsock 1998: 110). Doubt—not cynicism, but healthy scepticism—is an essential tool in this process, as the whole struggle to understand is grounded on seeking really good answers to the most basic questions, such as "How do I know?" These answers need to be sought through individual and collective processes of inquiry. We often think of learning as primarily an individual quest, in which someone accumulates knowledge in ways that can be measured through testing processes. Yet collective inquiry is crucial, in part because we need to learn from each other if we are ever to piece together the big picture. In a sense, each of us can only know the world from our own position within it. It is crucial, then, to listen to others who can inform us about how the world looks from their vantage point. Through this dialogue and effective inquiry, we can figure out the ways in which individual experiences are shaped by forces beyond our own personal lives, so we can more clearly understand the uneven workings of the complex whole of society.

Who Knows Better?

The democratic imagination can never be separated from issues around the politics of knowledge. The way you answer questions about whether people can ever really know what is good for them, or be trusted to act responsibly in the face of difficult choices, will deeply shape your views on democratic practices. The Greek crisis described at the beginning of this chapter is one striking example of the kinds of questions about knowledge and the character of democracy that always exist below the surface of everyday social life.

Developing your own democratic imagination involves thinking about knowledge not as a fixed body of facts that already exists "out there" but as the result of inquiries that are shaped by material and social relations and therefore capable of changing over time. The more effective you become at thinking through common sense assumptions that organize our ways of knowing, not only in schools but in other parts of the world, the better you will become at thinking about the relationship between knowledge and power in general. Understanding the power of knowledge involves examining the power struggles among different knowledges. The next chapter extends this discussion on the always-embodied character of knowledge. It focuses on the relationship between democracy and bodies.

7 DEMOCRACY AND BODY POLITICS

Richard Farkas (2007) argues that a long history of wars and occupations has left its mark on South Eastern Europe: "The body politic in the Balkans is clearly marked by scars from many centuries of trial and conflict" (p. 2). The past is present in this region, in part due to the legacy those marks represent: "scars invite memory." The political society of South Eastern Europe is likened to a human body, which bears scars that mark experiences from well before the lifespan of the current population and invokes collective memories today.

There are, in fact, important debates about the extent to which the ugly transition from state "communism" to capitalism in much of South Eastern Europe was the inevitable progression of history. Certainly, the resurgent and often violent nationalisms that marked the break-up of former Yugoslavia invoked history, and leaders of various stripes claimed to be seeking redress for longstanding grievances. However, commentators have to be cautious about stereotyping the Balkans as a place determined only by its history, composed of warring peoples where conflict is essentially inevitable. Misha Glenny (1999) notes that the Balkans are too often dealt with in stereotyped terms: "As Yugoslavia began to disintegrate in 1989, generalizations about the people who inhabit the region, and their histories, were spread by media organizations that have long ago outlawed such clichés when reporting from Africa, the Middle East or China" (p. xxi).

In his book, Farkas is not stereotyping but trying to help readers understand the vivid ways in which the past informs the present, using the human body as a metaphor for collective experience, which has physical (scars) and mental (memories) aspects. Farkas did not invent the term "body politic." The idea that political society can be compared to a human body with a scope and lifespan far exceeding that of individual humans is an old one. But the political significance of human bodies goes beyond the metaphor of "body politics."

Democracy is often seen as a grand ideal, sustained historically as it gets passed from mind to mind through education. It can also be understood as a set of practices, which involve bodies as well as minds in specific, deliberate activities aimed at making and remaking the world. At the level of practice, there are sharp debates about what real democracy looks like. In the official version, democracy is largely an animating ideal put into practice primarily through being a responsible citizen and making periodic visits to a polling station to vote in elections. In contrast, the democracy-from-below conception of self-government casts bodies in a more prominent role, for example, occupying streets, parks, workplaces, or schools to protest against the existing order and sow the seeds of a new one. It is now common during demonstrations, particularly in the face of a heavy police presence, to chant, "This is what democracy looks like." In this sense, democracy looks like bodies crowded in places they would not normally be, disrupting everyday reality and developing new practices of popular power.

In this chapter, we will explore the importance of body politics in the theory and practice of democracy. The body has provided an ongoing metaphorical reference point for understanding politics, but it is also at the centre of a variety of democratic practices. These practices are associated with contending visions of democracy, ranging from lining up on election day at a polling place to raising a hand to vote at a meeting, joining a protest, or, even, sustaining injury or dying for a cause. Because bodies play such a fundamental role in everything humans do, they are easily taken for granted or overlooked in discussions about politics. This chapter encourages you to reflect specifically on the embodied character of all political thought and action, as well as what it means for bodies to do democracy.

Body Politics and the Use of Metaphor

The cartoonist Garry Trudeau, the artist behind the long-running Doonesbury strip, told *Rolling Stone* magazine that comics can provide special insights into current events. "What's wonderful about a comic strip is the stories unfurl in such a tiny, incremental way that you can keep a story alive for weeks.... So I can insinuate some of these issues under the skin of the body politic" (Kidd 2010, par. 3). Comics, which at first sight seem to be a form of light entertainment, can provide powerful images of contemporary politics that the more sober and descriptive news articles cannot match. The capacity for insight comes both from the pace of comic strips, allowing characters and situations to develop over a long trajectory, and from the use of images.

Sometimes the richest insights into human affairs come not from literal description but from images that use humour and indirect references. Cartoons and graphics' have been used to analyze politics and to advocate, at least since the French Revolution. Of course, the use of imagery in politics goes well beyond cartoons, and metaphor is not restricted to comics or popular culture. Political theory draws deeply on metaphorical representations of social processes. A metaphor is defined as "a figure of speech in which a name or descriptive word or phrase is transferred to an object or action different from, but analogous to, that to which it is literally applicable" (OED Online 2011). A metaphor, then, uses one thing to suggest another, conjuring up some sense of related properties and parallel paths of development.

The use of the body as a metaphor for political society has a long history. A.D. Harvey (2007) found examples tracing back over 25 centuries, from sources as varied as Hindu texts, Aesop's fables, and Greek philosophy. The philosopher Al-Farabi, writing in the tenth century in Damascus and Baghdad, used the body as a metaphor for a well-run city:

> The excellent city resembles the perfect and healthy body, all of whose limbs co-operate ... there being among them one ruling organ .... The parts of the city which are close in authority to the rulers of the city perform the most noble voluntary actions, and those below them less noble actions, until eventually the parts are reached which perform the most ignoble actions ... although they may be extremely useful—like the action of the bladder and the lower intestine. (Al-Farabi, quoted in Harvey 2007: 13–14)

The body provides an extremely rich metaphorical source for understanding political society. In the Al-Farabi quotation, the theme of interdependence is combined with that of hierarchy—the parts of the city need to work together in balance, but that is only maintained through a clear hierarchy, which relies, ultimately, on having only one ruling organ. In a prominent biological metaphor for Victorian society, "the adult middle-class (or aristocratic) man, representing the governing or ruling group, was seen as the Head of the social system," while "middle-class women represented the emotions, the Heart, or sometimes the Soul, seat of morality and tenderness" (Davidoff 1995: 104–5).

Although the body has often been used as a metaphor for political society, its meanings have varied across time and space. The rise of democracy brought about a dramatically different conception of political society and therefore a great shift in its symbolic representation in terms of the human body. During the French Revolution, for example, the understanding of the body politic changed dramatically, as democracy supplanted the absolutist rule of the monarch. Indeed, dispute over cultural representations of politics in terms of the body played an important role in defining the new perspectives of those times (de Baecque 1997).

One of the great exciting challenges of a revolution is an opening up of culture, as many things that seemed fixed and taken for granted are suddenly in flux. Participants in the French Revolution reset the calendar to "Year One," so great did they see the changes they were making. They marked the emergence of a new era with a whole range of cultural activities, including festivals, songs, paintings, and sculptures. Democracy required a very different set of cultural representations than absolutist monarchy.

This was a turbulent time, associated with militant struggle and the intense battle of ideas, both directly in the form of political debate and indirectly in the form of literary, visual, and musical expressions. Specific images of bodies were used in particular ways as part of that political exchange. The nobility and the priests, for example, were commonly portrayed as fat, with their excess weight serving as a sign of their wealth and non-labouring lifestyle. One cartoon, called "The Patriotic Fat Remover," showed priests being stripped of their fat, which was then turned into gold for the revolutionary national treasury (de Baecque 1997: 1). Later, we will return to the question of body image and body politics, talking about the ways "fatness" and "leanness" are used to add specific moral and economic dimensions to these metaphors.

The emergence of modern democracy required a remaking of the body politic. In an absolute monarchy, the body of the king or queen represented the state. King Louis XIV of France is associated with the statement "*L'Etat c'est moi*," which means, "I am the state." This was literally true, as the monarch was basically cast as the origin of all state power and the ultimate earthly decision maker. The monarch as the absolute and only source of all legitimate political power is captured in an image crafted for the cover of Thomas Hobbes's book *Leviathan*, which shows a king whose body is made up of all the little bodies of the population.

The termination of the old state required the execution of the monarch and his heirs, who were the embodiment of absolute rule. Indeed, the importance of execution in the French Revolution, which is strongly associated with the use of the guillotine as an efficient machine for removing heads, derives in part from the fact that, in the old order, the bodies of the hereditary nobility and their absolute power were inseparable. If the body of the king literally was the state, then only his execution could permit the rise of a new state. Yet execution was also used by revolutionaries against each other in the Terror that followed the early years of revolution. The period of revolutionary terror undercut the democratic claims of the emergent order because, in a democracy, political power and the body of any given individual are separable in principle, allowing individuals to pass into and out of office through election or appointment rather than through hereditary privilege or the claim to rule by the will of god. In other words, democracies do not rely on executing leaders to transfer political power.

Violence and Political Bodies

One of the important ways bodies appear in political action is through violence that maims them. Revolutionary violence, in the specific sense of harming or killing people as part of the process of transforming society, is one of the most complex and vexing issues in democratic theory. The official view of democracy repudiates violence as a means of change, at least once democracy has been accomplished. This view takes for granted the official state-sanctioned violence of authorities such as the military or the police, whose actions are defined as the legitimate pursuit of order in the interests of all. Indeed, Max Weber (1958) influentially defines the state as "a human community that (successfully) claims the monopoly of the legitimate use of physical force within a given territory" (p. 78). State violence is defined as uniquely legitimate as it is in the national interest, while private violence by individuals or non-state organizations threatens to disrupt order in the public realm.

The official view of democracy, therefore, disavows violence by anyone other than agents of the state. Yet, to some proponents of democracy from below, non-violence in the face of armed force can simply mean acquiescence. It is hard to imagine that we would have trade unions today, for example, if workers simply accepted the legitimacy of state violence and eschewed the use of force for themselves. For example, the 1937 sit-down strikes in Flint, Michigan, were crucial in getting General Motors and the automobile industry to recognize union rights. Workers literally sat down at their workstations and occupied the plants, which is, of course, illegal, as the factory is the property of its owners. Eventually, the police attacked those occupying the plants and those picketing outside, working in cooperation with private company security forces. As participant Genora Johnson Dollinger recalls, "The police were using rifles, buckshot, firebombs, and tear-gas canisters" (Dollinger and Dollinger 2000: 133). Yet workers did not simply withdraw in the face of this "legitimate" state violence; they fought back: "Workers overturned police cars to make barricades. They ran to pick up the fire bombs thrown at them and hurl them back at the police" (Dollinger and Dollinger 2000: 133). The struggle continued, and, ultimately, General Motors recognized the union.

Even if revolutionary violence can be justified, however, there is sure to be an uneasy fit between violence and democracy. A regime of violent rule and democracy are incompatible, as power will tend to devolve to those who control the use of force. Genuine democracy must include the voices and actions of all, and this universality is surely undercut by violence, which tends to concentrate power in the hands of those who dominate physically, mentally, or through the use of weapons.

The historical record clearly shows that the establishment of democracy has tended to involve some degree of violence, as the old order does not

---

EXERCISING YOUR DEMOCRATIC IMAGINATION
Civil Disobedience

In 1930, Mahatma Gandhi led a 380-kilometre march as part of the Indian independence movement to overthrow British colonial rule. The march clearly and deliberately broke British law. Colonial authorities used every means at their disposal to try to stop it, including firing machine guns into unarmed crowds, killing hundreds of demonstrators. Today, most people, including most British officials, recall the march as an act of heroism. Yet, at the same time, contemporary demonstrations against democratic governments are routinely broken up by authorities, often through the use of police violence.

The *Oxford English Dictionary* defines civil disobedience as "refusal to obey the laws, commands, etc., of a government or authority as part of an organized, non-violent political protest or campaign" (OED Online 2011). Environmental activists blocking logging vehicles, students occupying administrative offices, and workers illegally striking in solidarity with other workers are all examples of civil disobedience. The civil rights leader Dr. Martin Luther King, Jr. (1963/1981) reasoned that to disobey unjust laws is not only appropriate but the responsibility of people who believe in democracy: "To accept an unjust system is to cooperate with that system, and thereby to become a participant in its evil" (p. 18). Yet, when explaining why police needed to tear down the Occupy Toronto encampment in St. James Park in 2011, the deputy mayor repeatedly said, "The law is the law."

History includes many examples of laws passed by democratic governments that would offend most people today. Slavery in the United States was enforced by law. Women were prevented by law from participating in politics. Homosexuality was illegal in many democracies until very recently.

Should anti-racists, feminists, and queer activists have gone on obeying these laws?

What makes breaking the law legitimate in one case and illegitimate in another?

usually give up and hand over power to the people unless forced. It is not an accident that the rise of democracy is associated with revolutions or civil wars in England, France, Germany, and Russia and with anti-colonial uprisings in the Americas, Asia, and Africa. As C.L.R. James (1980) writes, "Those in power never give way, and admit defeat only to plot and scheme to regain their lost power and privilege" (p. 127).

There are also important ways that the violence of the old regime frames the transition to a new social order, even as a newer and more just way of living is emerging. The French Revolution precipitated a successful slave revolt in Haiti, the colony that was the greatest single source of wealth for monarchist France. Slavery involved intense brutalization of the bodies of captives, as subordination did not result automatically from legal owner-ship but had to be beaten into people who continued to resist in many ways. The colonial landowners in Haiti had developed a regime that included the routine use of many forms of physical punishment and murder. The slaves who overthrew their colonial masters destroyed property and killed many landowners. As C.L.R. James (1980) writes in *The Black Jacobins,* his great history of the Haitian slave revolt, "From their masters they had known rape, torture, degradation and, at the slightest provocation, death. They returned in kind.... Now that they held power they did as they had been taught" (p. 88).

Yet, James (1980) argues, the violence of the slave revolution was far more contained than that of the old colonial slaveholders. The insurgent slaves were "far more humane than their masters had been, or ever would be, to them.... Compared to what their masters had done to them in cold blood, what they did was negligible" (pp. 88–89). The routinized violence of the slaveholding regime was far more brutal and sustained than the revolutionary violence as the slaves rose up.

Revolutionary moments, in short, are a complex interplay between the conditions of the old order that is being overthrown and those of the new world arising. They are moments when symbols and even words are highly contested, as new meanings begin to emerge associated with new experiences and ways of living. The French Revolution created an important transition from the representation of the body politic as the "body of the king" to a conception of it as the great "body of citizens" (de Baecque 1997: 8). The "body of citizens" was represented in various ways, ranging from masses in the streets to symbolic representation through new images. Specifically, the image of a woman, often armed, became a core symbol of the new Republic, a symbol associated with liberty (de Baecque 1997: 320). At the same time, festivals that actually brought masses into the streets were an important part of revolutionary commemoration in France and Russia.

Democracy and Bodies in Action

One of the great challenges of democracy from below is that it requires the people, and indeed each person, to value their own ability to partake in collective self-rule. Clearly, this requirement involves a massive shift from absolute monarchy, in which the natural order of things is that a tiny minority is born to govern, and the majority is born to work for that minority. In other words, in feudal societies some bodies were born to rule and others to be ruled. Even in a representative democracy, most people are expected to participate only in limited ways, helping to choose the active decision makers through elections, for example. Institutions like schools and workplaces certainly do not prepare people for active self-government.

It is not automatic that those who have been told their whole lives that they are a lesser category of humans, ill-suited to rule, will spontaneously develop the propensity to participate in self-government through democracy. That is one of the reasons why Marx, among others, believed that revolution was an important part of the process of achieving democracy from below. The key feature of revolution, in this sense, is a mass uprising in which large segments of the population mobilize to take over the streets, occupy workplaces, and seize control of community sites. It is not about small conspiracies of armed militants taking action but rather about active participation by the mass of the people, who take power with their own hands.

Marx and Engels (1976) argue that revolution is necessary because those currently in power will not give it up without an uprising, but also because the people who become activists and make the revolution transform themselves through the process:

> The revolution is necessary, therefore, not only because the *ruling* class cannot be overthrown in any other way, but also because the class *overthrowing* it can only in a revolution succeed in ridding itself of all the muck of ages and become fitted to found society anew. (P. 60)

Revolution has an important educational dimension, as people get rid of the "muck of ages" through their own activism. The world looks different as everyday life is disrupted by demonstrations, occupations, and strikes (Camfield 2011: chap. 1). Activism provides a new perspective on reality, and even familiar streets are transformed by the presence of masses of people. Activism also fires up the hunger for knowledge and the sense of responsibility for knowing. People cast in the position of voting for or against a strike, for example, which can involve tremendous risk and sacrifice as income is cut off and jobs threatened, will often want to know more about the collective agreement and bargaining process than they might have previously.

In these situations, the circulation of such knowledge speeds up, as people carry on a new level of discussion and debate with others. When your body is on the line, your need to know is intensified. Politics is no longer a distant activity by specific actors to be watched on television but an immediate part of shared life experience in one's own communities. Visitors to the city of Petrograd during the Russian Revolution noted the vibrancy of political discussion and debate everywhere they went, even among people who, not long before, would not have ventured an opinion. New levels of active participation can lead to a new need to know.

The American radical John Reed was an eyewitness to the 1917 revolution in Russia. He commented on the excitement around the exchange of ideas, which included a passion for reading that for many meant acquiring basic literacy. "All Russia was learning to read, and *reading*—politics, economics, history—because the people wanted to know.... Russia absorbed reading matter like hot sand drinks water, insatiable" (Reed 1919: chap.1). And all that reading was accompanied by endless discussion: "Lectures, debates, speeches—in theatres, circuses, school-houses, clubs, Soviet meeting-rooms, Union headquarters, barracks. Meetings in the trenches at the Front, in village squares, factories" (Reed 1919: chap.1). He summed this up by saying, "For months in Petrograd, and all over Russia, every street-corner was a public tribune. In railway trains, street-cars, always the spurting up of impromptu debate, everywhere" (Reed 1919: chap. 1).

Historically, democracy has developed only when people chose new forms of active participation and put their bodies on the line. Wendy Parkins (2000) writes that many feminist campaigns have "deployed forms of protest which emphasized female embodiment in their contestation of the political domain" (p. 72). People make and remake democracy with their own minds and bodies, moving from being spectators to actors by demonstrating, refusing, seizing, storming, speaking out, or listening. John Berger (1968) argues that the core of a mass demonstration is a show of potential force: "it *demonstrates* a force that is scarcely used" (p. 754). Even if the potential force is not deployed, large demonstrations get at least some of their power from the transformative potential of masses who dramatically outnumber police and can grind the city to a halt simply through filling the streets. Perhaps part of the let-down from a completely ritualized demonstration, in which participants feel they are going through the motions of walking from here to there, is that people recognize the gap between the potential power of the moment and what they actually achieve.

Nurturing Democracy

The capacities developed through mass participation in a revolutionary situation will fade over time, particularly if the postrevolutionary society does not nurture democratic capacities. The American poet Walt Whitman, writing more than 70 years after the American Revolution, was deeply concerned about enhancing democratic capacities that were withering in the climate of official representative democracy. The 1850s and 1860s were a time of flux, as the United States headed toward civil war between the slaveholding south and the north in the context of industrialization, the growth of cities, increased immigration, and the perceived corruption of political institutions. In this context, Whitman's work was a vibrant articulation of democracy from below, a celebration of the people and their capacities as part of a project of "democratic regeneration" (Frank 2007: 403). In Martha Nussbaum's words, "Walt Whitman is a political poet, a poet who holds that poetry has an essential role to play in the life of the American democracy" (Nussbaum 2011: 96).

His writing celebrates the democratic capacities of the everyday people, a power reflected in their bodies, voices, and spirits. Whitman's poem "I sing the Body Electric" proclaims, "The man's body is sacred and the woman's body is sacred / No matter who it is, it is sacred." This includes the lowly as well as those of high station, and he gives particular examples of labourers and recent immigrants: "Each belongs here or anywhere just as much as the well-off, just as much /as you" (Whitman 1940: 108). Even today, this claim challenges the anti-immigrant and anti-poor rhetoric that seems to be resurgent in twenty-first-century politics: "Each has his or her place in the procession."

The idea that democracy is a procession rather than a fixed set of institutions is central to Whitman. Indeed, a walk through the streets of New York provided more democratic energy for Whitman (1860/2002) than reading a newspaper or listening to a politician, as is evident in his poem "Mannahatta," for example. At a time when the cities were growing rapidly, and with them the social problems associated with poverty, overcrowding, lack of sanitation, and intense inequalities, Whitman celebrated New York as a place of the people (Berman 2011: 149–50).

In Whitman's writing, genuine democracy includes a passion for each other—and that passion is inherently embodied. As Nussbaum (2011) writes, "For Whitman, the democratic vision is, ultimately, a vision of love" (p. 96). His loving eye elevates those he describes so that democratic participation is driven by mutual passion: "Underneath it all is the Expression of love for men and women" (Whitman 1940: 196). This passion is multidimensional and distinctly erotic. Vivian Pollak (2000) describes this view as Whitman's "sexually marked body politic" (p. xiii).

In "Song of Myself," Whitman (1940) links euphoric passion and the body of a presumed stranger who leaves quietly at sunrise. "I am satisfied—I see, dance, laugh, sing; / As the hugging and loving bed-fellow sleeps at my side through the night, / and withdraws at the peep of the day with a stealthy tread" (p. 37). Although the gender of this "bed-fellow" is not defined, Whitman included same-sex eroticism in his writing at a time in the 1800s when this was not widely socially acceptable.

The frank and erotic presence of the body is central to Whitman's democratic imagination, including its commitment to equality: "Welcome is every organ and attribute of me, and of any man hearty and clean / Not an inch nor a particle of an inch is vile, and none shall be less familiar / than the rest" (Whitman 1940: 37). By emphasizing the always-embodied character of human life, Whitman challenges the line dividing political and private worlds, raising possibilities for developing democracy in new directions. As Nussbaum (2011) explains, "Focussing on the body, we reveal ourselves to ourselves as equally needy and finite and mortal, and also equally noble and beautiful; we find a foundation for both equal support and equal respect and love" (p. 111).

Keep Your Laws off Our Bodies

The link we find in Whitman's work between democracy and bodies and eroticism was echoed prominently almost 100 years later with the emergence of second-wave feminism and lesbian-gay liberation in the 1960s. One of the important aspects of these movements was investigating the hidden histories of gender and sexuality, including the ways of life and struggles that traditional accounts rendered invisible. People began to look back to see when and where same-sex relations had been practised and what women had done to make history.

One theme in some of these hidden histories is the role that the emergence of capitalism had in making a new politics of sex and gender possible. On the one hand, capitalism, unlike the other economic relations underpinning class societies, allows the productive classes (working-class employees) to own their own bodies, breaking the ties to the slaveholder or landowner that had shaped the life experiences of slaves and peasants. On the other, it separates the core relationships of social production (going to work) from those of **social reproduction** (making and sustaining life at home)

(D'Emilio 1992). In contrast, in pre- and non-capitalist societies, people tended to hunt, fish, and farm in the same village and kin relationships as they raised children, ate, rested, and enjoyed leisure. The separation between the public life of work and school and private life, a separation that many take for granted in contemporary capitalism, does not exist in the same way in other forms of society, which unite work, play, and household in a single set of relationships.

The ownership of one's own body and the separation of working relationships from social reproduction created new possibilities for choice in the realm of what we might call "private life." Yet state policymakers and advocates for social reform in the nineteenth century saw this choice as a problem that threatened the social reproduction of the working class. A crisis that was described in terms of "degeneration" was seen as the result of unregulated sexuality and blurred gender roles. New forms of moral regulation were introduced, ranging from the prohibition of prostitution and male homosexuality to social assistance programs such as mother's allowance to support a particular household structure (Gordon 1990; Weeks 1990).

Beginning in the 1960s, second-wave feminism and lesbian-gay liberation fought in new ways to open up possibilities for real freedom in the realms of gender and sexuality. These included a reclaiming of control over our own bodies as a fundamental condition for shaping our destinies, as in the important feminist classic *Our Bodies, Our Selves* (Boston Women's Health Collective 1971). The politics of choice in contraception and abortion was expressed in the chant "keep your laws off my body." These new liberation politics included a celebration of the erotic as emancipatory, perhaps most strongly in particular gay-libertarian politics in which sexual activity was celebrated as a practice of freedom (Sears 2005). Indeed, a trailblazing newspaper for gay liberation published first in Toronto in 1972 was called *The Body Politic*. Yet, as the formal rights of women and of lesbians and gays were expanded, these themes of reclaiming our bodies and radical eroticism faded in favour of social inclusion and equal rights.

So it is a challenge now to re-imagine what hot democracy might look like. The official version of democracy is a rather cold, rational idea. There is another version, however, that sees democracy as not only a product of but also a guideline for our most powerful human relationships. The meeting point of democracy and desire is one that can inspire a deepening of democratic practices and better ways of conducting personal relations.

This theme is raised in Angela Y. Davis's analysis of African American women and the blues, in which she discusses the impact of emancipation from slavery on the daily lives of those former slaves who were freed and on the lives of their descendants. Racism was not eliminated, and former slaves remained impoverished. However, they did win increased freedom in the realm of personal relations. As Davis (1999) writes, "For the first time in the history of the African presence in North America, masses of black women and men were in a position to make autonomous decisions regarding the sexual partnerships into which they entered" (p. 4).

The explicit sexuality in the lyrics of women blues artists reflected the celebration of the only meaningful realm of freedom they had gained since the abolition of slavery. Artists Gertrude "Ma" Rainey, Bessie Smith, and Billie Holiday crafted musical performances that combined pain and suffering with very suggestive sexual references. Their work is a powerful example of the ways sexual freedoms are deeply attached to all other forms of liberation, and this example provides a powerful insight into the potential depth of democratic practices.

The Body Politic in Lean Times

In the late twentieth and early twenty-first centuries, the body politic has been diagnosed as having a weight problem. The goal of putting it on a diet seems to be shared by politicians of many stripes. Indeed, with the accumulation of state debt due to the massive bailout of corporations after the global slump of 2008, the body politic may be put on a *crash* diet. We may be moving rapidly out of the realm of dieting and toward an eating disorder that leads to starvation.

The use of the lean body as a model for an efficient and productive organization began in the automotive industry in the 1980s with the language of "lean production." The concept of lean production generalized practices introduced in the Japanese automotive industry in the 1960s and 1970s. Lean production methods basically focused on the elimination of "waste" associated with previous mass production systems through the reorganization of labour processes and the restructuring of labour–management relations (Elger and Smith 1994; Moody 1997). The introduction of new information-age technologies and the reorganization of workers into teams, combined with the shift away from traditional union–management relations with their adversarial character and focus on job ownership, were to create a more flexible and efficient workplace.

The lean production model soon moved beyond the automotive sector into a wide range of workplaces. It soon began to have an impact on state policymaking as well, providing new tools for imagining a social policy compatible with neo-liberalism (discussed in Chapter 3). Just as mass production methods were cast as wasteful to innovation, so the social programs of the welfare state were characterized as an obstacle to social innovation and economic prosperity.

In the French Revolution, the priests and nobles were caricatured as fat and seen as obstacles to a just society. Now, it is state employees, unionized workers, and the poor. In contemporary society, which constructs fatness as a moral failing, leanness is held up as the model of taking care of yourself. Social policy today is based on this ethos, on the lean person who is "driven to maintain herself or himself at peak levels of fitness and generally organizes his or her life around lean principles, avoiding waste and dependence" (Sears 1999: 103).

Programs that were won democratically, for example, ones that provide help to individuals and families with limited incomes and that range from social assistance to public housing, are now cast as obstacles preventing these people from taking control of their own destinies. Public-sector workers are routinely cast as "fat bureaucrats," particularly given that they have maintained better pay, pensions, and benefits while unions in private-sector workplaces have made many concessions in these areas. The fight over whether the body politic is being made lean and efficient or is, in fact, being starved of the vital nourishment needed to sustain it has raged in the political realm over the past 20 years, and these battles continue.

Consumption and Body Politics

It is interesting to note that the era of lean production in the late twentieth and early twenty-first centuries has also seen the rise of the lean, muscular body as the standard for physical fitness and the ideal to which we are all supposed to aspire. The dominance of this body type has corresponded with the development of a lean ethos, which downloads responsibility for our well-being onto our own shoulders, as services and benefits are cut (Sears 1999). The rise of the lean ethos has gone along with a tremendous stigmatization of body fat.

Interestingly, the stigmatization of fat and the celebration of the lean, muscular body has little to do with specific health considerations. Sweeping generalizations about the health effects of excessive body mass are based on very limited scientific evidence that shows only narrow correlations in specific conditions (see Gard and Wright 2005). The rise of the lean, muscular ideal since the 1960s has less to do with health concerns than with social and cultural changes that influenced the conception of the ideal body type, including the increased impact of consumerism on our daily lives, changing work processes, and shifting gender relationships.

One dimension of this change is a shift in what is considered the desirable male body type for stars. If you compare pictures of a 1950s male movie star such as Rock Hudson or Marlon Brando to shots of contemporary actors, you see a notable difference in their conditioning. Today, many male actors have highly defined muscles, including six-pack abs, and are so lean that their veins are visible. The standards for these bodies are influenced by body-building, which has gone from being a marginal and stigmatized activity to a mainstream influence on modern views concerning how an athletic male body should look (Heywood 1997: 165). The built body has become an ideal, and that body must be produced through a deliberate process of transforma-tion, which includes gym training, diet, supplements, shaving, and tanning, as well as specific photographic techniques. The rise of the "designed body" is associated with the increasing influence of the consumption of commodi-ties in our everyday lives and the triumph of marketing of "every element of bodily need and desire including the medical, the cosmetic, the athletic, the sexual, the erotic—everything and anything to which can be attached a price in the flow of exchange" (Prosono 2008: 650).

The cult of the lean, muscular male body is also a result of changing gender relations. The past 30 years have seen the rise of a consumerist masculinity engaged with fashion and grooming, even though previous standards of masculinity had identified concern about personal appearance with feminin-ity (Mort 1996). Women's bodies have been measured against established aesthetic standards for much longer. This consumerist masculinity is deeply racialized, as the images of idealized built bodies are often associated specifi-cally with whiteness to the extent that companies such as Abercrombie and Fitch have actually engaged in employment practices that discriminate against people of colour, for example prohibiting hairstyles associated with black men (McBride 2005).

The consumption of commodities has influenced not only our feelings about our own bodies but also our sense of democracy. Lizabeth Cohen (2004) argues that consumerism and citizenship became deeply interconnected in the United States after World War II, as working people organized and fought for rights (such as union rights and civil rights) that allowed them to increase their standards of living and gain access to the market as consumers of more than just necessities. This trend has led to an equation of democracy and consumerism that influences politics in the "developed" capitalist economies of the Global North.

The consumerist vision of democracy is evident in the motion that Minnesota Republican Michele Bachmann presented to the US House of Representatives in March 2011, called the "Light Bulb Freedom of Choice Act." This motion aimed to repeal environmental legislation, passed a few years earlier, to phase out incandescent light bulbs in favour of more sustainable and energy-efficient alternatives. As Bachmann explains in a press release, "The government has no business telling an individual what kind of light bulb to buy" (Montopoli 2011). The notion that one has a right to make certain consumption decisions is connected to a vision of democracy that identifies it deeply with the choice between products for sale on the market. This notion is connected with the idea that citizens should be treated as customers in relation to government services, such as schools or social programs.

It is easy to see how people seeking services or university students dealing with their institution could consider it a step up to be treated as a customer rather than being subjected to impersonal bureaucratic processes that leave them feeling powerless. Yet the rights of a customer are ultimately highly constrained, limited, basically, to choosing between available products and enforcing the promises associated with warranties and guarantees. As consumers, we are often confronted with the limited choice between nearly identical products from rival firms, which may not actually meet our needs. Democracy might offer a richer model for these interactions, in which the self-defined needs of citizens, students, and service users actually shape the institution and its web of social relations.

Virtuality, Democracy, and Body Politics

On Saturday, August 6, 2011, riots broke out in London and then elsewhere in Britain. The five-day riots originated with a group of people protesting the police killing of Mark Duggan in Tottenham, a lower-income area of London with a high proportion of residents of colour. Indeed, the riot sparked by police violence against low-income members of visible minorities is a recurrent theme in Europe and North America. Riots erupted under similar situations in England in the 1980s.

One of the distinguishing features of the events this time was the role of social media. An article in the *Guardian* newspaper contrasted the 2011 events with a similar (though ultimately more contained) riot decades earlier in the Tottenham area (Halliday 2011a). In 1985, a riot took place in the Broadwater Farm area of Tottenham after the death of Cynthia Jarret at the hands of the police. At an open-air mass meeting, a community leader rose with a megaphone and yelled, "You tell them that it's a life for a life from now on. This is war" (Halliday 2011a: par. 2).

In 2011, a Facebook page began to upload pictures of events as they unfolded, while tweets called people to action. The role of BlackBerry Messenger may have been even more important. It apparently played a prominent role in organizing actions not only because of its popularity among younger people but also because messages are encrypted and cannot be traced by the police. The security features, which are a major selling point in the business market, are alleged to have offered a new way of organizing insurgency.

It seems that Research in Motion, the parent company for BlackBerry, is not planning to use this feature as a sales pitch in its heated battle with Apple's iPhone. As stories about the role of BlackBerry Messenger circulated quickly around the global media, the company announced that it would cooperate with the police investigation, which could include handing over the personal information of people using the network to encourage participation in insurgency. A warrant would be required to hand over the message content, but identifying information can be shared in the interest of national security or to prevent crime (Halliday 2011b).

There is no doubt that social media offer new opportunities for mobilization, as well as for community formation on a global scale. It is possible to distribute analysis and information very quickly and to keep interested parties apprised of events as they develop. These possibilities have made some analysts very optimistic that social media can play an important role in nurturing democracy in the twenty-first century.

Indeed, some writers argue that the way social media are structured provides a model for a more democratic kind of dissident organizing. Judy Rebick (2009) calls for new forms of networked politics, tracing out a model that combines specific types of bottom-up activist organizing with the characteristics of the online communities many of us participate in (such as Facebook, Google+, or issue-based forums). There is no formal leadership, so anyone can initiate an action and invite those who agree to participate, for example, by starting a Facebook page (leaving aside for the purposes of this discussion that some of these online operations are in fact mega-corporations making big bucks through advertising and imposing unilateral managerial decisions). This model "does manage to liberate the genius and talents in ordinary people by using open space, horizontal structures, and self-organization" (Rebick 2009: 143).

Certainly, formal and informal networks play an important role in activist mobilization, one that has often been underestimated through lenses that direct attention to formal organizations such as political parties, unions, and advocacy groups. It would be possible to argue that network politics does not completely supersede more formal organizations but might, in fact, complement them; however, in this chapter, we cannot fully develop this debate.

Nick Dyer-Witheford (2009) discusses these developments using the concept of "the commons," a term initially applied to community-held agricultural areas that were expropriated and replaced by fenced-off private land. The commons belongs to all, and Dyer-Witheford argues that open source and peer-to-peer models begin to develop elements of the commons as oppositional spaces, even within a capitalist society. These proliferating information technologies are valuable tools for activists, and there is certainly interesting thinking about the extent to which they might provide new models for organizing. However, the communities that form through information technologies still need to be connected to bodies in motion to achieve change.

The Egyptian revolution of January 2011 drew heavily on the use of social media to call out activists for protests and communicate about developments. But the impact of social media can be overstated:

> Commentators in the West have been quick to credit online social networking with empowering the protests. But the revolution that started in January 2011 in Cairo has provided powerful evidence that the virtual is not enough: in the course of several historic days in Tahrir Square it became decisively clear that the occupation of physical urban space was, and continues to be, crucial to the success and continuity of the revolution. (Elshahed 2011: par.4).

Information technologies clearly offered enhanced communication capacities, but, ultimately, the success of the revolution depended on bodies taking action, people seizing the square and sustaining their occupation in the face of brutalizing, repressive force. That required the development of the collective capacity to sustain the occupation by nourishing the bodies and minds of those who filled Tahrir Square:

> People sold food and drinks, set up recycling bins and portable toilets, organized the logistics of daily life.... Throughout the square bloggers were streaming comments and images onto the Internet. Doctors and nurses were providing free healthcare in impromptu clinics. Filmmakers were interviewing protesters and creating an instant archive, a visual and oral record of history as it was unfolding. Musicians, professional and amateur, wrote songs and tested them on eager audiences. There were poets, puppeteers and comedians. Art teachers provided supplies and then displayed the artworks that resulted on a public wall. (Elshahed 2011: par. 10)

This activism, including the development of methods of sustenance, became even more important when the government shut down access to information technologies. The potential for new forms of democracy to be unleashed through virtual connectivity is something that we will be able to assess fully only as movements emerge. However, the project of democracy from below requires the actions of bodies in motion, as the dominant forms of power continue to rely on physical force as a crucial component of social control, through the actions of police, jail guards, soldiers, immigration officers, and security guards.

Democracy and Embodied Inequality

Actual existing democracies have not treated all bodies equally. Indeed, the unequal treatment of bodies is one of the core elements of persistent oppression, even in a situation of democratic rights. Democratic rights have coexisted with slavery, for example, in the United States. There is a real contradiction between the notion that "all men are created equal," in the words of the United States Constitution, and the persistence of the most brutal form of inequality: the enslavement of some by others. If one of the central ideas of capitalism is that people own their own bodies, democratic capitalism would seem incompatible with the practice of slavery. Ellen Meiksins Wood (1995) argues that this contradiction was resolved by intensifying racism. The institution of slavery was justified in a capitalist democracy "by excluding slaves from the human race, making them non-persons standing outside the normal universe of freedom and equality" (p. 259).

As stated previously, under feudalism, the bodies of the king and the nobility were seen as completely different from those of the people: nobility was born to rule. This view changed after the rise of democracy because, at least in principle, formal equality reigned. Even those with tremendous economic power and wealth were, in principle, cast as equal to those with lower incomes—all were citizens. Yet just beneath the surface of this formal equality lurked a brutal inequality based on the disqualification of some as fully human due to their specific characteristics (for example, the superficial traits such as skin colour, nose shape, and hair type that are used to mark "race").

Women were also disqualified as fully human and therefore excluded from the vote and from many other rights. Barbara Ehrenreich and Deirdre English (1979) point out in their pioneering work that science played a major role in the disqualification of women from full humanity, treating their bodies as a natural artefact: "Woman's body, with its autonomous rhythms and generative possibilities, appears to the masculinist vision as a 'frontier,' another part of the natural world to be explored and mined" (p. 19).

Of course, slavery was eventually abolished in the United States and formal human rights have been extended to include women and people of colour. Still, the disqualification of some bodies as fully human (and therefore eligible for equality) persists. Nikhil Pal Singh (2004) argues that, for African Americans, "whatever value accrues to formal citizenship depreciates under the pressures of inegalitarian distribution and is remanded under the auspices of excessive policing and punishment" (p. 216). The disproportionate policing and imprisonment of African Americans, the spatial segregation that operates in cities, the racialized division of labour in workplaces, and the persistently high unemployment of people of colour are evidence of a persistent exclusion of some bodies from full humanity. Patterns of racialization deeply shape the body politics of contemporary democracies, even if they refer to themselves as multicultural and colour blind.

The hierarchical organization of formally equal people on the basis of bodily characteristics persists. One of the most important forms that this inequality takes is the everyday presence of barriers to the participation of people with disabilities, in schools and workplaces, homes, commercial sites, leisure activities, and public spaces. Legislation has created some pressure to remove certain barriers under specific conditions, but the overall picture remains one of exclusion marked by the occasional exception.

There are many dimensions to this exclusion. Catherine Frazee (2006) reflects on the painful experience of being shooed away from a store that she could not physically enter: "The store manager has invoked … an aesthetic injunction, an assertion that people like me should remain outside of his visual field, should not be seen in or in proximity to his domain" (p. 359). This aesthetic apartheid runs deep, even if those who practise it do not consciously recognize the choices they are making and the implications of these choices for others. Frazee (2006) describes this circumstance as "layer upon layer of presumption, judgement, stereotype, erasure" (p. 360).

There have been important steps in the elimination of barriers to inclusion for people with disabilities, including legislation such as the Americans with Disabilities Act (ADA), which requires the elimination of barriers to access. The past few decades have seen an increase in the construction of ramps and many other changes to facilitate access for people with disabilities. But Marta Russell (1998) argues that more is required to foster genuine social inclusion:

> It would be revolutionary to force corporate America to hire disabled
> people and it would be revolutionary to prevent corporations from firing
> employees upon disablement. It is the economic arena, beyond ramps,
> that is central to breaking out of the underclass that has kept us on the
> bottom socio-economic rungs of the capitalist pyramid. (Pp. 118–19)

This does not mean that the apparatus of access is irrelevant or that these gains do not matter. As Russell (1998) argues, "To move beyond ramps, we must first agree that ramps are indisputably necessary" (p. 233). However, the goal of full democratic participation and social justice points beyond ramps to a whole set of changes, ranging from attitudinal change to improved social programs to the reorientation of paid work around workers' needs. In the early 1990s, before some of the current treatments were in place, some people living with HIV required frequent washroom visits and occasional rest periods during the working day (Adam and Sears 1996). In workplaces, however, the worker is expected to fit employers' needs rather than the other way around. Disability rights push us to ask penetrating questions about whom the workplace is for and why that might be so. Similar questions will also be asked about schools, stores, and public spaces—and across the whole range of human activities.

This approach pushes in the direction of universalistic solutions that anticipate the needs of the whole range of people who seek to use a particular space. It would mean moving beyond the problematic presumption that "disability disadvantage is both natural and inevitable" (Frazee 2006: 369). Schooling, for example, would be reconfigured around the needs of students rather than offering an education only to those who already fit in with the way the system is organized.

> It is time that children with disabilities are treated to the advantage of learning, through the implementation of educational innovation that recognizes the diversity of children in any classroom and encourages and rewards universal pedagogy that accommodates a variety of learning styles and needs. (Rioux and Pinto 2010: 639)

Embodied Democracy

The question of embodied democracy, then, pushes us to ask troubling questions about the extent to which existing practices fully meet the needs of people in their real diversity. The official view of democracy sees the (always-embodied) inequalities that persist in spite of the extension of full citizenship as a problem that can be remedied within the system, though there is tremendous debate among advocates of this perspective about the extent to which those facing disproportionate poverty and imprisonment are to be held responsible for their own situation. In contrast, the lens of the from-below perspective would see the persistence of embodied inequalities as a sign of the limitations of actually existing democracy.

8 THE STRUGGLE CONTINUES

Democracy in Crisis

In a quirky movie made in 2009 called *The Trotsky*, the lead character is a present-day high-school student who believes he is the reincarnation of the great Russian revolutionary Leon Trotsky. Leon the student explains that his destiny is the same as his namesake's: to help organize a mass rebellion against an oppressive ruling order so that the people may rise up and set themselves free. The key difference is that, whereas, in the case of the Russian Revolution of 1917, Trotsky was leading a workers' army against the Russian monarchy, in 2009, Trotsky's reincarnation seeks to mobilize his fellow students to overthrow the school's ruthless principal. The problem that the second coming of Trotsky continually runs up against is that the students don't seem to care enough to take action. No matter how many leaflets he distributes explaining the potential power of the student body or how many fiery speeches he gives against the evil principal, most students just shrug their shoulders and go about their day. Leon is continually confronted with why students are so tuned out. In several scenes, he faces this question: Is it boredom or apathy?

Leon's problem in the movie is not altogether different from problems in democracies today. On the one hand, there are relatively few highly politically active people who do work in community organizations, student groups, political parties, and so on, and, on the other hand, there are large numbers of people who appear not to care much about politics and who avoid political activity whenever possible.

Because few people today would claim to be actively involved in public decision making, it's no surprise that many people view democracy as something that happens at a distance. Nevertheless, one of the main ideas this book has suggested is that, even when democracy feels like something that's being done *to* us rather than *by* us, we reproduce democracy on a daily basis: renewing a driver's licence, relaxing in a public park, filing a workers' compensation claim, watching sports on the public broadcasting network, going to school. Each action, in itself, may be fleeting and seemingly inconsequential, and these latently political moments may take place within a narrow, incomplete, or even distorted democratic system. Yet democracy is only ever maintained through the consent of the people living under it. In that sense, we do the work of democracy all the time. Consent doesn't necessarily mean active or deliberate participation. Inaction and apathy are also ways of consenting. The point is that reflecting upon your role in a democracy does not require that you leap onto totally new terrain. It means recalibrating your view somewhat so that things that were once unclear begin to come into focus.

The previous chapters have encouraged you to reflect in more rigorous ways upon processes in which you're already deeply involved. The aim of this final chapter is to emphasize why we think it is especially important that people work to broaden their democratic imagination at this moment in history. It's up to you to choose what to do with the insights that flow from your reflections. Ideally, thinking about them in the context of some of the historical struggles we've discussed in this book will help you to reconsider the limits of what is politically possible today, as well as how you might fit into the struggles that lie ahead. When people begin to understand the ways in which their everyday actions are crucial to reproducing the current social system, they are more likely to inquire into what they can do to bring about positive change. The recognition of human agency—the capacity of humans to act upon the world to change it—can be very powerful.

As a starting point for our concluding discussion on the need to reopen democratic debate, it is worth being reminded that recent years have been marked by severe economic and political crises. In the words of President Obama, the economic crisis that started in 2008 "just keeps on going" (Sparrow 2011: par. 79). Banks and corporations have received trillions of public dollars in bailouts at the same time as governments around the world have slashed spending on social programs, cut minimum wages and pensions, introduced user fees on public services that used to be publicly funded, raised postsecondary tuition, and fired public sector workers. The social safety net of the welfare state period is being eroded at the same time as banks foreclose on record numbers of homes and unemployment rates soar. Around the world, different movements have emerged to resist the age of austerity; and students and young people are at the forefront of these movements in many places, including Egypt, Chile, Greece, the United Kingdom, the United States, and Quebec.

Government approaches to the economic crisis have sharpened many of the tensions long felt in contemporary democracies. There are growing gaps between promises of equality and the lived experience of inequality. The chance to participate meaningfully in public decision making is tightly restricted by representative institutions. James Laxer (2009) argues that running an election campaign has become so expensive that credible candidates must either be independently wealthy or backed by rich companies and organizations. "Voters feel less inclined to trust politicians, less inclined to participate in elections, and more willing to believe that political power is slipping out of democratic control into the hands of supranational bureaucrats or companies" (Buchanan and Conway 2002: 12). Government bureaucracies are massive, complex, and often unresponsive. They operate in ways that tend to discriminate against marginalized groups. These trends raise questions about whether the people are truly trusted to know what's good for them.

In fact, the political crisis of our time has become so severe that some political observers have concluded that democracy has been vanquished altogether. John Wallach (2010), for example, does not dispute that democracy is broadly celebrated and widely assumed to have been achieved, but he concludes that "we do not live in democracies." In Wallach's eyes, actually existing democracies today are not controlled by the people in any substantive way.

This statement is certainly provocative, but Wallach's argument may seem less than outlandish when considered in light of your own experiences. To what extent do you play a significant role in making decisions about the things that matter most in your life? No doubt you've had some say over whether or not to stay in school, what jobs to apply for, what friends you have, and the kinds of things you do in your spare time. But there are certain aspects of life that are easily taken for granted that you might not have chosen if the choice were up to you. For example, it is difficult to imagine most students choosing to pay thousands of dollars in tuition every year if they had the option of choosing to go to school for free. Similarly, most people would prefer to live in clean, comfortable, affordable housing, yet many hand over significant portions of their pay to live in cramped, rickety buildings because they can't afford to choose otherwise. Surely people would choose to hold stable, well-paying, interesting jobs with good benefits rather than short-term contracts to do gruelling work from which they might be fired at any moment.

In Western democracies today, all citizens have the right to vote and equal protection under the law. Wallach raises the question of whether these features are sufficient for a country to be considered a democracy. At a time when elections are ignored by 1 in 3 people, and seem to be meaningless mudslinging matches fought by elites even in the eyes of those who do bother to vote, their capacity to serve as solid cornerstones of a whole democratic order is debatable.

Similarly, although the principle of equality before the law is a cherished democratic value, in practice, certain groups of people are far more likely to be arrested and incarcerated than others. As Nikhil Pal Singh (2004) writes, "today, more than one million black persons are in prisons and jails, making blacks approximately 50 percent of the entire U.S. prison population," despite the fact that they make up only about 12% of the population as a whole (p. 10). Angela Y. Davis (1998) notes that "the vast populations of incarcerated people of color is dramatic evidence of the way racism systematically structures economic relations" (p. 66). Davis is an activist-scholar of colour who was herself jailed for her political activism in the 1970s. (She was acquitted of the charges against her after a massive public campaign to free her.) Davis explains that the racialized character of the prison system reflects political and economic systems that reproduce white and middle-class privilege while marginalizing people of colour. Although behaviour that gets defined as criminal may indeed be high in areas populated largely by people of colour, the problem, says Davis, is that crime in these communities is not "recognized as evidence of structural racism, but rather is invoked as a consequence of the assumed criminality of black people" (p. 64). In other words, rather than asking what is wrong with the basic structures of a society that so poorly supports communities of colour, the question becomes how to police more tightly areas with high concentrations of crime. Between 1979 and 1990 in the United States, prison construction increased 612% (Marable 2000: 58).

In contrast to white, middle-class sections of major cities, where belief in achieving prosperity and happiness is the norm, are the communities of people of colour, "where the norm is that young men will spend time in jail, where the entire communal life orients around gray stone buildings—institutions dedicated to the physical control of human bodies. This is the Land of Liberty, yet some class/race-defined segments of the society literally live in a police state" (Loury 2002: 81). Critics argue that a criminal system that separates populations along lines of race and class is incompatible with democracy. As Joy James (2007) writes, "when one considers the historical black and indigenous presence on American soil, this nation has never known democracy in the absence of some form of institutional captivity" (p. xiv). Racialized inequality is not merely a recent departure from the democratic norm but a longstanding institutionalized component of existing democracies in the Global North. Manning Marable (2000) writes that the racialized "prison industrial complex" is one of the core obstacles to fulfilling the dream of black liberation—a dream that "has been so long delayed, corrupted, and compromised that many black folk question the viability of the entire political project called 'American democracy'" (pp. 58, 53).

EXERCISING YOUR DEMOCRATIC IMAGINATION
Free at Last?

The African American poet Langston Hughes wrote his poem "Democracy" in 1949 (Hughes 1959: 285). The poem makes it clear that Hughes regards American democracy as an incomplete and compromised project: "Democracy will not come / Today, this year / Nor ever / Through compromise and fear." Hughes expresses anger at the idea that African Americans should wait patiently: "I tire so of hearing people say, / Let *things take their course. / Tomorrow is another day. / I do not need my freedom* when I'm dead. / I cannot live on tomorrow's bread."

Hughes uses freedom, specifically the unfreedom of African Americans, as a measure of the reality of American democracy. People tend to associate freedom and democracy, seeing these as complementary concepts. Yet, in practice, countries that operate fully within the norms of liberal democracy often have substantial populations of people who face limited freedom as a result of structural inequalities.

Given the changes since he wrote this poem, has the freedom that Hughes sought as part of American democracy now been won?

Ways of Seeing Democracy

These and other contradictions explain why democracy is so difficult to pin down. In this book, we have suggested that contending democratic ideals and vastly different conceptions of democracy in practice make democracy a contested concept. Democracy is complex, contradictory, and unsettled in the sense that its meaning at any given moment in history reflects struggles among different social groups who view and do democracy very differently. In light of democracy's contested character, the most illuminating ways of learning about democracy will not be about simply memorizing the inner workings of existing political institutions. On the contrary, they will involve developing the conceptual tools necessary to navigate key debates about the meaning of rule by the people. Many people across the political spectrum agree that existing democratic systems are in trouble. If democracy is not only to be saved but also to be reinvigorated for the benefit of all, it needs more people with the skills and confidence to enrich and expand the vital debates about democracy, which have been narrowing and hollowing out in recent decades.

"Virtually all contemporary political thinkers may claim to be democrats, but the distinctions between their understandings of democracy can make all the difference in the world" (Myers 2010: 84). In this book, we have focused on two contrasting poles along the spectrum of democratic perspectives. We've called these two positions *official democracy* and *democracy from below*. Although they disagree on a wide variety of points, it is important to keep in mind that both the official-democracy and democracy-from-below approaches begin with the assumption that the best political system will be the one rooted in the principle of popular sovereignty. What distinguish the two views are their differing conceptions of what democracy means: what its objectives are, how it ought to function, and the forces that risk weakening democratic projects.

The view of official democracy is that the core of democratic government has already been achieved in many countries, even if its specific forms might need some fine-tuning. In this view, the democratic ideal of "rule by the people" is embedded in the institutions, norms, and practices of existing democracies. The principle of popular power operates through a system in which electors choose the leaders who will represent them in legislatures and govern over them with their consent. Citizenship rights are guaranteed to everyone who qualifies and protected by a constitution. Special legal provisions protect the rights of minorities. All are equal in the eyes of the law, and the law rules over the arbitrary power of political leaders and the state. The right to own property and carry out private business transactions is also protected by law.

Of course, even people who assume that democracy has been accomplished will often argue that the system can still improve. Elected representatives are encouraged to seek new and creative ways of connecting with their constituents to better learn from them and transmit information. Bureaucracies are told to become more streamlined, so citizens can access services with less trouble and business and trade can carry on more efficiently. Government is told to develop ways of engaging citizens more effectively in the democratic process in order to counteract popular apathy and declining civic intelligence. Experts seek to fine-tune the legal system in order to provide greater security during a time of global instability while, at the same time, honouring basic citizenship rights. It is not that the official-democracy perspective refuses to admit that there are problems with the current political landscape; it's just that it views the existing institutional framework of democratic government as the best possible tool for addressing such problems.

By contrast, the democracy-from-below perspective views democratic government as being an inherently unfinished project, one that can never be finally achieved in a system based upon fundamental social inequalities. According to this view, although putting in place the processes and structures by which Western democracies operate was an important first step, the most basic institutions organizing democracy today—representative government, large bureaucracies, and free-market economies, to name a few—are forms of government *over* the people and risk being antidemocratic when measured against collective self-government in all areas of life. The democracy-from-below perspective is critical of contemporary democratic government for many reasons, but all stem from the assumption that, in order for government to be legitimate and effective, it must, as fully as is realistically possible, be conducted by the people themselves through their own knowledge and action. Institutions and practices run contrary to the democratic spirit when they shift decision-making power out of the people's hands and into specialized governmental bodies or an economic sphere that is placed outside the control of everyone except a tiny group of major property owners and industry executives.

From this perspective, democracy is not only a type of government in the sense of involving leaders, parliaments, and constitutions but a way of organizing social relations in all areas of society: legislative councils and juries, for sure, but also workplaces, schools, mass media, and the provision of essential services such as food, water, shelter, health care, and so on. Thus, in this view, democracy is not simply a pre-established model that a country either has or doesn't have. It is always a work in progress, a guiding spirit realized to greater and lesser degrees depending upon the extent to which robust practices of collective self-governance take hold throughout all aspects of society. Writing from this perspective, Wallach argues that, despite what today's political leaders say, we are not all democrats now; and yet "most of us still would *like* to be." Addressing his comments to people who believe in a radically new model of democracy and desire its creation, Wallach writes, "we must engage in continual and concrete imaginings, and then action, to make it real" (Wallach 2010: par. 17).

The history of democracy over the past two centuries can be seen as the clash of these two core perspectives—official democracy and democracy from below. Struggles between them have occurred not only in academic debates but also in workplaces, parliaments, farming communities, and city streets. Although these debates can take on the air of academic navel-gazing when they are carried out in institutions of formal education, scholars did not invent these struggles. On the contrary, they emerged in real human experience during battles over the control of material conditions and the ability to make political-economic decisions.

Of course, in the everyday rough-and-tumble of political and social life, these two perspectives are rarely found as the highly developed, coherent models that we have presented here in this book. People's actual political practices tend to be much messier and draw on different, at times even contradictory, ideas. However, contrasting two broadly representative models helps us think about the fundamental tensions running through the major democratic struggles of the past centuries, as well as the ones that will be central to struggles in the years ahead. Getting better at identifying traces of these two perspectives in everyday experiences can help to reveal elements of democratic life that are not always apparent at the surface level of day-to-day political debate.

Struggles, Settlements ... and More Struggles

One way to broaden the democratic imagination is to reflect on how experiences in your own life connect up with one or another of these two main frameworks. That's because part of strengthening the democratic imagination is being able to articulate more clearly what democracy is, what it looks like, in its various forms. This ability involves analyzing competing depictions of democracy. For example, the leaders of the wealthy Group of Eight (G8) countries have declared their "profound commitment to the values of freedom and democracy, and their universality" (G8 2011: par. 1). The G8 frames its policies as being legitimate expressions of popular demands. Yet protestors at G8 summits condemn these governments for acting in antidemocratic ways. In efforts to resist the G8 version of democracy, protestors have organized street demonstrations, staged sit-ins, occupied buildings, and, at times, carried out targeted property damage.

You might view these tactics as being either inherently threatening to democratic order or the potentially effective actions of a vibrant democratic movement, depending in large part on whether you tend to view the world through the lens of official democracy or democracy from below. These debates around the G8 help to illustrate the fact that actually existing democracies are made and remade through ongoing tensions between competing forces in society. Whether consciously or not, people respond to the G8 protests and police actions within frameworks that draw on understandings of democracy as a form of government with consent (official) or as a struggle for self-government (from below). By providing tools for analysis and reflection, this book aims to elevate that unconscious deliberation about the character of democracy to the level of conscious discussion and debate.

Thinking about democracy as a series of relationships that are made and remade through social struggles helps to guard against the risk of assuming that democracy is static. The familiar experiences we've all had of the rigidities of democratic government make it easy to assume that democracy is frozen in time. This book has urged you to take up the more difficult task of imagining democracy as being always in motion: a system whose very stability requires constant deliberate actions and at least semi-conscious consent on the part of huge numbers of people. Becoming more alive to the ways in which democracy is constantly being reproduced, even when it appears as though it isn't changing at all, is a crucial step toward imagining what would need to happen in order to deliberately change the course of democracy in one direction or another.

Democracy is dynamic, developed by the processes through which contending forces with different perspectives mobilize to shape society. In various ways, workers, women, indigenous peoples, lesbians and gays, people of colour, students, and many others have resisted and made demands. These movements often do not win everything they seek but settle for some gains or, at times, minimal losses. Richard Johnson and his colleagues use the term temporary political "settlement" to describe the situation in which relative stability prevails over open conflict between contending forces in a capitalist democracy (Education Group 1981: 32). David Harvey (2006) talks about the postwar "compromise ... between capital and labor" to refer to the relative political calm established during the welfare state period (p. 14). The useful thing about the language of settlements and compromises is that it draws attention to the fact that democracy in the Global North, despite appearing as though it were a coherent and neatly finalized political system, is, in fact, constituted by deeply contradictory tensions—even when it appears as though no great struggle is going on.

Pluralists conceive of these disputes as competition between interest groups that may disagree over government policy, all pressuring state policymakers fully within the parameters of the existing political system (see Chapter 5). In contrast, Johnson and Harvey are more aligned with a democracy-from-below perspective; they investigate the ways in which the demands of these contending groups get contained within the existing system despite their potential to disrupt it and go beyond current dominant ideas of democracy. Just one example is the movement for lesbian and gay liberation, launched in the late 1960s. It had bold ideas of transforming relations of gender and sexuality. This movement made a real difference in the lives of many, yet its vision has shrunk so that the focus is much more on fitting in with the dominant relations (for example, winning the right to marry) rather than challenging the overall structure of gender and sexuality in this society. That is an example of a settlement: the political movement declines after strategic gains that fall far short of the bold visions animating it at earlier moments.

In the case of the welfare state period discussed in Chapter 3, a compromise or settlement could be said to have been established to the extent that employers recognized the new rights of workers to bargain collectively, and workers agreed not to strike except for when in the legal position to do so. The state would become a more active participant in processes of social reproduction, regulating industry more tightly and guaranteeing a minimum standard of living for the workforce. This settlement did not end the conflict between owners and workers once and for all, but it did establish widely agreed upon mechanisms for addressing disputes, which in turn led to the emergence of new forms of common sense about what was politically possible to achieve. Broadly speaking, democracy was composed and held in place through a range of contending forces—but contained by an overall system that sought to subsume tensions within the state rather than allow them to break out into open conflict (Neocleous 1996).

The labour unions and other radical political organizations pushing for a more expansive democratic order did not see their dreams fully realized in the welfare state, but neither were the forces of democracy from below demolished by the settlement. To think of democracy at any given moment as a settlement or compromise is to recognize that power is not vested only in governments but moves in multiple directions. The concept of democratic settlements also helps us understand the ways in which even a seemingly stable political system not only is capable of housing deep-seated tensions among social groups but is actually reflective of this discord.

Nevertheless, settlements can be broken—either from above (through revisions in government policy) or from below (through surges in mass militancy). And indeed, as discussed in Chapter 3, the welfare state compromise was smashed during the 1970s. Social programs were cut, and business was deregulated. When a settlement is broken, opportunities emerge for substantive political change to take place (Sears 2003). The whole democratic universe can move in one direction or another. The outcome cannot be known in advance but will be decided only through struggle between contending forces. In Harvey's words, "the whole history of the [welfare state] compromise and the subsequent turn to neo-liberalism indicates the crucial role played by class struggle" in structuring relations of power between social groups (Harvey 2006: 64).

Currently being debated is whether the neo-liberal period of the early twenty-first century can be characterized as a political settlement. Although neo-liberal policies have been implemented by democracies around the world, many governments are imposing even deeper cuts to public services and weakening further the ability of labour unions, community organizations, and other groups to organize on behalf of working people. It seems inaccurate to call this situation a "settlement," then, as the neo-liberal assault is intensifying in many ways. Furthermore, although resistance from below has been beaten back to historically low levels, it has not been annihilated. In fact, as the next section emphasizes, even while democratic debate and practice have been narrowed in some respects under neo-liberalism, there is no shortage of cases that see people pushing for social change through popular power from below. Remarking on the sudden emergence of the global Occupy movement in 2011, Francis Fox Piven says, "I think we may be on the cusp, at the beginning of another period of social protest" (Piven 2011). The future of democracy is an open question.

Another World Is Possible

The 2012 student strike in Quebec certainly opened up the question of democracy in important ways. In response to a government-imposed tuition fee increase of 75% over five years, Quebec students launched what turned out to be the longest and largest of the nine general strikes Quebec college and university students have mounted since 1968. The strike lasted over 100 days, with more than 170,000 students opting for an unlimited strike mandate to stay out until the government settled, while another 130,000 took limited strike action for a specific time period.

Contending visions of democracy lie at the core of this strike. The Quebec student movement can be seen as a model of democracy from below, building people power in the streets and founded on participatory decision-making processes through general membership meetings on campuses. Lafrance and Sears (2012) argue that this strike provides a model of "democratic, activist student unionism," which helps students develop "capacities to analyze their situation, communicate with each other and act in concert, confident that others will also join the fight" (pars. 6, 14). The Quebec student movement centres on general membership meetings at every campus, where students come together to debate and decide on actions up to and including strike mandates. The strike is not called by a central body, nor can it be ended by the Quebec-wide student organizations, but is mandated campus by campus (or at times faculty by faculty) on the basis of open and participatory general membership meetings. Quebec students and their allies have also expressed popular power in the streets, holding massive demonstrations of over 200,000 on March 22 and May 22, mass pickets in defiance of injunctions on campuses, and regular night marches.

On the other hand, the same strike can be seen from an official democracy point of view as an example of mob rule and a threat to collective decision making. As *Sun News* correspondent Brian Lilley (2012) writes, "People's lives have been put at risk by the mob that is attempting to overthrow democratic rule in Quebec—that may sound like a stretch to call it that but that is what this is. The student mob is trying to overthrow democracy" (par. 9). From this official perspective, the government elected by the people has been challenged by an uprising in the streets that threatens the rule of law. This argument that the strike is undemocratic has been used to justify the introduction of extraordinary legislation (Bill 78) by the Charest government in Quebec, legislation that creates new regulations for street protests and will impose sharp penalties on those who impede study on campus when classes resume. In contrast, opponents of Bill 78 see it as a violation of fundamental democratic rights, and they have responded by making pot-banging protests in the streets—to symbolize their defiance of the law.

The resilience of the mass mobilization by Quebec students in 2012 reframes questions of democracy, providing new possibilities and challenges. In 2005, as a result of the massive disruption caused by the student strike of that year, the Quebec government was forced to abandon several of its planned changes, including "the programme of rebates on student debt linked to performance and ... its long-term project of abolishing student grants" (Bazin 2005: par. 3). The 2012 strike will have even deeper consequences, posing for students in Quebec, their allies, and others who have paid attention the question of what democracy really looks like and how we need to conduct ourselves to build and preserve it.

Similarly, the question of democracy was opened up in Los Angeles in 1993, when a group of workers of colour, many of whom were women, organized a Bus Riders Union (BRU). The purpose of the BRU was "to address the environmental racism of auto-based pollution, to establish a first-class, bus centered mass transit system, and to fight for mobility for the working class of color to get to schools, jobs, hospitals, and recreation" (Mann 2001/2009: par. 12). Historically, unions have been organized at the workplace. However, the organizers of the BRU saw an opening to do popular education and build collective action on public buses, as buses are one of the few places where a diverse group of working-class people regularly congregate.

From the start, the BRU has worked to raise awareness and resist the racially structured "two-tiered" transit system funded by the Los Angeles Metro Transit Authority: "an opulent rail system for a significantly white, significantly suburban small group of 'choice' rail riders (26,000 a day) and a dilapidated bus system for an overwhelmingly black, Latino, Asian, and low-income white 'transit dependent' population—400,000 daily riders, 94% of all the MTA's passengers" (Mann 2001/2009: par. 12). The BRU has used a wide range of tactics to press for its demands, including fare boycotts, poster campaigns, occupying busy intersections, and mounting legal challenges. It has forced the MTA to take some action. For example, the BRU claimed victory when the transit authority reversed its decision to buy cheaper carcinogenic diesel buses and instead purchased a fleet of compressed natural gas buses. Yet, even though the BRU has not won all of its demands, it has brought together thousands of workers in a collective effort to improve their transit system. At the same time as tangible gains have been fought for and won, the BRU has helped to build political capacity, generating *"new structures of leadership run by people of color, workers, immigrants, and women"* (Mann 2001/2009: par 19, italics in original). The BRU's members did not come into their democratic activism through elite education or from a history of social privilege. But when an opening emerged to act with others to make a real difference in their daily lives, many people who did not consider themselves "political" took political action.

David McNally (2011a) describes numerous cases in which people in the Global North have resisted austerity measures brought down in the wake of the 2008 economic crisis. For example, mass demonstrations in Iceland forced an unresponsive government to resign. In the United States and Ireland workers occupied factories to fight lay-offs and demand better severance packages. Although successful in securing fairer severance deals for laid-off workers, they were unable to keep the factories from closing. However, in France, where workers engaged in the more militant tactic of "boss-napping," real gains were achieved:

> This tactic first emerged when workers at FCI Microconnections in Mante-la-Jolie seized their plant in order to stop layoffs. Seven weeks later, a group of strikers converged on company headquarters in Versailles, where they set up barricades and prevented the chief executive officer and his staff from leaving. In the face of this mobilization, management eventually agreed to keep the factory open until 2014 and to pay the workers for twenty-seven of the thirty-four days they had spent occupying their workplace. (McNally 2011a: 148)

McNally interprets these mobilizations and more recent ones—such as those of the indignados in Spain, the massive student protests in Chile and the United Kingdom, the strikes in Wisconsin and Greece, as well as the Occupy movement in many countries—as hopeful signs that the democracy-from-below spirit may yet be rejuvenated in the Global North. He also sees important lessons in developments in the Global South. In Bolivia, for example, the government was forced to cancel a contract to privatize the water system—a policy that doubled the cost of water for citizens virtually overnight—after "one hundred thousand people [in a city of 600 000] were in a state of semi-insurrection" (McNally 2011a: 156).

Yet McNally's optimism is not without limits. He is hopeful about the rise of democratic struggle in the wake of the most recent economic crisis, but his conclusion about the state of popular power is also sobering. In his words, "this wave of opposition" has been "courageous and inspiring," but it has also been "inadequate to the tasks of the moment" (p. 146). Recognizing this inadequacy does not diminish the incredible campaigns waged to date, but we must be honest about the force of the trends that threaten democracy and what would be required to reverse them and strengthen popular power. As people face high unemployment and cuts to government services, many have become more aware of the instability of the political order. It remains to be seen whether this realization will lead people into further inaction because the problem seems simply too big, or whether it will inspire the formation of new movements aiming to strengthen popular power.

Building Democratic Capacities

Our hope is that this book has got you thinking about your own role in making and remaking democracy. This does not mean that the weight of being the next Trotsky is on your shoulders. It does mean recognizing that democracy is and always has been a project in the making, one that depends upon at least the latent consent of most people—and one that has only ever expanded through the actions of groups of people dreaming of a better world. There is no recipe for starting or growing a democratic movement. Some people get involved in their unions or join political parties, others start reading groups with friends, others form community networks because of the way a government policy affects life in their neighbourhood. In all of these cases, what starts small has the potential to become larger—to involve new people, to link up with like-minded groups. The exact way in which democratic organizing begins and flourishes is only ever apparent when it's figured out through action.

As you become more aware of the democratic processes in which you're embedded and maybe even begin to take more deliberate political action, we encourage you also to think about how well the structures of government described in this book are living up to their democratic promises. Similarly, David Harvey (2006) has urged people to consider what rights ought to be guaranteed in a democratic society. He asks whether a political framework based upon the right to private property is a sufficient basis for a system in which the people rule, or whether there are "different conceptions of rights to which we may appeal" (p. 57). For his part, Harvey imagines a stronger democratic future based upon "alternative bundles of rights" that include "the right to life chances, ... to a decent and healthy living environment, ... to collective control of common property resources, ... to the inviolability and integrity of the human body," and to "control over production by the direct producers" (p. 66).

Democracy remains a contentious topic in the early twenty-first century. This book is intended to stimulate the democratic imagination by asking readers to situate themselves in these ongoing processes rather than casting themselves as observers. You might find David Harvey's expansive vision of rights inspiring, or you might strongly disagree with it. Ultimately, you need to decide and take action; or someone else will do it in your name.

Glossary

This glossary includes terms with broad social-science relevance that play active roles in core discussions but are not developed in the body of the book.

Absolute monarchy: The system of rule by nobility in which the sovereign's decision-making power is not limited by constitutional or other constraints.

Anarchist: A proponent of anarchy or anarchism. Anarchism is a political philosophy that rejects all forms of hierarchy and coercive power. It is especially critical of the state as a form of social control. Anarchists argue that democracy consists of cooperative, non-hierarchical, self-organized political activity.

Austerity: Something having an austere quality. The word "austere" means severe, sombre, strict. Government austerity refers to a program of severe cuts to government spending. In the wake of the economic crisis of 2008, governments around the world seem to be moving toward a new age of austerity. Austerity policies rolled out in recent years include massive cuts to welfare programs, public pensions, public sector wages, and health and education budgets, as well as mass firings of public sector workers.

Capitalism: An economic and social system in which society's key productive resources (for example, land, factories, patents) take the form of capital, which can be bought and sold. Under capitalism, these resources are owned or controlled by employers and investors, while the core labour is performed by formally free working people hired as wage labourers.

Class: A group formed by reason of common attributes. Class is one of those difficult terms that have many meanings. In everyday speech, it tends to refer to groups formed because of the distribution of resources among the population, which is divided into the wealthy, poor, and middle orders. In a more technical sense, it is used in theories of inequality to discuss the division of society between the producers who do the key work in society and the rulers who live off the proceeds of the labour of others.

Cold war: The rivalry after World War II between the Soviet Union and the United States and their respective satellites or allies. As the action of World War II cooled down, the ongoing struggle between the United States and the Union of Soviet Socialist Republics intensified. These superpowers were not only the centre of competing power blocs. They also identified with contending ideologies: capitalism vs. socialism. The cold war ended with the fall of the Berlin Wall in 1989 and the rapid collapse of the Soviet bloc.

Collective action: An attempt to make change through the coordinated efforts of groups of people working toward a common goal. Examples of collective actions include labour strikes, boycotts, occupations, and flash mobs.

Conservative: A supporter of political policies that seek to preserve or sustain the existing order. At times, this aim may mean that conservatives favour specific changes required to maintain the social relations that support the dominant order, for example, in the face of economic or political uncertainty.

Feminist: A person who fights to improve the situation of women in society. While some feminists concentrate on winning equal rights for women, others have fought for an end to male privilege and oppression of all forms.

Global North: A broad sociological term referring to the collective identity and power of the world's advanced industrial economies. Most of the countries comprising the Global North are in Europe and North America; however, wealthy and powerful countries such as Australia are also included, notwithstanding their geographical position. The term deliberately links the military, economic, and cultural power of the imperial countries of the Global North to the exploitation and marginalization of countries in the Global South.

Global South: A broad sociological term referring to most of the countries in Latin America, Africa, and Asia. Many countries in the Global South were formally colonized by countries in the Global North. Although formal colonial relations were overthrown by national liberation movements, the global power system continues to be oriented around the military, economic, and cultural dominance of the Global North.

Industrialization: The spread of industrial production methods reorganizing work, migration, transportation, and commerce around the use of machines in fields, factories, mines, and cities. Historically, industrialization has allowed for a greater output of cheaper goods. The rise of industrialization was associated with many other social changes, such as the shift of population from the countryside to the cities and development of extensive transportation and communications networks.

Key productive resources: The natural resources, machines, processing plants, patents, and other tools used to reproduce human life on a daily basis. Factories, harvesting equipment, communication systems, and land are among society's key productive resources. In a capitalist society, the key productive resources are privately owned by employers and investors.

Liberal: Generally, a person in accord with the principles of liberalism or favourable to reform and the maximization of individual liberty. This term, though, has many meanings. Broadly speaking, it is often associated with freedom. In a more narrow sense, it is associated with the freedom of property owners to use or exchange their private resources without interference, whether in the form of state regulation or the constraint of trade. This narrower sense of liberal describes those who seek to reduce obstacles to the capitalist market economy, in part by implementing state policies that support this economic system.

Liberal democracy: The democratic practices of government that have been associated with the liberal or pro-capitalist state, which are based on such rights as freedom of speech, electoral participation, and property rights.

Marginalization: The systematic silencing, discrimination, and exclusion of non-dominant people by socially and economically privileged groups.

Marxist: An advocate of Marxism, a political-economic theory derived from the works of Karl Marx. Marxism emphasizes the need for revolution to overthrow capitalism and create new forms of socialism based on workers' control. Marx's contribution was to track the key dynamics of capitalism in a period when the system was still developing and its core features were more clearly visible.

Material conditions: The environmental circumstances that shape the possibilities for action. Assessments of material conditions focus on the fundamental human interchange with nature, which is always mediated through technological development, as well as legal and political relationships.

Moral regulation: The social policies implemented by governments that seek to shape the population in particular ways, whether through education, law enforcement, health care or social assistance.

Neo-liberalism: The contemporary form of liberal (see *Liberal*) policy that emerged in response to the growth of the welfare state. **Neo-liberal**

policies tend to see the regulation of labour markets and state expenditure on health, education, or social assistance as constraints on the freedom of investors and employers and, hence, as obstacles to the operation of the capitalist market economy.

Political spectrum: The range of political opinions understood as a continuum from anti-capitalists on the left, who, at their most radical, seek to overthrow the existing system, to pro-capitalists on the right, who seek to preserve the system at all costs.

Popular power: The ability of vast numbers of people to control collectively the political, economic, and social conditions under which they live. Although democracy is rooted in the principle of popular power (i.e., *rule by the people*), in practice, this power takes a variety of forms (for example, representative democracy or direct democracy). Activists, scholars, politicians, and other public figures continue to debate what forms of democracy most effectively enable the exercise of popular power.

Postmodern (or significatory) perspectives: Theoretical frameworks for understanding social life that reject scientific-style universal assumptions and explanations. Postmodern perspectives emphasize the fragmented, localized, and fluid aspects of the human condition. They presume that reality itself is composed through the never-ending interplay of representation, meaning that humans have no direct access to reality but only know their surroundings through the mediation of cultural representation.

Privilege: Unearned advantages held by some groups of people in society on the basis of dominant relations of power. For example, a society organized around white privilege refers to social relations rooted in racial hierarchies that afford special authority and opportunities to white people, advantages not afforded to people of colour.

Profitability: The potential or capacity to generate benefit, gain, or profit, or the degree to which some thing or relationship yields profit. A business is profitable to the extent that the amount of money it brings in exceeds its costs. In a capitalist economy, all businesses must make profits if they are to survive for long. Profits are the source of revenue used to invest in the new technologies required to compete with other profit-making businesses. Under capitalism, the drive for profits has meant that owners are constantly seeking ways of driving down the cost of labour.

Racialize: The ways in which dominant social norms and institutions work to uphold the belief that certain biological differences (specifically, skin colour) reflect substantive differences in the personalities and capabilities of human beings. This technical term is used to indicate that, even though races in the biological sense do not exist in the human species, characteristics assumed to be associated with "race" are used as a basis for discrimination and oppression in contemporary society.

Radical: The quality of favouring or effecting fundamental or revolutionary change, or a person advocating this sort of change. The word radical derives from the word "root." To propose radical social change, therefore, means to advocate changing the very roots of the current social order.

Relations of power (or power relations): The ways in which dominant social values and control over key resources systematically privilege some people and marginalize others.

Revolution: The overall transformation of the social, economic, and political system through the overthrow of the existing rulers and the creation of new forms of government or self-government.

Settler societies: Societies that have experienced or are experiencing particular forms of colonial domination in which people from the imperial homeland settle in the "new" world, violently displacing the indigenous peoples living there. Examples of countries that have experienced settler colonialism include Canada, the United States, Australia, Israel, and South Africa.

Social democracy: The political perspective and program historically associated with the working-class movement that seeks to use existing mechanisms within capitalist society, such as running for office, to obtain reforms to improve the lives of working people. Social democracy is the core political perspective of parties such as the New Democratic Party in Canada and the Labour Party in Britain.

Social relations: See *Relations of power*.

Social reproduction: The perpetuation or maintenance of society and social life or of particular social characteristics, structures, or traditions over time. Human life requires an ongoing interchange with nature that uses up energy, which must be restored to carry on the work. On an individual level, we must reproduce ourselves by resting and eating, among other things. On a social level, society must be sustained by nurturing the productive population, caring for the unwell, and raising the next generation. This process is called "social reproduction," and it is associated with "social production," which is the interchange with nature to generate resources to meet wants and needs.

Socialist: A person, concept, or party advocating socialism or something that is characteristic of or related to implementing socialism. **Socialism** is a political philosophy aiming to achieve substantive social equality through the democratic ownership and control of society's key productive resources by the majority of the people.

Stalinist regime: A bureaucratic, authoritarian form of government that developed in the Soviet Union (USSR) and its satellites under the rule of Joseph Stalin (leader of the USSR from 1928 to 1953). Stalinist regimes are characterized by a high level of centralized decision making and the prohibition of political dissent. Stalin directly and indirectly oversaw the imprisonment, exile, and execution of tens of millions of people living under Soviet rule.

Substantive equality: Equality in outcomes and material conditions as well as in access to opportunities and rights. In contrast to the formal equality provided to citizens by legal rights in liberal democracies, substantive equality refers to the relative equity of actual living conditions. Substantive equality involves equal access to basic necessities of human life, such as food, shelter, and control over labour processes. This approach also necessitates a consideration of the effects of discrimination and disadvantage, and it acknowledges that, because of historical inequities, treating all people the same *is not* treating them as equals.

Technocratic: Having the characteristic of being ruled by experts who are supposedly disinterested, unbiased, and apolitical.

Third World: A term associated with the non-aligned movement, which began as newly decolonized states sought to create a third force in world politics free of the two dominant superpowers in the cold war (see also *Global South*).

Tributary mode: An economic system in which the owners of the key productive resources (mainly land) live off the proceeds of the work of peasants or slaves who are bound to the land or to the landowner and do the key productive labour in society.

Undocumented workers: Working people (waged, unwaged, or unemployed) whose status is not recognized by the state under which they live. Because their labour is officially illegal in the eyes of the state, undocumented workers are not protected by labour, health, and safety standards or guaranteed a minimum wage. Nevertheless, many economists point out that major economies in the Global North, such as the US economy, rely heavily upon undocumented labour and would not be able to function without it.

Welfare state: A state in which the welfare of the people, especially in matters such as social and economic security, health, education, housing, and working conditions, is a major responsibility of government. In the period following World War II, social policy in most countries in the Global North shifted to offer a wide range of programs to provide for the well-being of the population, programs in areas of social assistance, education, and health care, for example. These programs, introduced in response to extensive union struggles, have been cut back as a consequence of austerity offensives since the late 1970s. In the Global South, welfare states tend to be less extensive, but countries often provide state subsidies on specific necessities of life, such as flour and cooking oil.

Western: A broad sociological term referring to the economically advanced and politically powerful countries of Western Europe and North America.

Working class, working people (or workers): The individuals or a segment of society that is composed of most human beings who do not own key productive resources (such as factories, mines, computer patents, industrial farms) and therefore must try to sell their capacity to work to an employer or live in a household that earns employment income or has access to social benefits, such as unemployment insurance. The term working people applies not only to people presently employed but also to underemployed and unemployed people, unwaged labourers, undocumented workers, and homeless people.

References

Adam, Barry D., and Alan Sears. 1996. *Experiencing HIV: Personal, family, and work relations*. New York: Columbia University Press.

Alfred, Gerald R. 1995. *Heeding the voices of our ancestors: Kahnawake Mohawk politics and the rise of native nationalism*. Toronto: Oxford University Press.

Ali, Tariq. 2011. "Anti-imperialism and the New Left, revolt and retrenchment [Interview by Sasha Lilley]." In *Capital and its discontents: Conversations with radical thinkers in a time of tumult*, ed. S. Lilley, 210–19. Oakland: PM Press.

Allen, Lillian. 1993. *Women do this every day: Selected poems of Lillian Allen*. Toronto: Insomniac Press.

Alvarez, Mike, Jose Antonio Cheibub, Fernando Limongi, and Adam Przeworski. 1996. "Classifying political regimes." *Studies in Comparative International Development* 31 (2): 3–36. http://dx.doi.org/10.1007/BF02719326.

Amin, Samir. 1993. "The issue of democracy in the contemporary Third World." In *Low intensity democracy: Political power in the new world order*, ed. Barry Gills, Joel Rocamora, and Richard Wilson, 59–79. London: Pluto.

Amnesty International. 2010. UK: Amnesty deeply concerned over Cable's comments on the importance of human rights in China trip. http://www.amnesty.org.uk/news_details.asp?NewsID=19072 (accessed 30 November 2011).

Arblaster, Anthony. 1987. *Democracy*. Milton Keynes: Open University Press.

Arblaster, Anthony. 1994. *Democracy*. 2nd ed. Buckingham: Open University Press.

Arblaster, Anthony. 2002. *Democracy*. 3rd ed. Buckingham: Open University Press.

Asante, Molefi. 2005. *Race, rhetoric, and identity: The architecton of soul*. Amherst, MA: Humanity Press.

Bannerji, Himani. 2000. *The dark side of the nation: Essays on multiculturalism, nationalism, and gender*. Toronto: Canadian Scholars' Press.

Bannerji, Himani. 2011. *Demography and democracy: Essays on nationalism, gender, and ideology*. Toronto: Canadian Scholars' Press.

Barber, Benjamin. 1984. *Strong democracy: Participatory politics for a new age*. Berkeley: University of California Press.

Bartleman, James K. 2005. *Strengthening Ontario's economic advantage: Address of the Honourable James K. Bartleman, Lieutenant Governor of Ontario on the opening of the Second Session of the Thirty-Eighth Parliament of the Province of Ontario.* 12 October 2005. http://www. premier.gov.on.ca/news/event.php?ItemID=5227&Lang=EN (accessed 29 October 2009).

Battistoni, Richard. 1985. *Public schooling and the education of democratic citizens.* Jackson: University Press of Mississippi.

Bazin, Jose. 2005. "Quebec students' strike: A battle won, a struggle that must continue." *International Viewpoint* 367. http://www. internationalviewpoint.org/spip.php?article780 (accessed 21 August 2011).

Beetham, David. 1996. *Bureaucracy.* 2nd ed. Minneapolis: University of Minneapolis Press.

Beetham, David. 2005. *Democracy: A beginner's guide.* Oxford: Oneworld.

Benhabib, Seyla, and Judith Resnik. 2009. "Citizenship and migration theory engendered." In *Migrations and mobilities: Citizenship, borders, and gender*, ed. Seyla Benhabib and Judith Resnick, 1–44. New York: New York University Press.

Berger, John. 1968. "The nature of mass demonstrations." *New Society* 295: 754–55.

Berger, Mark T. 2004. "After the Third World? History, destiny, and the fate of Third Worldism." *Third World Quarterly* 25 (1): 9–39. http:// dx.doi.org/10.1080/0143659042000185318.

Berger, Stefan. 2002. "Democracy and social democracy." *European History Quarterly* 32 (1): 13–37. http://dx.doi.org/10.1177/0269142002032001560.

Berman, Marshall. 2011. "'Mass merger': Whitman and Baudelaire, the modern street and democratic culture." In *A political companion to Walt Whitman*, ed. John E. Seery, 149–54. Lexington: University of Kentucky Press.

Birch, Kean, and Vlad Mykhnenko. 2010. "Introduction: A world turned right way up." In *The rise and fall of neo-liberalism: The collapse of an economic order?* ed. Kean Birch and Vlad Mykhnenko, 1–20. London: Zed Books.

Bookchin, Murray. 1999. *Anarchism, Marxism, and the future of the left.* San Francisco: AK Press.

Boston Women's Health Collective. 1971. *Our bodies, our selves.* Boston: Boston Women's Health Collective.

Boycott the Elections 2011. 2011. About. http://boycottelections2011. blogspot.com/p/about_09.html (accessed 28 April 2011).

Braverman, Harry. 1974. *Labor and monopoly capital.* New York: Monthly Review Press.

Brecht, Bertolt. 1964. *Brecht on theatre: The development of an aesthete*, ed. and trans. John Willett. London: Methuen.

Bringuier, Jean Claude. 1980. *Conversations with Jean Piaget*, trans. Basia Miller Gulati. Chicago: University of Chicago Press.

Brito Vieira, Mónica, and David Runciman. 2008. *Representation*. Cambridge: Polity.

Broad, Dave. 2011. "The productivity mantra: The profit motive versus the public good." *Social Studies* 7 (1/2): 65–94.

Bruni, Frank. 2012. "Snowe's sad retreat." *The New York Times*, 3 March 2012. http://www.nytimes.com/2012/03/04/opinion/sunday/bruni-snowes-sad-retreat.html (accessed 26 March 2012).

Buchanan, Tom, and Martin Conway. 2002. "The politics of democracy in twentieth-century Europe: Introduction." *European History Quarterly* 32 (1): 7–12. http://dx.doi.org/10.1177/0269142002032001559.

Burke, Edmund. 1774/1987. "Speech to the electors of Bristol." In *The Founders' Constitution*, vol. 1, chap. 13, doc. 7. Chicago: University of Chicago Press. http://press-pubs.uchicago.edu/founders/documents/v1ch13s7.html (accessed 29 March 2011).

Burke, Marc E. 1993. *Coming out of the blue: British police officers talk about their lives in "the job" as lesbians, gays, and bisexuals*. London: Cassell.

Butts, Robert Freeman. 1978. *Public education in the United States: From revolution to reform*. New York: Holt, Rinehart and Winston.

Callaghan, John. 2000. *The retreat of social democracy*. Manchester: Manchester University Press.

Callinicos, Alex. 2004. "Marxism and politics." In *What is politics: The activity and its study*, ed. Adrian Leftwich, 60–74. London: Polity.

Cameron, David. 2011. PM's speech at London Conference on Libya. http://www.number10.gov.uk/news/pms-speech-at-london-conference-on-libya/ (accessed 31 July 2012).

Camfield, David. 2006. "Neoliberalism and working-class resistance in British Columbia: The hospital employees' union struggle, 2002–2004." *Labour/Le Travail* 57 (Spring): 9–41.

Camfield, David. 2011. *Canadian labour in crisis: Reinventing the workers' movement*. Halifax: Fernwood.

Cappella, Joseph N., and Kathleen Hall Jamieson. 1997. *Spiral of cynicism: The press and the public good*. New York: Oxford University Press.

Carnoy, Martin. 1984. *The state and political theory*. Princeton: Princeton University Press.

Carroll, William K. 2005. "Introduction: Social democracy in neoliberal times." In *Challenges and perils: Social democracy in neoliberal times*, ed. William K. Carroll and R.S. Ratner, 7–24. Halifax: Fernwood.

Catt, Helena. 1999. *Democracy in practice*. London: Routledge.

CBC News. 2011. "Leaders make debate pitches, trade barbs." *Canada Votes 2011*, 12 April 2011. http://www.cbc.ca/news/politics/canadavotes2011/story/2011/04/12/cv-election-debate-main.html (accessed 13 April 2011).

Cheney, George. 2002. "Mondragon cooperatives." *Social Policy* (Winter): 4–9.

Chomsky, Noam. 2011. "Anarchism, council communism, and life after capitalism [Interview by Sasha Lilley]." In *Capital and its discontents: Conversations with radical thinkers in a time of tumult*, ed. S. Lilley, 237–45. Oakland: PM Press.

Citizen Watch Co. 2011. Citizen history. http://www.citizenwatch.com/COC/English/history.asp (accessed 15 June 2011).

Clarke, George Elliott. 2011. "For a multicultural, multi-faith, multiracial Canada: A manifesto." In *Home and native land: Unsettling multiculturalism in Canada*, ed. May Chazan, Lisa Helps, Anna Stanley, and Sonali Thakkar, 51–57. Toronto: Between the Lines.

Clarke, Simon. 1983. "State, class struggle, and the reproduction of capital." *Kapitalistate* 10/11:113–30.

Coates, Ken. 1964. "Workers' control." *New Left Review* 1 (23): 69–71.

Cohen, Lizabeth. 2004. *A consumers' republic: The politics of mass consumption in postwar America*. New York: Vintage Books.

Collins, Nick. 2010. "*WikiLeaks: Guilty parties 'should face death penalty.'*" *The Telegraph*, 1 December 2010. http://www.telegraph.co.uk/news/worldnews/wikileaks/8172916/WikiLeaks-guilty-parties-should-face-death-penalty.html (accessed 30 November 2011).

Congressional Hispanic Caucus Institute. 2011. CHCI and CHLI welcome Hispanic members of the 112th Congress. http://www.chci.org/news/pub/chci-and-chli-welcome-hispanic-members-of-the-112th-congress (accessed 19 September 2011).

Connell, R.W. 1995. *Masculinities*. Berkeley: University of California Press.

Contenta, Sandro, and Laurie Monsebraaten. 2009. "How we're creating an illegal workforce." *Toronto Star*, 1 November 2009, A1. http://www.thestar.com/news/investigations/article/719355--how-we-re-creating-an-illegal-workforce (accessed 8 June 2012).

Corporate Citizenship Limited. 2011. What we believe. http://corporate-citizenship.co.uk/about-us/what-we-believe (accessed 15 June 2011).

Corwin, Norman. 1945. "On a note of triumph." CBS, May 8. MP3 audio file, http://www.radio4all.net/index.php/program/33233 (accessed 14 May 2012).

Cowan, Deborah. 2008. *Military workfare: The soldier and social citizenship in Canada*. Toronto: University of Toronto Press.

Cowan, Deborah, and Emily Gilbert. 2008. "The politics of war, citizenship, territory." In *War, citizenship, territory*, ed. Deborah Cowan and Emily Gilbert, 1–30. New York: Routledge.

CP24. 2011. "Hudak says he'd scrap 'wasteful bureaucracy' at OPA." *CP24.com*, 22 March 2011. http://www.cp24.com/servlet/an/local/ CTVNews/20110322/110322_power_authority/20110322/ (accessed 13 June 2011).

Cunningham, Frank. 1987. *Democratic theory and socialism*. Cambridge: Cambridge University Press.

Cunningham, Frank. 2002. *Theories of democracy: A critical introduction*. London: Routledge.

Dahl, Robert A. 1989. *Democracy and its critics*. New Haven: Yale University Press.

Darlington, Ralph. 2002. "Shop stewards' leadership, left-wing activism, and collective workplace union organisation." *Capital and Class* 26 (1): 95–126. http://dx.doi.org/10.1177/030981680207600104.

Darlington, Ralph. 2010. "The state of workplace union reps' organization in Britain." *Capital and Class* 34 (1): 126–35. http://dx.doi.org/10.1177/ 0309816809353502.

Darnton, Robert. 1990. *The kiss of Lamourette: Reflections in cultural history*. New York: W.W. Norton & Co.

Davidoff, Leonore. 1995. *Worlds between: Historical perspectives on gender and class*. New York: Routledge.

Davis, Angela Y. 1998. "Race and criminalization: Black Americans and the punishment industry." In *The Angela Y. Davis reader*, ed. Joy James, 61–73. Malden: Blackwell.

Davis, Angela Y. 1999. *Blues legacies and black feminism: Gertrude "Ma" Rainey, Bessie Smith, and Billie Holiday*. New York: Vintage.

de Baecque, Antoine. 1997. *The body politic: Corporeal metaphor in revolutionary France*, trans. Charlotte Mandell. Stanford: Stanford University Press.

de Tocqueville, Alexis. 1835. *Democracy in America*. University of Virginia Hypertexts. http://xroads.virginia.edu/~HYPER/DETOC/ (accessed 27 November 2011).

D'Emilio, John. 1992. "Capitalism and gay identity." In *Making trouble: Essays in history, politics, and the university*, ed. John D'Emilio, 100–113. New York: Routledge.

Democratic People's Republic of Korea. 2011. Juche ideology. http://www. korea-dpr.com/juche_ideology.html (accessed 29 May 2012).

Dollinger, Sol, and Genora Johnson Dollinger. 2000. *Not automatic: Women and the left in the forging of the Auto Workers' Union*. New York: Monthly Review Press.

Dominion Institute. 2005. The 2005 annual Canada Day history quiz. http://www.dominion.ca/English/CanadaDayQuizFACTUM2005.pdf (accessed 26 July 2011).

Dovi, Suzanne. 2002. "Preferable descriptive representatives: Will just any woman, black, or Latino do?" *American Political Science Review* 96 (4): 729–43. http://dx.doi.org/10.1017/S0003055402000412.

Dovi, Suzanne. 2009. "In praise of exclusion." *Journal of Politics* 71 (3): 1172–86. http://dx.doi.org/10.1017/S0022381609090951.

Draper, Hal. 1974. "Marx on democratic forms of government." *Marxists Internet Archive*. http://www.marxists.org/archive/draper/1974/xx/democracy.html (accessed 25 February 2012).

Duverger, Maurice. 1954. *Political parties: Their organization and activity in the modern state*, trans. B. North and R. North. London: Methuen.

Dyck, Rand. 2008. *Canadian political: Critical approaches*. 5th ed. Toronto: Nelson.

Dyer-Witheford, Nick. 2009. The circulation of the commons. http://www.fims.uwo.ca/people/faculty/dyerwitheford/index.htm (accessed 16 August 2011).

Dylan, Bob. 1964/2011. "The times they are a-changin'." *bobdylan.com*. http://www.bobdylan.com/us/songs/times-they-are-changin (accessed 11 November 2011).

Eagleton, Terry. 1976. *Marxism and literary criticism*. Berkeley: University of California Press.

Eagleton, Terry. 2007. *Ideology: An introduction*. New ed. London: Verso.

Eagleton, Terry. 2011. *Why Marx was right*. New Haven: Yale University Press.

Ebert, Teresa L. 1986. "The crisis of representation in cultural studies: Reading postmodern texts." *American Quarterly* 38 (5): 894–902. http://dx.doi.org/10.2307/2712833.

Education Group, Centre for Contemporary Cultural Studies. 1981. *Unpopular education: Schooling and social democracy in England since 1944*. London: Hutchinson in association with the Centre for Contemporary Cultural Studies.

Ehrenreich, Barbara, and Deirdre English. 1979. *For her own good: 150 years of the experts' advice to women*. Garden City: Anchor Press.

Eichner, Carolyn J. 2004. *Surmounting the barricades: Women in the Paris Commune*. Bloomington: Indiana University Press.

Eley, Geoff. 2002. *Forging democracy: The history of the left in Europe, 1850–2000*. New York: Oxford University Press.

Elger, Tony, and Chris Smith. 1994. "Global Japanization? Convergence and competition in the organization of the labour process." In *Global*

Japanization? The transformation of the labour process, ed. Tony Elger and Chris Smith, 31–59. London: Routledge.

Ellis, Faron, and Heather MacIvor. 2008. *Parameters of power: Canada's political institutions*. Brief ed. Toronto: Nelson.

Elshahed, Mohamed. 2011. "Tahrir Square: Social media, public space." *The Design Observer Group*, 27 February 2011. http://places.designobserver.com/feature/tahrir-square-social-media-public-space/25108/ (accessed 16 August 2011).

Fahrmeir, Andreas. 2007. *Citizenship: The rise and fall of a modern concept*. New Haven: Yale University Press.

Fanon, Frantz. 1963. *The wretched of the earth*, trans. Constance Farrington. New York: Grove Press.

Farkas, Richard P. 2007. *Democratization in the Balkans: Prescription for a badly scarred body politic*. Boston: Northeastern University Press.

Fay, Brian. 1975. *Social theory and political practice*. London: George Allen and Unwin.

Finkel, Alvin. 1979. *Business and social reform in the thirties*. Toronto: Lorimer.

Foot, Paul. 2005. *The vote: How it was won and how it was undermined*. London: Viking.

Foucault, Michel. 1965. *Madness and civilization: A history of insanity in the age of reason*, trans. Richard Howard. New York: Pantheon Books.

Foucault, Michel. 1980. *Power/knowledge: Selected interviews & other writings, 1972–1977*, ed. Colin Gordon. New York: Pantheon Books.

Frank, Jason. 2007. "Aesthetic democracy: Walt Whitman and the poetry of the people." *Review of Politics* 69 (3): 402–30. http://dx.doi.org/10.1017/S0034670507000745.

Franzway, Suzanne, Dianne Court, and R.W. Connell. 1989. *Staking a claim: Feminism, bureaucracy, and the state*. Sydney: Allen and Unwin.

Frazee, Catherine. 2006. "Exile from the China shop: Cultural injunction and disability policy." In *Disability and social policy in Canada*, ed. Mary Ann McColl and Lyn Jongbloed, 2nd ed., 357–69. Toronto: Captus University Press.

Friedman, Thomas. 2011. "A progressive in the age of austerity." *The New York Times*, 15 October 2011. http://www.nytimes.com/2011/10/16/opinion/sunday/friedman-a-progressive-in-the-age-of-austerity.html (accessed 16 October 2011).

Fudge, Judy, and Fiona MacPhail. 2009. "The temporary foreign worker program in Canada: Low-skilled workers as an extreme form of flexible labor." *Comparative Labor Law & Policy Journal* 31 (5): 101–39.

Fukuyama, Francis. 1989. "The end of history?" *The National Interest* 15 (Summer): 3–18.

G8. 2011. "G8 declaration: Renewed commitment for freedom and democracy." *G20–G8, France 2011: Archives.* http://www.g20-g8.com/g8-g20/g8/english/live/news/renewed-commitment-for-freedom-and-democracy.1314.html (accessed 9 November 2011).

Gard, M., and J. Wright. 2005. *The obesity epidemic: Science, morality, and ideology.* New York: Taylor & Francis.

Ginsborg, Paul. 2008. *Democracy: Crisis and renewal.* London: Profile Books.

Glaberman, Martin, and Seymour Faber. 1998. *Working for wages: The roots of insurgency.* Dix Hills, NY: General Hall.

Glenny, Misha. 1999. *The Balkans, 1804–1999: Nationalism, war, and the great powers.* London: Granta.

Glover, Julian. 2011. "Europeans are liberal, anxious and don't trust politicians, poll reveals." *The Guardian,* 13 March 2011. http://www.guardian.co.uk/world/2011/mar/13/guardian-icm-europe-poll-2011 (accessed 15 March 2011).

Gluckstein, Donny. 2011. "Workers' councils in Europe: A century of experience." In *Ours to master and to own,* ed. I. Ness and D. Azzellini, 32–47. Chicago: Haymarket Books.

Golash-Boza, Tanya Maria, and Douglas A. Parker. 2006. "Immigration policy statement from Sociologists Without Borders: Dehumanizing the undocumented." *Counterpunch,* 15 May 2006. http://www.counterpunch.org/2006/05/15/dehumanizing-the-undocumented/ (accessed 11 November 2011).

Goldberg, David Theo. 2002. *The racial state.* Oxford: Blackwell.

Gordon, Lewis R. 1995. *Fanon and the crisis of European man.* New York: Routledge.

Gordon, Linda. 1990. "The welfare state: Towards a socialist-feminist perspective." *Socialist Register* 26:171–200.

Gordon, Todd. 2010. *Imperialist Canada.* Winnipeg: Arbeiter Ring Publishing.

Government of Canada. 2006. "Address by the Honourable James M. Flaherty, P.C., MP, Minister of Finance, to the Investment Dealers Association of Canada." *Department of Finance Canada: Archives.* http://www.fin.gc.ca/n06/06-006_1-eng.asp (accessed 28 June 2011).

Government of Canada. 2011a. Canada's Citizenship Award: Open for nominations. http://www.cic.gc.ca/english/department/media/releases/2011/2011-03-07.asp (accessed 11 November 2011).

Government of Canada. 2011b. *Discover Canada: The rights and responsibilities of citizenship* [Study guide]. Ottawa: Citizenship and Immigration Canada. http://www.cic.gc.ca/english/pdf/pub/discover.pdf (accessed 28 March 2011).

Government of the United States of America. 1791. *United States Constitution: Bill of Rights*. Washington, DC: National Archives. http://www.archives.gov/exhibits/charters/bill_of_rights_transcript.html (accessed 2 October 2011).

Graeber, David. 2002. "The new anarchists." *New Left Review* 13 (Jan.–Feb.): 61–73.

Graeber, David. 2011. "Occupy and anarchism's gift of democracy." *The Guardian*, 15 November 2011. http://www.guardian.co.uk/commentisfree/cifamerica/2011/nov/15/occupy-anarchism-gift-democracy (accessed 24 March 2012).

Gramsci, Antonio. 1971. *Selections from the* Prison Notebooks, ed. and trans. Quintin Hoare and Geoffrey Nowell Smith. New York: International Publishers.

"Greek politics and the Euro crisis: The back road to public consent [Editorial]." 2011. *The Globe and Mail*, 3 November 2011, A18.

Grundmann, Reiner. 2008. "What may the sheep safely know?" In *Knowledge and democracy: A 21st-century perspective*, ed. Nico Stehr, 85–103. New Brunswick, NJ: Transaction Publishers.

Hall, Alan, Anne Forrest, Alan Sears, and Niki Carlan. 2006. "Making a difference: Knowledge activism and worker representation in Joint OHS Committees." *Relations industrielles / Industrial Relations* 61 (3): 408–36.

Hall, Stuart. 1992. "The West and the rest: Discourse and power." In *Formations of modernity*, ed. Stuart Hall and Bram Gieben, 275–331. Cambridge: Polity Press in association with the Open University. http://dx.doi.org/10.1017/CBO9780511628092.

Hall, Stuart. 1997. "The work of representation." In *Representation: Cultural representations and signifying practices*, ed. Stuart Hall, 13–74. London: Sage.

Halliday, Josh. 2011a. "London riots: How BlackBerry Messenger played a key role." *The Guardian*, 8 August 2011. http://www.guardian.co.uk/media/2011/aug/08/london-riots-facebook-twitter-blackberry (accessed 16 August 2011).

Halliday, Josh. 2011b. "London riots: Police to track rioters who used BlackBerrys." *The Guardian*, 9 August 2011. http://www.guardian.co.uk/technology/2011/aug/09/london-riots-blackberrys-police (accessed 16 August 2011).

Hartsock, Nancy C.M. 1998. *The feminist standpoint revisited and other essays*. Boulder, CO: Westview Press.

Harvey, Arnold D. 2007. *Body politic: Political metaphor and political violence*. Newcastle: Cambridge Scholars Press.

Harvey, David. 2006. *Spaces of global capitalism: Towards a theory of uneven geographical development*. London: Verso.

Haudenosaunee Confederacy. n.d. What is the Confederacy? http://www. haudenosauneeconfederacy.ca/whatisconfederacy.html (accessed 5 April 2011).

Heywood, Leslie. 1997. "Masculinity vanishing: Bodybuilding and contemporary culture." In *Building bodies*, ed. Pamela Moore, 165–83. New Brunswick, NJ: Rutgers University Press.

Hmelo-Silver, Cindy E., and Howard S. Barrows. 2006. "Goals and strategies of a problem-based learning facilitator." *Interdisciplinary Journal of Problem-Based Learning* 1 (1): 21–39.

hooks, bell. 2000. *Feminist theory: From margin to center*. 2nd ed. Cambridge: South End Press.

"How to redesign a tired democracy." *The Globe and Mail*, 28 April 2011, A8. http://www.theglobeandmail.com/news/national/time-to-lead/ redesigning-a-tired-democracy/article2003072/ (accessed May 7, 2012).

Hughes, Langston. 1959. *Selected poems of Langston Hughes*. New York: Vintage.

Hyman, Richard. 1971. *Marxism and the sociology of trade unionism*. London: Pluto.

Jacob, Merle. 2003. "Rethinking science and commodifying knowledge." *Policy Futures in Education* 1 (1): 125–42. http://dx.doi.org/10.2304/ pfie.2003.1.1.3.

James, C.L.R. 1980. *The Black Jacobins: Toussiant L'Ouverture and the San Domingo Revolution*. London: Alison and Busby.

James, Joy. 2007. "Preface: The American archipelago." In *Warfare in the American homeland: Policing and prison in a penal democracy*, ed. Joy James, xi–xvii. Durham, NC: Duke University Press.

JapaneseCanadianHistory.net. 2011. The war years. http://www. japanesecanadianhistory.net/the_war_years.htm (accessed 2 October 2011).

Jay, Anthony, and Jonathon Lynn. 1980. "Open government." *Yes Minister*, Series 1, Episode 1. BBC Television, 25 February 1980.

Kahn, Kim Fridkin, and Patrick J. Kenney. 1999. "Do negative campaigns mobilize or suppress turnout? Clarifying the relationship between negativity and participation." *American Political Science Review* 93 (4): 877–89. http://dx.doi.org/10.2307/2586118.

Kakabadse, Nada, and Andrew Kakabadse. 2009. "Global governance considerations for world citizenship." In *Citizenship: A reality far from ideal*, ed. Andrew Kakabadse, Nada Kakabadse, and Kalu N. Kalu, 24–48. New York: Palgrave Macmillan.

Kalu, N. Kalu. 2009. "Postmodern citizenship: Logic and praxis in state and identity." In *Citizenship: A reality far from ideal,* ed. Andrew Kakabadse, Nada Kakabadse, and Kalu N. Kalu, 10–23. New York: Palgrave Macmillan.

Keane, John. 2009. *The life and death of democracy*. London: Simon and Schuster.

Kelley, Robin D.G. 1994. *Race rebels: Culture, politics, and the black working class*. New York: The Free Press.

Kelley, Robin D.G. 2002. *Freedom dreams: The Black radical imagination*. Boston: Beacon Press.

Khandor, Erika, Jean McDonald, Peter Nyers, and Cynthia Wright. 2004. *The regularization of non-status immigrants in Canada 1960–2004: Past policies, current perspectives, active campaigns*. Toronto: STATUS Coalition. http://action.web.ca/home/narcc/issues.shtml?x=105434 (accessed 11 November 2011).

Kidd, Chip. 2010. "Doonesbury turns 40." *Rolling Stone,* 11 November 2010. http://www.rollingstone.com/politics/news/doonesbury-turns-40-20101027 (accessed 16 August 2011).

King, Martin Luther, Jr. 1963/1981. *Strength to love*. Philadelphia: Fortress Press.

Kingwell, Mark. 2011. "Intellectuals and democracy." *Academic Matters,* May: 8–11.

Kohn, Margaret. 2011. "Colonialism." In *Stanford Encyclopedia of Philosophy,* ed. Edward N. Zalta. http://plato.stanford.edu/entries/colonialism/ (accessed 26 October 2011).

Lafrance, Xavier, and Alan Sears. 2012. "Red Square, everywhere: With Quebec student strikers, against repression." *New Socialist: Ideas for Radical Change,* 23 May 2012. http://newsocialist.org/index.php?option=com_content&view=article&id=630:red-square-everywhere-with-quebec-student-strikers-against-repression&catid=51:analysis&Itemid=98 (accessed 7 June 2012).

Laxer, James. 2009. *Democracy*. Toronto: Groundwood Books.

Le Blanc, Paul. 2010. "What do socialists say about democracy?" *International Socialist Review* 74 (Nov.–Dec.). http://www.isreview.org/issues/74/feat-socialismdemocracy.shtml (accessed 3 January 2011).

Leacock, Eleanor, and Richard Lee. 1982. "Introduction." In *Politics and history in band societies,* ed. Eleanor Leacock and Richard Lee, 1–20. Cambridge: Cambridge University Press.

Leblanc, Daniel. 2011. "Baird aims to balance trade, human rights on China trip." *The Globe and Mail,* 17 July 2011. http://www.theglobeandmail.com/news/politics/

baird-aims-to-balance-trade-human-rights-issues-on-china-trip/
article2100120/ (accessed 30 November 2011).

Lennon, John. 1970. "Working class hero." *John Lennon/Plastic Ono Band*,
track 4, 3:48. London: Apple/EMI.

Lenski, Gerhard. 1966. *Power and privilege*. New York: McGraw-Hill.

Leyton, Elliott. 1978. "The bureaucratization of anguish: The Workmen's
Compensation Board in an industrial disaster." In *Bureaucracy and world
view: Studies in the logic of official interpretation*, ed. Don Handelman
and Elliott Leyton, 70–134. St. John's: Institute of Social and Economic
Research, Memorial University of Newfoundland.

Lilley, Brian. 2012. "Thugs bullying democracy." *Lilley's Pad*, 18 May 2012.
http://blogs.canoe.ca/lilleyspad/byline/thugs-bullying-democracy/
(accessed 7 June 2012).

Lilley, Sasha. 2011. "Introduction." In *Capital and its discontents:
Conversations with radical thinkers in a time of tumult*, ed. S. Lilley, 1–23.
Oakland: PM Press.

Loury, Glenn C. 2002. *The anatomy of racial inequality*. Cambridge, MA:
Harvard University Press.

Luxemburg, Rosa. 1918. "The Russian Revolution—Chapter 8: Democracy
and Dictatorship." *Marxists Internet Archive*. http://www.marxists.org/
archive/luxemburg/1918/russian-revolution/ch08.htm (accessed 29
August 2011).

Lynn-Jones, Sean M. 1998. *Why the United States should spread democracy*. Discussion paper 98-07. Cambridge, MA: Center for Science and
International Affairs, Harvard University. http://belfercenter.ksg.
harvard.edu/publication/2830/why_the_united_states_should_spread_
democracy.html (accessed 1 October 2011).

MacLeavy, Julie. 2010. "Remaking the welfare state: From safety net
to trampoline." In *The rise and fall of neo-liberalism: The collapse of an
economic order?* ed. Kean Birch and Vlad Mykhnenko, 133–50. London:
Zed Books.

Macpherson, C.B. 1965. *The real world of democracy*. Toronto: House of
Anansi Press.

Malcolmson, Patrick, and Richard Myers. 2005. *The Canadian regime:
An introduction to parliamentary government in Canada*. 3rd ed.
Peterborough, ON: Broadview Press.

Manjoo, Farhad. 2008. *True enough: Learning to live in a post-fact society*.
Hoboken, NJ: John Wiley and Sons.

Mann, Eric. 2001/2009. "Building the anti-racist, anti-imperialist united
front: Theory and practice from the L.A. Strategy Center and Bus Riders
Union." *The Labor/Community Strategy Center*, 12 March 2009. Repr.

from *SOULS Magazine*, Fall 2001. http://www.thestrategycenter.org/article/2009/03/12/building-anti-racist-anti-imperialist-united-front (accessed 20 August 2011).

Mansbridge, Jane. 1999. "Should Blacks represent Blacks and women represent women? A contingent 'yes.'" *The Journal of Politics* 61 (3): 628–57.

Marable, Manning. 2000. "Black radicalism and an economy of incarceration." In *States of confinement: Policing, detention, and prisons*, ed. Joy James, 53–59. New York: St. Martin's Press.

Marlow, Iain, Andy Hoffman, and David Ebner. 2011. "Can China save the world again?" *The Globe and Mail*, 17 October 2011. http://m.theglobeandmail.com/report-on-business/international-news/can-china-save-the-world-again/article2178600/?service=mobile (accessed 20 October 2011).

Marshall, T.H. 1964. *Class, citizenship, and social development*. Chicago: University of Chicago Press.

Marx, Karl. 1867/1976. *Capital*. Vol. 1, trans. Ben Fowkes. London: Penguin Books.

Marx, Karl. 1977. *Economic and political manuscripts*. Moscow: Progress.

Marx, Karl, and Friedrich Engels. 1976. *The German ideology*. Moscow: Progress.

McBride, Dwight A. 2005. *Why I hate Abercrombie and Fitch: Essays on race and sexuality*. New York: New York University Press.

McClenaghan, William A. 1975. *Magruder's American Government*. Boston: Allyn and Bacon.

McNally, David. 2001. *Bodies of meaning: Studies on language, labor, and liberation*. Albany: State University of New York Press.

McNally, David. 2006. *Another world is possible: Globalization and anti-capitalism*. 2nd ed. Winnipeg: Arbeiter Ring.

McNally, David. 2011a. *Global slump: The economics and politics of crisis and resistance*. Oakland: PM Press.

McNally, David. 2011b. "Mubarak's folly: The rising of Egypt's workers." *David McNally: Activist, author, professor*. http://davidmcnally.org/?p=354 (accessed 11 February 2011).

Michels, Robert. 1962. *Political parties: A sociological study of the oligarchical tendencies of modern democracy*, trans. Eden Paul and Cedar Paul. New York: Free Press.

Mills, C. Wright. 1959. *The sociological imagination*. New York: Oxford University Press.

Montessori, Mario, and A.S. Neill. 1966. "Radical private schools." *This Magazine is About Schools* 1 (1): 5–19.

Montopoli, Brian. 2011. "Bachmann to Democrats—Don't tell Americans what light bulbs to buy." *Fox Nation*, 3 March 2011. http://nation.foxnews.com/michele-bachmann/2011/03/03/bachmann-democrats-dont-tell-americans-what-lightbulbs-buy (accessed 6 September 2011).

Moody, Kim. 1997. *Workers in a lean world: Unions in the international economy*. London: Verso.

Moody, Kim. 2011. "A general strike in the heartland?" *Labor Notes*, 18 March 2011. http://labornotes.org/2011/03/general-strike-heartland (accessed 30 November 2011).

Mooers, Colin. 1991. *The making of bourgeois Europe*. London: Verso.

Morgan, David, and Mary Evans. 1993. *The battle for Britain: Citizenship and ideology in the Second World War*. London: Routledge.

Mort, Frank. 1996. *Cultures of consumption: Masculinities and social space in late twentieth-century Britain*. London: Routledge.

Mosley, Ivo. 2000. "Introduction." In *Dumbing down: Culture, politics and the mass media,* ed. Ivo Mosley, 1–10. Bowling Green, OH: Imprint Academic.

Moss, Stephen. 2011. "Francis Fukuyama: 'Americans are not very good at nation-building.'" *The Guardian*, 23 May 2011. http://www.guardian.co.uk/books/2011/may/23/francis-fukuyama-americans-not-good-nation-building (accessed 18 August 2011).

Myers, Jason C. 2010. *The politics of equality: An introduction*. London: Zed Books.

Neocleous, Mark. 1996. *Administering civil society: Towards a theory of state power*. New York: St. Martin's Press. http://dx.doi.org/10.1057/9780230379978.

Ness, Immanuel, and Dario Azzellini. 2011. "Introduction." In *Ours to master and to own: Workers' control from the commune to the present*, ed. I. Ness and D. Azzellini, 1–7. Chicago: Haymarket Books.

No One Is Illegal—Toronto. 2011a. We demand. http://toronto.nooneisillegal.org/demands (accessed 11 November 2011).

No One Is Illegal—Toronto. 2011b. Regularization—Status for all! http://toronto.nooneisillegal.org/node/377 (accessed 11 November 2011).

Norris, Pippa. 2011. *Democratic deficit: Critical citizens revisited*. Cambridge: Cambridge University Press.

Nussbaum, Martha C. 2011. "Democratic desire: Walt Whitman." In *A political companion to Walt Whitman*, ed. John E. Seery, 96–130. Lexington: University of Kentucky Press.

Obama, Barack. 2011. "Speech on the Middle East May 19." *The Huffington Post*, 19 May 2011. http://www.huffingtonpost.com/2011/05/19/obama-middle-east-speech-_n_864153.html (accessed 8 June 2011).

OED Online. 2011. *Oxford English dictionary online*. Oxford: Oxford University Press.

Office of History and Preservation, Office of the Clerk. 2011. *Black Americans in Congress*. Washington, DC: US Government Printing Office. http://baic.house.gov/historical-data/representatives-senators-by-congress.html?congress=112 (accessed 19 September 2011).

Olson, Joel. 2002. "Whiteness and the participation-inclusion dilemma." *Political Theory* 30 (3): 384–409. http://dx.doi.org/10.1177/009059170203003006.

Omar, Mostafa. 2011. "Egypt's unfinished revolution." *International Viewpoint* 436, May. http://www.internationalviewpoint.org/spip.php?article2152 (accessed 12 July 2011).

Ontario Ministry of Education. 2005. *The Ontario curriculum, grades 9 and 10: Canadian and world studies*. Toronto: Ontario Ministry of Education.

Paine, Thomas. 1776. *Common sense*. 3rd ed. http://www.ushistory.org/paine/commonsense/singlehtml.htm (accessed 15 March 2012).

Palmer, Bryan D. 1983. *Working-class experience: The rise and reconstitution of Canadian labour, 1800–1991*. Toronto: Butterworths.

Palmer, Bryan D. 1987. *Solidarity: The rise and fall of an opposition in British Columbia*. Vancouver: New Star.

Pannekoek, Anton. 1948/2003. *Workers' councils*. Edinburgh: AK Press.

Parkins, Wendy. 2000. "Protesting like a girl: Embodiment, dissent, and feminist agency." *Feminist Theory* 1 (1): 59–78. http://dx.doi.org/10.1177/14647000022229065.

"The perils of extreme democracy." 2011. *The Economist*, 20 April 2011. http://www.economist.com/node/18586520/print (accessed 16 May 2012).

Pitkin, Hanna Fenichel. 1967. *The concept of representation*. Berkeley: University of California Press.

Pitkin, Hanna Fenichel. 2004. "Representation and democracy: Uneasy alliance." *Scandinavian Political Studies* 27 (3): 335–42. http://dx.doi.org/10.1111/j.1467-9477.2004.00109.x.

Piven, Frances Fox. 2006. *Challenging authority: How ordinary people change America*. Lanham, MD: Rowman & Littlefield.

Piven, Frances Fox. 2011. "From protest to disruption: Frances Fox Piven on Occupy Wall Street [Interview by Chris Maisano]." *The Activist*, 7 October 2011. http://theactivist.org/blog/from-protest-to-disruption-an-interview-with-frances-fox-piven (accessed 8 October 2011).

Pollak, Vivian R. 2000. *The erotic Whitman*. Berkeley: University of California Press.

Prashad, Vijay. 2007. *The darker nations: A people's history of the Third World*. New York: The New Press.

Prezworski, Adam. 1991. *Democracy and the market: Political and economic reforms in Eastern Europe and Latin America*. Cambridge: Cambridge University Press.

Prezworski, Adam. 2010. *Democracy and the limits of self-government*. Cambridge: Cambridge University Press.

Princeton University. 2011. "Mission statement." *Office of the Vice President for Campus Life*. http://www.princeton.edu/campuslife/mission/ (accessed 15 June 2011).

Prosono, Marvin. 2008. "Fascism of the skin: Symptoms of alienation in the body of consumptive capitalism." *Current Sociology* 56 (4): 635–55. http://dx.doi.org/10.1177/0011392108090946.

Reagan, Ronald. 1984. "Speech on the 40th anniversary of D-Day." *The History Place: Great speeches collection*. http://www.historyplace.com/speeches/reagan-d-day.htm (accessed 25 August 2011).

Rebick, Judy. 2000. *Imagine democracy*. Toronto: Stoddart.

Rebick, Judy. 2009. *Transforming power: From the personal to the political*. Toronto: Penguin Canada.

Reed, John. 1919. *Ten days that shook the world*. New York: BONI & Liveright, Inc. Transcibed in 2001 by David Walters for the *Marxists Internet Archive*. http://www.marxists.org/archive/reed/1919/10days/10days/index.htm (accessed 16 August 2011).

Rehfeld, Andrew. 2005. *The concept of constituency: Political representation, democratic legitimacy, and institutional design*. Cambridge: Cambridge University Press. http://dx.doi.org/10.1017/CBO9780511509674

Richardson, George. 2005. "Nostalgia and national identity: The history and social studies curricula of Alberta and Ontario at the end of empire." In *Canada and the end of empire*, ed. Phillip Buckner, 183–94. Vancouver: UBC Press.

Rinehart, James W. 1987. *The tyranny of work: Alienation and the labour process*. 2nd ed. Toronto: Harcourt Brace Jovanovich.

Rioux, Marcia H, and Paula C. Pinto. 2010. "A time for the universal right to education: Back to basics." *British Journal of Sociology of Education* 31 (5): 621–42. http://dx.doi.org/10.1080/01425692.2010.500094.

Rogers Brubaker, William. 1989. "The French Revolution and the invention of citizenship." *French Politics and Society* 7 (3): 30–49.

Rousseau, Jean-Jacques. 1762/1968. *The social contract*. Trans. Maurice Cranston. Harmondsworth: Penguin Books.

Rowbotham, Sheila. 1972. *Women, resistance and revolution: A history of women and revolution in the modern world*. New York: Pantheon Books.

Rudé, George. 1964. *The crowd in history, 1730–1848*. New York: John Wiley and Sons.

Russell, Marta. 1998. *Beyond ramps: Disability at the end of the social contract*. Monroe, ME: Common Courage Press.

Ruypers, John, and John Ryall. 2005. *Canadian civics*. Toronto: Emond Montgomery Publications.

Sanbonmatsu, John. 2011. "Postmodernism and the politics of expression [Interview by Sasha Lilley]." In *Capital and its discontents: Conversations with radical thinkers in a time of tumult*, ed. S. Lilley, 220–36. Oakland: PM Press.

Sandbrook, Dominic. 2011. "A damnable contempt for democracy." *Mail Online*, 3 November 2011. http://www.dailymail.co.uk/debate/article-2056870/Greece-referendum-crisis-A-damnable-contempt-democracy.html (accessed 9 November 2011).

Saunders, Doug. 2011. "Greece backs off referendum, dealing blow to euro-zone equality." *The Globe and Mail*, 3 November 2011. http://www.theglobeandmail.com/news/world/greece-backs-off-referendum-dealing-blow-to-euro-zone-equality/article2225004/ (accessed 4 November 2011).

Schouls, Tim. 2009. "Why group representation in Parliament is important." In *Crosscurrents: Contemporary political issues*, ed. Mark Charlton and Paul Barker, 6th ed., 252–64. Toronto: Nelson Education.

Schudson, Michael. 1996. *The power of news*. Cambridge, MA: Harvard University Press.

Schudson, Michael. 1998. *The good citizen: A history of American civic life*. New York: Martin Kessler Books.

Schweisfurth, Michele. 2006. "Education for global citizenship: teacher agency and curricular structure in Ontario schools." *Educational Review* 58 (1): 41–50. http://dx.doi.org/10.1080/00131910500352648.

Scott, James C. 2009. *The art of not being governed: An anarchist history of upland Southeast Asia*. New Haven: Yale University Press.

Sears, Alan. 1999. "The 'lean' state and capitalist restructuring: Towards a theoretical account." *Studies in Political Economy* 59 (Summer): 91–114.

Sears, Alan. 2003. *Retooling the mind factory: Education in a lean state*. Aurora, ON: Garamond Press.

Sears, Alan. 2005. "Queer anti-capitalism: What's left of lesbian and gay liberation?" *Science and Society* 69 (1): 92–112. http://dx.doi.org/10.1521/siso.69.1.92.56800.

Sears, Alan, and James Cairns. 2010. *A good book, in theory: Making sense through inquiry*. 2nd ed. Toronto: University of Toronto Press.

Sebestyen, Victor. 2011. "The K.G.B.'s bathhouse plot." *The New York Times* [Sunday Review], 21 August 2011, 4.

Singh, Nikhil Pal. 2004. *Black is a country: Race and the unfinished struggle for democracy*. Cambridge, MA: Harvard University Press.

Sitton, John F. 1987. "Hannah Arendt's argument for council democracy." *Polity* 20 (1): 80–100. http://dx.doi.org/10.2307/3234938.

Situationist International (and students of Strasbourg University). 1966. *On the poverty of student life*. http://www.bopsecrets.org/SI/poverty. htm (accessed 3 January 2011).

Sivanandan, A. 1985. "RAT and the degradation of black struggle." *Race & Class* 26 (4): 1–33. http://dx.doi.org/10.1177/030639688502600401.

Smith, Chris, David Knights, and Hugh Willmott, eds. 1991. *White-collar work: The non-manual labour process*. Houndmills: Macmillan.

Smith, Dorothy E. 1987. *The everyday world as problematic: A feminist sociology*. Toronto: University of Toronto Press.

Smith, Dorothy. 1990. *The conceptual practices of power*. Toronto: University of Toronto Press.

Sparrow, Andrew. 2011. "Politics live: G20-summit." *The Guardian*, 3 November 2011. http://www.guardian.co.uk/world/blog/2011/nov/03/g20-summit-live-coverage (accessed 3 November 2011).

Staggenborg, Suzanne. 2008. *Social movements*. Oxford: Oxford University Press.

Stehr, Nico. 2008. "Introduction: Is freedom a daughter of knowledge?" In *Knowledge and democracy: A 21st-century perspective*, ed. Nico Stehr, 1–6. New Brunswick, NJ: Transaction Publishers.

Stimmann Branson, Margaret. 1991. "The education of citizens in a market economy and its relationship to a free society." Paper presented at the International Conference on Western Democracy and Eastern Europe: Political, Economic, and Social Changes, Spree Hotel, East Berlin, Germany. 14–18 October. http://www.civiced.org/papers/education.html (accessed 28 June 2011).

Svensson, Palle. 1995. *Theories of democracy: The Brno Lectures*. Aarhus, Denmark: Department of Political Science, University of Aarhus.

Taras, David. 2001. *Power and betrayal in the Canadian media*. Peterborough, ON: Broadview Press.

Tilly, Charles. 1996. "The emergence of citizenship in France and elsewhere." In *Citizenship, identity and social history*, ed. Charles Tilly, 223–36. New York: Cambridge University Press. http://dx.doi.org/10.1017/S0020859000113653.

Tombs, Robert. 1999. *The Paris Commune 1871*. London: Longman.

The Trotsky. 2009. Directed by Jacob Tierney. 120 minutes. Alliance Films.

Tsai, Kellee S. 2007. *Capitalism without democracy: The private sector in contemporary China*. Ithaca, NY: Cornell University Press.

Turpin, Colin, and Adam Tomkins. 2007. *British government and the constitution: Text and materials*. Cambridge: Cambridge University Press.

US Citizenship and Immigration Service. 2011. *Learn about the United States: Quick civics lessons for the naturalization test*. http://www.uscis. gov/portal/site/uscis/menuitem.749cabd81f5ffc8fba713d10526e0aa0/?v gnextoid=c242df6bdd42a210VgnVCM100000b92ca60aRCRD&vgnextc hannel=c242df6bdd42a210VgnVCM100000b92ca60aRCRD (accessed 30 November 2011).

Vallance, Elizabeth. 1983. "Hiding the hidden curriculum: An interpretation of the language of justification in nineteenth-century educational reform." In *The hidden curriculum: Deception or discovery*, ed. H. Giroux and D. Purpel, 9–27. Berkeley, CA: McCutcheon Publishing. http:// dx.doi.org/10.2307/1179123.

Van Der Hout, Eliora, and Anthony J. McGann. 2009. "Proportional representation within the limits of liberalism alone." *British Journal of Political Science* 39 (4): 735–54. http://dx.doi.org/10.1017/ S0007123409000684.

Wald, Alan M. 1992. *The responsibility of intellectuals*. New Jersey: Humanities Press.

Walia, Harsha. 2011. "Letter to Occupy Together movement." *rabble.ca*, 14 October 2011. http://rabble.ca/news/2011/10/acknowledgement-occupations-occupied-land-essential (accessed 15 October 2011).

Wallach, John R. 2010. "None of us is a Democrat now." *Theory & Event* 13 (2). http://muse.jhu.edu/ (accessed May 15, 2012).

Weale, Albert. 2007. *Democracy*. 2nd ed. New York: Palgrave Macmillan.

Weber, Max. 1958. *From Max Weber: Essays in sociology*, ed. and trans. H.H. Gerth and C. Wright Mills. New York: Oxford University Press.

Weeks, Jeffrey. 1990. *Coming out: Homosexual politics in Britain from the nineteenth century to the present*. Rev. ed. London: Quartet.

Weldon, Laurel. 2011. *When protest makes policy: How social movements represent disadvantaged groups*. Ann Arbor: University of Michigan Press.

The White House. 2009. Administration launches comprehensive Open Government plan. http://www.whitehouse.gov/the-press-office/ administration-launches-comprehensive-open-government-plan (accessed 28 June 2011).

Whiteley, Paul. 2009. "Is the party over? The decline of party activism and membership across the democratic world." Paper presented at the Political Studies Association Meeting, University of Manchester. April.

http://www.psa.ac.uk/2009/pps/Whiteley.pdf (accessed 28 October 2011).

Whitman, Walt. 1860/2002. "Mannahatta." http://www.poemhunter.com/poem/mannahatta/ (accessed 11 August 2011).

Whitman, Walt. 1940. *Leaves of grass*. Ed. Christopher Morley. New York: Doubleday and Doran.

Wilfrid Laurier University. 2003. "Values, vision, mission and guiding principles." *Laurier Office of the President*. https://www.wlu.ca/page.php?grp_id=2295&p=13531 (accessed 15 June 2011).

Wiseman, Nelson. 2006. "Get out the vote—not: Increasingly effort, declining turnout." *Policy Options* (February): 18–23.

Wolf, Eric R. 1982. *Europe and the people without history*. Berkeley: University of California Press.

Wood, Ellen Meiksins. 1995. *Democracy against capitalism: Renewing historical materialism*. Cambridge: Cambridge University Press. http://dx.doi.org/10.1017/CBO9780511558344.

Wrigley, Terry. 2003. *Schools of hope: A new agenda for school improvement*. Stoke on Trent: Trentham Books.

Wrigley, Terry. 2004. "'School effectiveness': The problem of reductionism." *British Educational Research Journal* 30 (2): 227–44. http://dx.doi.org/10.1080/0141192042000195272.

Young, Iris Marion. 2002. *Inclusion and democracy*. Oxford: Oxford University Press. http://dx.doi.org/10.1093/0198297556.001.0001.

Youngs, Richard. 2003. "Linking free trade and democracy: The European Union's experience in the Middle East." *Sada*, 25 September 2003. http://carnegieendowment.org/2008/08/25/linking-free-trade-and-democracy-european-union-s-experience-in-middle-east/6frs (accessed 30 November 2011).

Zeitlin, Irving M. 1997. *Rulers and rule: An introduction to classical political theory from Plato to the Federalists*. Toronto: University of Toronto Press.

Zimmer, Ben. 2010. "Truthiness." *The New York Times*, 13 October 2010. http://www.nytimes.com/2010/10/17/magazine/17FOB-onlanguage-t.html (accessed 16 May 2012).

Zweifel, Thomas D. 2002. *Democratic deficit: Institutions and regulation in the European Union, Switzerland, and the United States in comparative perspective*. Lanham, MD: Lexington Books.

Index